TRUST IN GOD

Finding Peace Amidst Life's Storms

by,
Joseph C. Stemple

Copyright © 2024 Joseph C. Stemple

All rights reserved.

BOOK DEDICATION

First and foremost, I humbly dedicate this book to God, the author of my faith, and the very breath that sustained me through this spiritual journey. "Trust in God" is a testament to God's unwavering grace during the highs and lows that marked its creation. With a grateful heart, I dedicate it first to Him.

Heavenly Father, I owe everything - the very breath in my lungs and the ability to put pen to paper. This book is not mine but yours. It was conceived in prayer, written through spiritual inspiration, and belongs fully to your purposes. May these words minister your truth, touch hearts, and bring readers into a deeper experience of your unfailing love. I am merely the vessel, and all praise belongs to you. Apart from your grace, I am nothing. So, with fear and trembling, I present this work to you, praying it will accomplish your desires - to strengthen faith, deepen devotion, and magnify your name in the hearts of all who read it. To you alone be the glory. It is my prayer that as readers experience these stories, they will awaken more fully to the reality of your presence, nearness, and transforming power.

To my wife of 33 years, Daniella Stemple, who has been at my side every step of our marriage and this journey with God. She is the love of my life, best friend, and soul mate, and this book exists because of her unconditional support and inspiration in our friendship and marriage.

For my parents, Martha/Allen (Moraes) and Charles H. Stemple, whose boundless love and sacrifices paved the way for all my successes.

To my siblings, Charles A/ (Nury) Stemple, Margaret/ (Oscar) Stevens, Micheal J. Stemple, Sylvia/ (Tony) Ramirez, Mary/ (Paul)Vasques, Martha Perez, my first friends and forever allies. Thanks for always having my back.

Dedicated To The Memory Of:

Martha/Allen Moraes

Charles H. Stemple

Charles A. Stemple. Jr

TABLE OF CONTENTS

BOOK DEDICATION 1
PREFACE 1
INTRODUCTION 1

CHAPTER 1 "Trust in God" 1
Rest In God's Promises: Trusting God's Plan For Tomorrow 1
Walking By Faith: Finding Strength For The Journey 1
The Power Of Surrender: Letting Go And Finding Inner Peace 1
Rise Above: Conquering Fear And Doubt With Confidence 1
Finding Peace In The Storm: A Guide To Navigating Life's Turbulence 1
Walking By Faith: Trusting God's Timing Along Your Journey 1
The Faithful Journey: Cultivating A Perspective Of Purpose 1
Finding Peace In Surrender: Trusting God's Will 1
Peace In The Storm: Trusting God's Presence Amid Uncertainty 1
The Power Of Trust: Embracing Faith In Action 1

CHAPTER 2 "Embracing the Way, the Truth, and the Life" 1
The Journey Within: Exploring The Depths Of Meaning .. 1
Journey Through Faith: A Story Of Jesus Christ 1
The Way, The Truth, And The Life: Understanding Jesus' Teachings 1
Miracles Unveiled: Witnessing The Power Of Jesus 1
The Heart Of Sacrifice: Understanding The Power Of Love 1
Risen: Exploring The Power Of The Resurrection 1

Living The Way Of Christ: Nurturing A Christ-Centered Lifestyle 1
Amidst The Storm: Seeking Solace And Serenity 1
Heart-To-Heart: Building Authentic Connections 1
A Path To Fulfillment: Embracing Way, Truth, And Life's Calling 1

CHAPTER 3 "Put God First" 1
Guided By Grace: Understanding Divine Priorities 1
Beyond The Noise: Finding Peace By Letting Go 1
In God's Hands: Seeking Divine Guidance for Decision Making 1
Let Go, Let God: Surrendering Control And Finding Peace 1
Purposeful Living: Embracing Service As A Way Of Life 1
The Soul's Compass: Navigating Towards Spiritual Growth 1
Walking With God: Deepening Your Relationship Daily .. 1
Hope In The Storm: Navigating Life's Challenges With Faith 1
Spiritual Harmony: Embracing God's Priorities In Love ... 1
Walking In Grace: Embracing God's Plan For Us Every Day 1

CHAPTER 4 "The Power Of Forgiveness" 1
Forgiveness: The Key To Empowerment And Inner Peace 1
The Heart Of Forgiveness: Embracing Understanding And Compassion 1
Freeing Yourself: Unpacking Emotional Baggage For A Lighter Journey 1
Healing Begins From Within: Embracing Personal Responsibility 1
Shackles Of The Heart: Understanding And Releasing The Blocks To Forgiveness 1
Compassionate Living: Empathy As The Key To Fulfillment 1

The Art Of Forgiveness: Techniques For Cultivating Peace And Freedom 1
Pathways To Forgiveness: Embarking On The Journey Of Healing 1
Embracing Grace: Forgiving Others, Forgiving Ourselves 1
The Path To Self-Forgiveness: Acknowledging And Embracing The Journey 1
Embracing Renewal: Healing And Moving Forward With Purpose 1

CHAPTER 5 "God's Unconditional Love" 1
God's Unconditional Love 1
Embracing Imperfection: Finding Beauty in Brokenness ... 1
Embers Of The Soul: Confronting The Darkness Within ... 1
Love's Guiding Light: A Journey Of Encountering God ... 1
From Bitterness To Blessings: Unveiling The Transformative Power Of Forgiveness 1
Perfectly Imperfect: Embracing Grace Amidst Flaws 1
Pathways To Purpose: Navigating The Divine Blueprint ... 1
Healing Hearts: The Journey Of Redemption In Relationships 1
The Promise Of Tomorrow: Holding Onto Hope In Suffering 1
Restored Faith: Nurturing Resilience And Restoration 1
Forgiven And Free: Embracing Redemption 1

CHAPTER 6 "Letting go of Judgment" 1
Letting Go Of Judgment 1
Breaking The Chains Of Judgment: Finding Freedom Within 1
Looking Inward, Seeing Outward: Recognizing Judgment's Impact 1
Finding Peace Within: Navigating The Path Of Self-Judgment 1
Embrace Your Uniqueness: Breaking The Cycle Of Comparison 1

The Compassionate Heart: Cultivating Self-Love And Understanding 1
Heart Wide Open: Embracing Vulnerability 1
Letting Go and Living: Liberating Yourself from Perfectionism 1
Unbreakable: Cultivating Resilience For Life's Trials 1
Living In The Moment: Practicing Mindfulness For Inner Peace 1
True To You: Embracing Authenticity In A World Of Expectations 1

CHAPTER 7 "Embracing the Heart of God: Finding love in every moment" 1
Embracing The Heart Of God: Finding Love In Every Moment 1
Unveiling Your Intrinsic Value: Understanding Our Worth 1
Embracing Boldness: Letting Go Of Fear And Doubt 1
Daily Delights: Finding Joy In Every Moment 1
Forgiveness: The Pathway To Healing 1
The Heart Of Togetherness: Nurturing Relationships 1
Passionate Living: Embracing Purpose With Zeal 1
Gratitude Attitude: Rewiring Your Brain For Happiness.... 1
Rising Above: Overcoming Life's Challenges 1
The Path To Purpose: Embracing A Meaningful Life 1

CHAPTER 8 "Embracing Hope: Finding Light in the Darkness" 1
Embracing Hope: Finding Strength And Purpose In Every Moment 1
God's Saving Grace: Exploring The Depths Of Redemption 1
Fearless: Conquering Doubt And Fear 1
In His Word We Trust: Finding Strength In Biblical Promises 1
Letting God Lead: Surrendering Control For Spiritual Growth 1

The Power Of Forgiveness: Healing From Within 1
Walking With God: Nurturing Your Relationship 1
The Faithful Path: Embracing Trust 1
Unshakable Hope: Triumphing Over Life's Trials 1
Whisper Of Hope: Encounters With God's Salvation 1

CHAPTER 9 "The Prayer Warriors Guide" 1
The Prayer Warrior's Call: Igniting The Flame Of Spiritual Battle 1
Prayer: A Pathway To Inner Peace 1
Unshaken: Standing Firm Through Life's Storms Of Fear And Doubt 1
Rising Strong: Embracing Resilience To Bounce Back Stronger 1
The Power Within: Cultivating A Resilient Positive Mindset 1
The Power Of Faith: Strengthening Your Relationship With God 1
Embrace The Journey: Transforming Through Change 1
Raising A Village: Fostering Supportive Communities 1
Weathering The Storm: Overcoming Obstacles Together In Your Relationship 1
Unleashing The Warrior Spirit: Overcoming Obstacles With Tenacity 1

CHAPTER 10 "Trust And Surrender" 1
Embrace Your Story: A Journey Of Self-Exploration 1
Breaking Chains: The Art Of Liberating Your Life 1
The Stillness Within: Finding Peace Amidst The Unknown 1
Finding Courage: Navigating Through Fear's Terrain 1
Resilience: The Power Within 1
Perfect Timing: Embracing the Divine Plan Titles 1
Through The Storm: Finding Silver Linings 1
Faith In The Unknown: Nurturing Belief Amidst Uncertainty 1

Unstoppable: Rising Above Resistance To Achieve 1
Mission Accomplished: Living With Purpose And Fulfillment.. 1

ABOUT THE AUTHOR 1

PREFACE

In the cacophony of our modern lives, where uncertainty seems to reign supreme and the pressures of daily existence weigh heavy on our shoulders, the concept of trust can feel like a distant echo from a forgotten era. Yet, it is precisely in these tumultuous times that the essence of trusting in God becomes most crucial.

In this book, "Trust in God," I embark on a profound exploration of what it means to place our trust in a higher power. Through the lens of faith, we navigate the complexities of our world, seeking solace and guidance in the divine presence that surrounds us.

Drawing upon the wisdom of scripture, the insights of spiritual leaders, and the lived experiences of individuals who have traversed the depths of despair to find solace in faith, this book invites readers on a transformative journey of introspection and discovery.

We delve into the very essence of trust itself, examining its roots, its manifestations, and its transformative power to uplift and sustain us through life's trials and tribulations. Through stories of courage, resilience, and unwavering faith, we witness the profound impact that trusting in God can have on our lives.

As the author of "Trust in God," it is my sincere belief that this book will serve as a guiding light for all those who seek to deepen their connection with God and cultivate a sense of trust that transcends the challenges of our time. May it offer comfort to the weary soul, inspiration to the searching heart, and renewed hope to all who dare to trust in God's unfailing love.

In a world filled with uncertainty and turmoil, the concept of trust often feels elusive. We grapple with doubt, fear, and the complexities of life, seeking solace and stability amidst the chaos. In this book, "Trust in God," we embark on a journey to explore the profound power of trust and faith in God.

Drawing upon timeless wisdom from various spiritual traditions, personal anecdotes, and reflections, and certainly my relationship with God. This book serves as a beacon of hope and guidance for those navigating the vicissitudes of life. Through the pages that follow, we delve into the essence of trust—what it means, how it is cultivated, and why it is indispensable on our spiritual path.

Regardless of one's religious affiliation or spiritual beliefs, the message of trust resonates universally. It is a reminder that, despite the uncertainties that surround us, there exists a source of unwavering support and guidance— a divine presence that beckons us to surrender our worries and place our trust in something greater than ourselves.

As the author of "Trust in God," it is my sincere hope that this book serves as a source of inspiration and encouragement for all who seek to deepen their trust in God and, ultimately, find peace amidst life's storms.

With humility and gratitude, I invite you to embark on this journey with an open heart and a steadfast trust in the power of God's grace. And may the words within these pages illuminate your path and strengthen your faith as you embark on the journey of trust in God.

INTRODUCTION

A relationship with God is a deeply personal and spiritual connection that individuals cultivate through faith, prayer, and devotion. It's a journey of seeking guidance, finding comfort, and experiencing a sense of purpose and fulfillment in life. Whether through organized religion or personal spirituality, it's about fostering a sense of connection to something greater than oneself and finding meaning in that connection.

A relationship with God embodies this pursuit, offering solace, guidance, and a sense of belonging in a world often fraught with uncertainty. It's through prayer that a relationship with God serves as a beacon of hope, inviting individuals to explore the depths of their spirituality and connect with a divine presence that transcends earthly boundaries.

A relationship with God is an invitation to connect with Him, to seek and find solace, wisdom, and purpose in a world that often leaves us searching. It's through prayer we find a pathway toward a deeper understanding of ourselves and our place in the universe.

Imagine having a constant companion who listens without judgment, provides guidance in times of uncertainty, and offers boundless love and support. This is the essence of a relationship with God. It's about forging a spiritual connection that transcends the mundane aspects of life and taps into something infinitely profound. Whether you're seeking solace, purpose, or simply a deeper understanding of existence, having a relationship with God will be a transformative journey.

In a world often fraught with uncertainty and challenges, the concept of trust is a beacon of hope and resilience. "Trust in God" is not merely a book; it is a journey, a testament to the enduring power of faith. Through these pages, we embark on a voyage of introspection guided by the wisdom of centuries and the eternal truths that anchor our souls.

Within these chapters, I find solace in my relationship with God, the experiences of seekers, and the timeless teachings that have shaped countless lives. Through stories of triumph over adversity, moments of doubt transformed into unwavering conviction, and the quiet whispers of the heart, we discover the essence of trust: surrendering to a higher purpose beyond our understanding.

As we delve into these pages, may we be reminded that trust is not a passive surrender but an active choice, a leap of faith into the unknown, buoyed by the certainty of God's providence. I pray this book serves as a guiding light on your journey toward deeper trust, resilience, and, ultimately, a closer connection with God.

In a world often tangled in the webs of doubt and uncertainty, there exists a beacon of unwavering strength and solace, trust in God. This book is not merely a collection of words, but a guiding compass for the soul's journey through the tempests of life.

Within these pages, you will find the echoes of faith that have resonated through the corridors of time, the stories of those who found refuge in the embrace of God's providence. It is a testament to the resilience of the human spirit and the transformative power of unwavering trust.

As you embark on this profound exploration, may you discover that trust is not blind submission but a conscious choice to surrender to God and his plans for us. Through the trials and triumphs shared within these chapters, may you find strength in the midst of adversity, clarity in moments of doubt, and hope in the face of despair.

May this book be a companion on your journey, a source of inspiration and comfort when the storms rage and the path ahead seems uncertain. May it illuminate the pathway to a deeper trust in God with you, leading you closer to his presence that guides and sustains us all. I pray that in the pages that follow, you find not just words but a sanctuary for the weary soul, a haven where trust blooms eternal.

In the tapestry of life, woven with threads of joy and sorrow, triumphs and tribulations, there exists a profound truth that transcends all challenges: trust in God. This book is a humble offering, a testament to the transformative power of faith in navigating the complexities of existence.

In these pages, we embark on a journey of exploration and discovery, guided by the timeless wisdom of spiritual traditions and the lived experiences of those who have walked the path of trust. It is an invitation to delve deep into the heart of faith, to unearth the treasures of resilience, hope, and surrender that lie therein.

As we journey together, let us remember that trust in God is not a passive acquiescence to fate but a dynamic relationship rooted in love, devotion, and surrender. It is a steadfast anchor amidst life's storms, a beacon of light illuminating the darkest nights of the soul.

Through scripture, anecdotes, reflections, and timeless teachings, we will unravel the mysteries of trust, learning to cultivate it amidst uncertainty, nurture it in times of abundance, and cling to it in moments of despair. For in trust, we find not only solace for the present moment but also a guiding light for the journey ahead.

May this book serve as a companion on your quest for deeper meaning and purpose, a source of inspiration and consolation when the path seems obscured. May it ignite within you the flame of trust, empowering you to face life's challenges with grace, courage, and unwavering faith. A journey with God, is a journey of trust, a journey that transcends time and space, leading us ever closer to his heart.

As we immerse ourselves in these narratives, may we be inspired to deepen our own relationship with God to cultivate an intimacy that transcends words and concepts. May we learn to listen to the whispers of the heart, to recognize the signs of God's presence in the ordinary moments of life, and to surrender to the transformative power of God's love.

Ultimately, this book is an invitation – an invitation to embark on a journey of exploration and revelation, to discover the beauty and mystery of the relationship with God that lies at the very core of our being. May it be a source of inspiration, comfort, and guidance as we navigate the sacred terrain of the human soul.

May your hearts be open, your minds receptive, and our spirits uplifted as we embrace the timeless message of "Trust in God."

Joseph Christopher Stemple

CHAPTER 1
"Trust in God"

Dark clouds rolled in rapidly, blotting out the warm spring sun. Ten-year-old Sammy watched apprehensively from his bedroom window as the winds picked up, whipping the trees violently back and forth. He had weathered many storms in his young life, but there was something particularly ominous about this one.

The first clap of thunder made Sammy jump, followed shortly by a brilliant flash of lightning splitting the sky. As the rain started pelting down in sheets, Sammy bowed his head and offered a silent prayer. "Lord, I'm scared. But I know you are always with me. Help me to trust in your strength during this storm."

The tempest raged for what seemed like hours. Sammy sat silently in his room, and the lightning illuminated from his parents' Bible, which rested on his desk with each flash of light. He recalled his mom reading her Bible in church and during mass. Sammy reached for his own Bible, which immediately opened to Psalm 89:9, and began to read. The Scripture declares, "You rule over the surging sea; when its waves mount up, you still them," speaking to God's power over the elements. Though the thunderous noise was deafening at times, Sammy felt a strange inner calm. He reminded himself that his heavenly Father was in control, no matter how fierce the tempest.

Psalm 89:9 reflects the acknowledgment of God's sovereignty and power over nature, specifically over the tumultuous sea. The "surging sea" symbolizes the chaos, instability, and unpredictable elements of life that confront us. However, the Psalmist affirms that God is in control even amidst chaos. God's authority extends over the waves of the sea, which metaphorically represent the challenges and trials that we encounter. The imagery suggests that just as God can calm the turbulent waters, he can also bring peace, order, and stability to the lives of those who trust in him.

When the worst had passed, Sammy stepped outside and observed the aftermath of what was now a calm storm, with the sky clearing and the sun breaking through. The storm had subsided. Tree branches littered the yard, and outdoor furniture was strewn about, but his home remained standing. He breathed a sigh of relief mingled with gratitude. Though he had momentarily felt overwhelmed by the fury of the storm, his trust in God and his word had sustained him. God was his rock, his shelter in the midst of life's wildest storms.

From that day forward, as Sammy grew older, whenever he found himself in a turbulent season of life, he recalled the lessons of that powerful thunderstorm. He clung tightly to God's promises, knowing that just as God ultimately calmed the raging winds and rains, He would bring peace to every struggle faced. His Trust in God was anchored in the One who commanded even the stormy waters.

Romans 8:28 serves as a cornerstone of the Christian faith, offering solace and hope during moments of uncertainty and adversity. This verse underscores the profound belief in God's providence and sovereignty, affirming that all circumstances, whether good or bad, work together for the ultimate good of those who love God and are called according to His purpose and plan for us. It showcases the transformative power of faith, guiding believers to place their trust in God's unfailing wisdom and care, even in the face of trials and hardships. It encourages believers to persevere in their faith, knowing that God is actively orchestrating events for their benefit, ultimately leading them toward His divine intentions.

Faith teaches us to acknowledge that God has a divine plan and purpose, even when we may not grasp it immediately. Trusting in God's plan entails having faith that He works everything out for the greater good, even amidst challenging circumstances. It requires patience, perseverance, and surrendering one's will to God's greater will and timeline.

Proverbs 3:5- 6 tells us, "Trust in the Lord with all your heart and lean not on your own understanding; in all your ways submit to him, and he will make your paths straight." This verse encourages complete reliance on God rather than attempting to figure everything out ourselves.

Trusting God's plan in the midst of trials or unanswered prayers offers the assurance that He has not abandoned us, even if His plan unfolds differently than we anticipated. It entails believing in the perfection of God's wisdom, love, and timing, even when circumstances seem imperfect.

Ultimately, trusting God's plan requires faith that He knows what is best and possesses a greater perspective than our limited human understanding. It provides peace, strength, and hope, even amidst life's most daunting challenges.

Beyond a mere concept, trusting God's plan represents a lifestyle anchored in indescribable peace, divine purpose, and unwavering hope amidst life's storms. It involves actively choosing to focus on the unseen spiritual realities that our almighty Father orchestrates sovereignty behind the scenes.

As we delve into the depths of trusting in God's plan, we embark on a journey toward deeper faith, courage, and profound existential freedom. This journey liberates us from the chains of worry and human striving, guiding us to embrace the resplendent adventure of resting in the inexhaustible wisdom and love of our heavenly Father.

In the pages ahead, we will unpack the profound existential impact of this spiritual stance of trust, along with strategies to nurture it more fully in our daily lives. Our journey begins with the conscious decision to choose faith over fear.

Rest In God's Promises: Trusting God's Plan For Tomorrow

Our lives are often filled with unexpected twists and turns, surprising us with both joyous moments and challenges that shake us to our core. In those moments when things don't go as planned, it is natural to feel disoriented and question our purpose. Yet, it's precisely during these challenging times that our faith is tested, prompting us to seek an understanding of God's path for us rather than questioning His intentions.

What if I told you that these unexpected detours and disappointments in our lives are not meant to shatter us but rather to shape us? What if we embraced the idea that each setback and disappointment is intricately woven into God's plan for our lives, crafted with love and purpose to draw us closer to Him and ensure we are living a life aligned with His will?

Trusting in God's plan requires a shift in perspective, an understanding that acknowledges that his ways are higher than ours. As adults navigating life's complexities, it's natural to desire control over our circumstances and to want everything to align with our desires. Yet, finding solace and comfort in the familiar, anything that deviates from our expectations can feel like a personal failure. However, this is precisely the time to recognize that God's plan is at work in our lives, making adjustments to keep us aligned with his divine purpose. Though we may not fully comprehend his plan, living with trust in God opens our eyes to the grandeur of his plan.

However, by surrendering our plans and desires to God, we open ourselves up to the possibility of something greater — things we never envisioned and certainly the grace of God we never anticipated. It takes strength and courage to trust in God. I understand that, especially when the path ahead seems shrouded in darkness, as has been your experience, living in shadows. In these moments, we must remember that God's plan often unfolds in mysterious ways, leading us to destinations we never imagined possible. But here is the key: you have to have faith in God. You must be willing to release the illusion of control and allow God to lead you to his kingdom and keep you secure.

From my own journey, I can attest that I once dwelled in darkness, lost, and besieged by countless struggles. I couldn't fathom when God would "make it right." Yet, I was ensnared by Satan's deceit. I couldn't discern what God was guiding me toward, merely seeking to align my heart with his.

Now, I comprehend. Not to dwell on my past but to reflect on my past transgressions and marvel at how I overcame those dire times. Why did I succumb to the darkness that ensured me? God necessitated my trials and tribulations, aware that my pursuit would inevitably lead me to him.

Trusting in God's plan means refraining from questioning him and acknowledging that his timing is impeccable. We inhabit a world driven by instant gratification and immediate results. We crave success, happiness, and fulfillment on our terms and schedules. However, God's plan often demands patience and resilience as we await its unfolding. True success is not instantaneous; only Satan promises much, and it results in fleeting gratification, leaving us stranded in darkness.

Take a moment to reflect on the times in your life when things didn't unfold as expected. Perhaps you encountered a job loss, a broken relationship, or a health challenge. In those instances, it may have felt as though your world was crumbling, and you couldn't comprehend why God would allow such pain. However, looking back, you can discern how those experiences molded your character, instilled resilience, and drew you nearer to God —that's just how he operates. God desires our safety and yearns for us to lead lives filled with fulfillment and success. Trusting in God and his plan will infuse you with hope, joy, and the strength to pursue your dreams. Amidst it all, maintaining peace is pivotal for preserving your joy, strength, and hope.

When we trust in God's plan, we embrace uncertainty. It means letting go of our need for control and placing our trust in the One who knows what lies ahead. It requires faith that even amidst chaos, God is working behind the scenes, orchestrating every detail for our ultimate good. As I often say, "Life is full of secrets, and all secrets belong to God." He has blessed me with many great secrets and has opened my heart to love those around me unconditionally.

Embarking on a journey of trusting in God's plan, we must remember that it won't always be easy; in fact, there will be difficult times. Yet, God's plan ensures our safety and provides us with our portion. Doubts and fears may arise, threatening to unravel our faith. But just as a tree's roots grow stronger when faced with strong winds, our faith can deepen through the storms of life.

Let us hold on to the blessed assurance that God is with us every step of the way, guiding us through the unknown secrets of our lives. In our darkest moments, when doubt seeks to consume us, we can find solace in the promise that God's plan surpasses our own. Let's take this leap of faith together, trusting in the One who holds our past, present, and future.

Scripture tells us in Matthew, "And Jesus said unto them, 'Because of your unbelief: for the verily I say unto you, if ye have faith as a grain of mustard seed, ye shall say unto this mountain, Remove hence to yonder place, and it shall be removed, and nothing shall be impossible unto you."

I pray you find strength in your faith, whether through this book, Scripture, to nourish and replenish your faith or the hope as you journey with God and his plan, leaving you on the precipice of discovering the profound ways in which his plan unfolds. As we eagerly await may our hearts remain open to his leading, ready to embrace the beautiful surprises yet to come. Trust in God's plan; He will guide and protect your heart.

Standing on the precipice of discovering the profound ways in which God's plan unfolds, it's crucial to remain open to his leading and ready to embrace the beautiful surprises yet to come. Trusting in God's plan means surrendering our limited understanding and relying on his infinite wisdom.

As we travel a journey through life, especially through the depths of uncertainty, it's comforting to know that we are never alone. Even when our faith falters, God remains steadfast, unwavering in his commitment to guide us through the unknown. His love is boundless, and his mercies are renewed every morning. His promise to us is simple: trust in his plan, and he will never forsake us.

Trusting in God's plan requires us to resist the temptation to rely solely on our own strength and understanding. Instead, it calls us to loosen our grip on our lives and place our trust in the One who holds our past, present, and future. By doing so, we invite God to transform our lives in ways we could never have envisioned. The past is immutable, and the future is veiled in secrecy—all secrets belong to God. He only asks that we live in the present moment, and he will guide our paths.

On this journey of trust in God, we'll inevitably encounter obstacles and challenges that seek to shake our faith. In such moments, we must remind ourselves of God's promises. He assures us that his plan surpasses our own, and he has a purpose for every twist and turn in our lives.

In our relationship with God, it's imperative to trust him wholeheartedly, not just intermittently. We must place our trust in him unconditionally. While we may not always comprehend why God permits certain hardships, we can find solace in knowing that he orchestrates all things together for our ultimate good. This assurance empowers us to persevere when the road ahead appears uncertain or difficult.

Trusting in God's plan also necessitates openness to his gentle guidance and divine interventions. Sometimes, his direction may come as a soft, reassuring whisper or through the actions and words of others, reminding us of his boundless love and care. God has set his plan in motion, and as a result, we encounter individuals in our lives who may seem incidental. However, God's plan is not random; it brings others into our lives to safeguard us, guide us, and draw us closer to him. His angels surround us —they may appear as ordinary people, but they, too, are part of his divine plan.

As we journey through life, let's not overlook the importance of patience. God's timing is impeccable, even when it doesn't align with our own desires or objectives. We must embrace the understanding that waiting isn't synonymous with idleness; rather, it presents an opportunity for growth, transformation, and a deepening of our relationship with God.

While we may yearn for immediate answers and swift resolutions, it is crucial to remember that God's plan operates on his eternal timetable. In the waiting, we learn to trust him more completely, fostering perseverance and resilience in our character. Despite my failings, God has never forsaken me; he's the same God who won't let me falter, so I rely on him to guide me through each day according to his plan.

Trusting in God's plan fosters growth and encourages us to adopt an attitude of gratitude. Reflecting on past experiences, setbacks, and disappointments often unveil themselves as pivotal moments that shaped and molded us into the individuals we are today. My commitment to God's plan has undeniably transformed me into the person I am today. Through pain and uncertainty, we discover God's faithfulness to his promise of using all things for our benefit.

For many believers, strength in God's plan offers solace and direction during trials, aiding them in persevering through adversity. It also bestows a sense of peace and purpose, reminding them that they are part of a divine design greater than themselves.

This belief encourages individuals to remain unwavering in their faith, trusting that God's plan for their lives ultimately leads to their benefit, even amidst uncertainty or hardship. It fosters resilience and hope, empowering individuals to navigate life's challenges with courage and determination.

As we journey through this chapter, let's strengthen our trust in God's plan. Trials may arise, but our faith will deepen, knowing that God is with us and we are integral to his plan. We are not alone on this journey; we have a loving Father who leads us, guiding each step along the way.

May your heart find encouragement and your spirit uplifted as you trust wholeheartedly in the One who holds your life in his hands. Though the path ahead may still be veiled in mystery, with unwavering trust in God, you can rest assured that his plan will unfold in marvelous ways. He will reveal his miracles and purpose for you.

With hope as our anchor and trust as our compass, let us march forward, confident in God's plan for our lives. And as we do, may our faith in his goodness and love continue to grow, lightening our path and drawing us nearer to the abundant life he has prepared for us.

Walking By Faith: Finding Strength For The Journey

In our journey through life, we inevitably encounter challenges that test our resilience and push us to our limits. At times, these trials can leave us feeling overwhelmed and defeated. Yet, it's precisely in these moments that our faith in God transcends mere belief; it becomes our anchor, offering the strength and guidance necessary to navigate life's storms.

Our faith serves as a powerful force that uplifts us when life's burdens weigh heavily upon us. It reassures us that we are not alone in our struggles; there is a higher power watching over us, guiding us toward a brighter tomorrow. When we place our trust in God, we access an infinite wellspring of strength that enables us to confront adversity with unwavering resolve.

One of the most remarkable aspects of faith is its independence from our circumstances. It doesn't hinge on having all the answers or a perfect understanding of life's mysteries. Instead, it calls us to surrender control and trust in the divine plan unfolding before us. In doing so, we find solace in knowing that every trial we face serves a purpose greater than ourselves.

Our faith can offer hope and optimism, even amidst adversity. Believing in something greater than oneself enables individuals to look beyond their current circumstances and maintain a positive outlook for the future.

Faith communities foster a sense of belonging and support for individuals. Being part of a faith community provides encouragement, guidance, and companionship, strengthening individuals through shared beliefs and experiences. Faith serves as a wellspring of strength for many people.

Throughout history, countless individuals have found solace and strength in their faith when confronted with seemingly insurmountable challenges. Their stories serve as a testament to the transformative power of belief. Consider the journey of Joseph in the Bible. Despite being sold into slavery by his own brothers and facing unjust accusations, Joseph clung to his trust in God. He believed that his suffering served a greater purpose. Ultimately, his unwavering faith led him to become a notable leader in Egypt, where he was reunited with his family and imparted a powerful lesson in forgiveness and resilience.

Faith not only provides the strength to endure but also grants the wisdom to see beyond our present circumstances. It allows us to view life's challenges as opportunities for growth and transformation. By surrendering to a higher power, we open ourselves up to the possibility of miracles and extraordinary outcomes that transcend our limited human understanding.

Moreover, faith offers a sense of peace amidst chaos and uncertainty. It reminds us of the comforting truth that we are cherished and watched over by a divine presence. When faced with despair, our faith becomes a guiding light, reassuring us that hope endures even in the darkest moments.

For many, faith in God becomes a steadfast anchor during times of profound difficulty, pain, or loss. In such moments, individuals often turn to their faith for solace, guidance, and strength to navigate through their most challenging times.

As we journey through our individual paths, it is vital to recognize the inherent strength within each of us to overcome life's trials. Our faith in God serves as a guiding beacon, illuminating our way and reminding us of the reservoir of inner strength we possess. Even when life's tumult threatens to engulf us, let us stand steadfast in our trust in God and his divine plan, drawing from our faith to rise above any adversity.

As we delve deeper into this exploration of faith and its capacity to fortify us, we will encounter Tales of triumph and perseverance that inspire and uplift our spirits. Through the lens of faith, we will uncover how God's guiding hand can transmute even the most difficult circumstances. Now is the time to remain anchored in faith, adhering to God's plan as we embark on our journey into the limitless power of our faith. In our continued exploration of faith's boundless power, we encounter stories of individuals who have drawn strength and inspiration from their unwavering trust in God and his plans for them. These stories exemplify how faith can metamorphose even the most arduous situations, demonstrating that amidst life's challenges, we can discover solace and resilience through our connection to something greater than ourselves.

Consider the story of Esther in the Bible, a courageous woman who found herself in a precarious situation. As a Jewish woman in Persia during a time of great turmoil and persecution, she could have easily succumbed to fear and hopelessness. Instead, Esther chose to embrace her faith and trust in God's plan. With wisdom and courage, she risked her own life to save her people from oppression, illustrating the remarkable strength that stems from a profound belief in a higher power.

Similarly, the life of Nelson Mandela serves as a testament to the transformative nature of faith. Incarcerated in a prison cell for 27 long years, Mandela delved deep within himself to discover strength and resilience through his unwavering faith in his purpose. His steadfast trust in God fueled his determination to fight for justice and equality, inspiring millions around the world to have faith in the power of forgiveness and the potential for a brighter future.

Faith is not a passive; it is an active force that inspires us to take action, even when faced with daunting odds. With each step we take, faith propels us, reminding us that we are never alone in our struggles. It breathes life into our dreams and helps us confront the fear of failure, assured that God's guidance will lead us toward our destiny.

Conquering the fear of failure through faith is a journey many undertake as they align their beliefs with their actions and perspectives.

Faith encourages trust in a higher purpose, fostering acceptance that failure is not the end but rather a step toward fulfilling our purpose. Yet, Faith is not exclusive to extraordinary circumstances. It is a constant companion for all, guiding decisions, offering solace in difficult times, and fostering an unshakable belief in the goodness of life. Even in mundane moments, faith imbues our lives with meaning, reminding us that every challenge is an opportunity for growth and transformation.

The strength derived from faith is a boundless well within us, accessible to all. It is not limited to a chosen few but a birthright waiting to flourish in our hearts.

So, amid life's storms, remember faith as your anchor, signaling that after the darkest nights, dawn emerges. It assures us of our resilience and inner strength to overcome any obstacle that comes our way.

Let us hold firm to our trust in God and his plans for us; knowing faith gives us the courage to face adversity head-on. May the stories of those who have walked this path inspire us and uplift our spirits. May we embrace an unwavering faith guiding us through challenges, enabling triumph, and fostering wisdom to become our best selves.

In this chapter and book, we embark on new journeys, exploring gratitude's transformative power. Until then, hold on to your faith as your guiding light, leading towards a life of purpose, joy, and unwavering strength against life's challenges.

The Power Of Surrender: Letting Go And Finding Inner Peace

In our life's journey, we often encounter uncertainties and challenges that test our ability to navigate them. We often strive to control every aspect of our lives, thinking it will ensure security and happiness. But what if I told you that surrendering control to God can bring greater peace and fulfillment?

Recognizing the need to relinquish control is the first step towards experiencing the freedom of surrendering to a higher power. It acknowledges our human limitations and life's complexity, making complete control impossible. While humbling, it leads to a deeper understanding of faith's power.

Surrendering control is not a weakness; it is a strength. It takes courage to let go of our need to control every outcome, trust in God's plan, and believe in a greater purpose. Embracing this mindset allows God's guidance into our lives, guiding us through the twists and turns of our journey.

Letting go of control does not mean apathy or inaction. It is not abandoning responsibility but releasing our attachment to specific outcomes. We pursue our goals while surrendering fears, knowing that God's wisdom surpasses our own.

In moments of surrender, our hearts experience beautiful transformation. We feel liberated as the burden lifts. This surrender opens up to divine guidance, leading us on unexpected paths.

Trusting God to guide our paths requires unwavering faith. Even amid chaos, we must believe there is a purpose behind it all. We trust God is aware of our struggles and working for our good, allowing us to surrender confidentially, knowing that we are not alone in this journey.

As you journey through these chapters, I invite you to reflect on your relationship with control. Are there areas where letting go feels difficult? Release those burdens, surrender to God's guidance, and witness the wonders in your life.

Remember, true beauty lies in surrendering, in relinquishing control to a higher power. In this book, I aim to explore practical methods for nurturing trust and strengthening our bond with God, embracing the liberating concept of letting go and anticipating the extraordinary that awaits us. We will also delve deeper into practical strategies for fostering trust and enhancing our relationship with God. Surrendering control is not always simple, especially when we are accustomed to relying solely on our own strength. Yet, with God's guidance, we can learn to release our grip and submit to His will.

I share with those around me the belief that God is closer than we realize; all we need to do is call out to Him through prayers. One way to cultivate trust in God is through prayer and meditation. Prayer and meditation are instrumental in cultivating trust in God. By quieting our minds and seeking His guidance, we open ourselves up to receiving His wisdom and direction. Through prayer, we can express our fears, worries, and desires, knowing that God is listening and ready to lead us. As we engage in this intimate dialogue with Him, we foster a deeper connection and trust, assured that He is always present to listen and provide.

Another practical step in letting go of control is to seek wisdom from others. There are many individuals around you who have faced similar struggles in relinquishing control. It is part of God's plan to bring these individuals into your life to aid you in this aspect of your journey. We are not meant to navigate life alone. Surrounding ourselves with a supportive community of like-minded individuals who share our faith can offer guidance, perspective, and encouragement. Sharing our struggles and fears with trusted friends, mentors, or spiritual leaders can provide fresh insights and bolster our trust in God's plan for our lives.

Moreover, practicing gratitude is vital on this journey of surrendering control. Setting aside time each day to contemplate the blessings and miracles in our lives shifts our focus from what we lack to what we have been given. Gratitude serves as a reminder of God's faithfulness and His constant presence. It nurtures a spirit of trust and contentment, reinforcing the notion that we are not alone and that God is continually working for our good.

As you continue on your journey with God and surrender control, it is crucial to remember that setbacks and challenges are not signs of God's absence or indifference. Instead, they present opportunities for growth and transformation. In these moments, we can choose to lean into our faith, trusting that God is orchestrating every circumstance for our ultimate benefit. While we may not always comprehend the reason behind our trials, through faith, we can find solace in the knowledge that God is guiding us toward a greater purpose.

Throughout my life, I have encountered numerous struggles, many of which left me wondering how I would overcome them. I came to the realization that God is in control. Understanding what that entails and what it feels like was imperative. I knew that if I did not relinquish control of my life to God, the cycle of failures and struggles would persist, leading me into my darker days with no improvement in sight. Acknowledging that I wasn't in control for the longest time, I finally engaged in an honest, open relationship with God. It was a pivotal moment when I felt liberated from my past, sensing the burdens being lifted from my shoulders. Through my journey and relationship with God, I've asked Him to guide me, and He has.

Patience is a virtue we must cultivate in our journey of relinquishing control. To trust in God's guidance necessitates letting go of our own timelines and agendas. Although, we may yearn for immediate answers or solutions, God's timing is always perfect. As we wait with patience and perseverance, we deepen our reliance on Him, confident that He will lead us precisely where we need to be at the right time.

Reflecting on the concept of letting go of control, we recognize that it is an ongoing journey marked by moments of surrender, trust, and growth. Through prayer, seeking wisdom from others, practicing gratitude, understanding setbacks as opportunities, and cultivating patience, we strengthen our connection and relationship with God, inviting Him to illuminate our life's path.

I encourage you to contemplate these practical steps and apply them to your own life. Embrace the transformative power of surrender and trust in God's guidance. As you do, may you experience the peace, fulfillment, and freedom that stems from relinquishing control and allowing God to work wonders in your life. Trust in His plan, knowing that He is by your side every step of the way. Keep the faith, my friends.

Rise Above: Conquering Fear And Doubt With Confidence

When it comes to following God's guidance, fear and doubt often act as significant roadblocks on our journey. We have all experienced moments when uncertainty creeps in, causing us to question our capability to trust in God's plan. These fears and doubts can hinder our progress, preventing us from fully embracing the path set before us.

So, how can we confront these obstacles and strengthen our trust in God's guidance? It begins with recognizing and acknowledging their presence. We must be honest with ourselves and identify the sources of our fears and doubts. Sometimes, they stem from past failures or disappointments, while other times, they arise from the unknown or the fear of stepping outside our comfort zones.

Once identified, it is essential to confront them with courage and faith. Instead of allowing our fears and doubts to paralyze us, we need to press forward, knowing God is with us every step of the way. Just as Moses found strength leading the Israelites out of Egypt, we, too, can find solace in God's guidance through challenging circumstances.

One effective strategy I have found in overcoming fear and doubt is immersing myself in God's word. The Bible is filled with stories of individuals facing fears and doubts, experiencing divine intervention. Studying these stories and reflecting on their lessons provides inspiration and encouragement. Stories like David facing Goliath or Abraham stepping out in faith remind us of God's strength to conquer our doubts and fears.

In addition to scripture, surrounding ourselves with a supportive community of believers is crucial. Sharing fears and doubts with trusted friends and mentors offers perspective and reassurance. Together, we can encourage one another, reminding each other of God's faithfulness and the power of trusting His guidance. Just as the early disciples formed a tight-knit community, we, too, can find strength and courage in the company of fellow believers.

As you grow in Christ Jesus and your relationship with God, you'll begin to notice changes unfolding in your life for the better. Surrounding yourself with a community of believers unveils the commonalities you share with them. Through this community, you'll encounter individuals who have embarked on a similar journey of transitioning away from self-control to surrendering to God's will. You will hear first-hand stories that resonate with your own experience, reaffirming the closeness of God to you.

As we confront our fears and doubts, prayer becomes our anchor. It serves as a direct connection to God, allowing us to pour out our hearts and seek His guidance and reassurance. Through prayer, we discover peace amidst the uncertainty and feel the embrace of our Heavenly Father's love. Sharing our fears and doubts with Him liberates our hearts and breaks the chains that once bound us in struggles.

Therefore, as you embark on this journey of overcoming fears and doubts, remember that trust in God's plan is an ongoing process. It demands strength, courage, and an unwavering commitment to relying on Him. Through this journey, you will find your relationship with God strengthening. Additionally, something remarkable occurs in your life — the relationships you once struggled to maintain are transformed.

Here, we will explore practical strategies to delve deeper into moving past our fears and doubts. Keep an open mind, prepare yourself for all the positive changes about to unfold in your life, and trust in God's plan for you.

Hold firmly to your faith, for there are greater things yet to come. Trust in God's unwavering love, and He will guide you through the storms of uncertainty, leading you to a place of immeasurable peace and joy. Amidst our journey towards overcoming fears and doubts, it is crucial to remember that God's love and guidance are ever-present, even amidst uncertainty. Therefore, take heart and be encouraged, for this chapter and book will equip you with practical strategies to conquer your fears and doubts and deepen your trust in God's guidance.

An effective strategy for overcoming fear and doubt is to nurture a mindset of gratitude. Gratitude possesses the power to redirect our attention from our worries and insecurities toward the blessings and provisions bestowed upon us by God. When we dedicate time to contemplate the goodness of God, our fears and doubts diminish, and we are reminded of His faithfulness in every season of our lives. Therefore, begin each day with a heart brimming with gratitude, and observe how your trust in God's guidance flourishes.

All that I discuss in this chapter and book stems from personal experiences and witnessing God's grace firsthand. From my struggles to encounters with countless others who share similar experiences, I discovered something profound – we all endure similar pain, face identical struggles, and confront real challenges. However, it's through surrendering control of our lives to God and allowing our hearts to embrace hope, strength, and love – both from God and those around us — that we experience an incredible transformation. Allowing God into our lives and fostering a relationship with Him and those we love truly is an extraordinary experience.

Another potent tool for conquering fear and doubt is the practice of meditation and mindfulness. Taking moments to be still, quieting our minds, and listening to the voice of God can offer the clarity and peace necessary to navigate through our fears and doubts. During these moments of tranquil reflection, we welcome God to communicate with us, to soothe our racing thoughts, and to guide our steps. Therefore, seek out a quiet space, breathe deeply, and open your heart to receive the wisdom and peace that God yearns to bestow upon you.

Just as you would welcome fear and doubt into your life, now is the time to relinquish your control and surrender it to God. The underlying principles remain the same; however, instead of inviting chaos, you invite God into the conversation. Invite Him to take away the chaos from your life and replace it with whatever He deems necessary to help you overcome your personal struggles, and rest assured, He will respond.

Moreover, it is essential to recognize that trust in God's guidance is not a solitary journey. Surround yourself with a community of believers who will uplift and encourage you on your path. Seek out individuals who have conquered their own fears and doubts, and let their stories serve as inspiration. Share your struggles and triumphs with one another, for in doing so, you will find strength in the knowledge that you are not alone. Together, in the company of fellow believers, you can overcome any obstacle that stands in your path. It's through this community of believers and followers that you will discover shared experiences and common ground. Open your heart and invite God into your life; it will never be the same for you.

Furthermore, remember that setbacks are an inevitable part of life, but they do not define our journey. When we stumble and falter in our trust in God's guidance, it is crucial to extend grace to ourselves. Our heavenly Father understands our human struggles and loves us unconditionally. So, be gentle with yourself when doubt creeps in, and trust that God's grace will carry you through even your lowest moments.

As we journey through this process and throughout the book, forgiveness will be a recurring theme. It is a crucial aspect to learn and practice, as it enables you to release the burdens that weigh heavy on your heart. Forgiveness may be challenging, but understanding its essence is vital for moving past your struggles and pain. Remember, forgiving yourself is equally important in fostering a relationship with God.

As we progress through this chapter, cling tightly to the assurance that God's love and guidance remain unwavering. Embrace the principles we have discussed: gratitude, meditation, community, and self-compassion. Through these practices, you will not only overcome your fears and doubts but also cultivate an unshakable trust in God's enduring love. As your relationship with God deepens, you will witness positive changes in your relationships with loved ones. Trust me, it will all begin to make sense.

Now, take a deep breath, and with each exhale, release your fears and doubts. Understand that you are capable of achieving great things, for you serve a mighty God who will never abandon you. Trust in His perfect timing, trust in His divine plan, and trust that He will guide you every step of the way. Know with certainty that He is only a whisper away from you.

As you progress on your journey, may your trust in God's guidance deepen, and may you experience the immeasurable peace and joy that result from surrendering your fears and doubts into His loving hands. Keep persevering, for the best is yet to come.

Finding Peace In The Storm: A Guide To Navigating Life's Turbulence

Our lives are journeys filled with ups and downs, unexpected twists and turns that can leave us feeling overwhelmed and helpless. The storms of life can come crashing down upon us, leaving us grasping for a lifeline amidst the chaos. During these challenging times, it is crucial to learn how to rely on God and find peace amid the storms. Often, we may find ourselves in the middle of a storm without even realizing it until it's too late. Trust in God and His plan for you to guide you through these moments should they arise.

Amidst our turmoil, it is easy to lose sight of the fact that we are never alone in our struggles. God accompanies us every step of the way, guiding us through the darkest nights and the fiercest storms. Just as a ship navigates through turbulent waters, we, too, can find our way through life's difficulties by surrendering our fears and placing our trust in God's loving hands.

When confronted with adversity, it is natural to question why such challenges have befallen us. We may wonder if there is a purpose behind our suffering or if God has abandoned us. It is during these moments that we must remind ourselves of God's unfailing love and faithfulness. He promises to be our constant source of strength and guidance, even in the midst of life's fiercest storms.

While I don't dwell on the past, I occasionally revisit it when facing tough times. I reflect on past struggles and wonder, "How did I get through that?" or "How did I survive that attack?" The answer remains the same each time: God.

He led me to it, and He brought me through it. I extend the same assurance to you. If God brought you to it, He will see you through it. You only need to trust Him with that struggle or storm.

Learning to rely on God during your storm requires a conscious decision to let go of our need for control. We must release the grip we have on our own plans and surrender them to His greater purpose. In doing so, we open ourselves up to the peace that surpasses all understanding, enabling us to weather any storm that comes our way.

Finding peace amid life's storms is not a passive endeavor. It requires active participation on our part. We must seek God wholeheartedly, turning to Him in prayer and through His word. By immersing ourselves in His truth, we find the anchor our souls desperately need. God's promises become our refuge, providing comfort and strength in the midst of life's trials.

One of the most powerful ways to find peace during turbulent times is by looking to the example of Jesus Christ. He, too, faced storms while on earth, enduring rejection, betrayal, and even death on the cross. Yet, he never wavered in his trust in God. Instead, he found solace in prayer, seeking His Father's guidance and strength.

Through Jesus' example, we learn that even when the storms of life rage around us, we can find peace by following His lead. Just as Jesus demonstrated unwavering faith in God, we, too, can find the strength to navigate life's storms, knowing that our Heavenly Father is guiding us every step of the way. I reiterate this point throughout this book because having a relationship with God is vital in facing the storms we encounter. We need to learn to entrust the storms to God and trust in His guidance through them.

So, as you face the storms of life, remember to lean on God's unwavering love and guidance. Trust in His promises and seek solace in His presence. Let go of your own plans and surrender to His greater purpose. By doing so, you will find the peace that surpasses all understanding, allowing you to navigate life's storms with unwavering faith.

In the midst of life's chaotic journeys, it is in God that we find our truest peace. As the winds howl and the waves crash around us, let us hold steadfast, knowing that God is our anchor in the storm. Though we may not see the full picture now, we can trust that God has a plan and purpose for every storm we encounter. I encourage you to cling to that hope as we venture through this book, where we will explore the ways in which God's guidance becomes even more evident in the aftermath of life's storms. Remain in faith, for the journey is far from over. In the aftermath of life's storms, we often find ourselves navigating through the remnants of what was once familiar. It is in these moments that we realize the true strength of our faith and the depth of our trust in God. Throughout this book, we'll delve into the ways in which God's guidance becomes even more evident as we emerge from the chaos.

When the storm finally subsides, we may be left feeling battered and bruised, unsure of how to move forward. It is during this time that God's presence becomes all the more palpable. You will just know his presence is near you. He gently whispers words of comfort and reassurance, reminding us that He has not abandoned us. In fact, He has been beside us all along, walking through the storm with us, guiding our every step. Who do you think was battling your storms before? If you think about it, it was God. Only now, you are accepting His plan and giving Him control of your life and storms.

As we gather the broken pieces of our lives, it is crucial to lean on God's unfailing love and guidance even when we feel lost or overwhelmed, He knows the way forward. Surrendering our plans, pains and our anxieties to Him allows space for miracles in our lives. Though the path may not be fully clear, we can trust that God is leading us in the right direction.

In this time of rebuilding, surrounding ourselves with a supportive community is vital. Seeking wisdom and encouragement from fellow believers can provide much-needed strength and perspective. Designed for connection, coming together in adversity allows us to find strength and solace in one other's stories of resilience and faith. Through these shared experiences, we begin to understand and see what resilience and faith truly mean.

Moreover, the lessons gleaned from navigating life's storms are not meant for solitary reflection. They serve as a beacon of hope for those amidst their own tempests. Sharing how we have leaned on God amid chaos offers inspiration to others, fostering growth within our faith and the wider community of believers. It is through extending a helping hand and guiding others away from their struggles that we manifest God's plan for ourselves and those around us.

In the aftermath of a storm, prioritizing healing and self-care is paramount. Enduring challenging times can exact a toll on our physical, emotional, and spiritual well-being. Hence, it is crucial to nurture our bodies, minds, and souls intentionally. Whether through prayer, meditation, physical activity, exercise, or communing with nature, we must engage in activities that replenish our spirits and cultivate inner peace. Restoration becomes our focus post-storm, transforming our struggles and pains into opportunities for personal growth and shared resilience among our community.

It is important to recognize that storms are an inevitable part of life's journey. However, our trust in God can remain steadfast and unwavering amidst the tempests. By leaning on His guidance, finding solace in His presence, and holding on to His promises, we can navigate through any storm that crosses our path.

Remember, you are never alone in this journey; God is with us, guiding us through every storm and leading us to calmer waters. Cling tightly to your faith, knowing that His love is unwavering and His plans for you are goodness. With God as your guide and compass, you can chart a course filled with purpose, peace, and unshakeable faith. As you emerge from life's storm, may you find solace in the knowledge that God's peace, strength, and hope will sustain you through those tough days.

May these words brings you comfort as you navigate life's storms. Embrace the lessons learned, share your experiences, and hold steadfast to the assurance that God will always lead you. For He is the Light that shines brightest in the darkest of nights, guiding you to a place of peace and wholeness.

Walking By Faith: Trusting God's Timing Along Your Journey

Patience, though often challenging, is a virtue that tests our trust in God's plan for our lives. In a world accustomed to instant gratification and immediate results, waiting and trusting in God's perfect timing can feel counterintuitive. Yet, as we traverse life's path, we come to realize that there are moments when patience and faith in God's timing are not only necessary but vital.

As adults, we have encountered countless situations where our impatience led us astray. We yearned for that dream job now, sought that promotion immediately, or longed for that special someone to enter our lives instantly. In such moments, it is easy to overlook the fact that God's plan unfolds with purpose and timing beyond our own desires. It is in these moments of waiting that we must remind ourselves that God's perspective surpasses our limited vision; He knows what's truly best for us. As we grasp the intricacies of God's plan, we gain clarity on our journey and understand why certain events need to unfold. We may even find ourselves reflecting, "If only I had known then what I know now." Yet, dwelling on regrets serves no purpose; instead, we must let them go and trust in the unfolding of God's plan.

Trusting in God's timing demands faith and comprehension. It entails acknowledging that we may not always possess the answers or grasp the bigger picture. Often, we find ourselves in situations where we feel stagnant and uncertain about what lies ahead. Yet, in these moments of ambiguity, we must lean on our faith and trust in the impeccability of God's timing.

The Bible abounds with tales of individuals who grasped the significance of trusting in God's timing. Abraham and Sarah patiently awaited their promised child. Joseph endured years in prison before ascending to the second most powerful position in Egypt. These stories serve as poignant reminders and while God's timing might not align with our own, it is always flawless.

Furthermore, God's timing teaches us valuable lessons and shapes our character. Through waiting, we cultivate patience, perseverance, and humility. We recognize that our plans do not always mirror with God's plans for our lives. By relinquishing our schedules and expectations, we undergo personal evolution and deepen our relationship with God.

Trusting in God's timing also entails relinquishing our fears and doubts. It involves releasing the urge to micromanage every aspect of our lives and embracing the notion that God's timing may encompass periods of waiting and uncertainty. Proverbs 3:5-6 reminds us, "Trust in the Lord with all your heart and lean not on your own understanding; in all your ways submit to him, and he will make your paths straight."

In our fast-paced society, where waiting is often dismissed as unproductive, it is paramount to remember that God's timing is never in vain. Every moment, every delay, and every setback serves a purpose in the grand design that God has for our lives. When we choose to trust in His perfect timing, we find peace and contentment amidst the waiting.

As we journey onward, let us welcome patience and trust in God's timing. Let us surrender our desires and expectations, knowing with full assurance that God discerns what is best for us. Though His timing may elude our comprehension, we can find solace in the assurance that He is in control. By entrusting ourselves to him, we release the burden of controlling every aspect of our lives.

In our ongoing journey of trusting in God's timing, we must learn to foster patience and embrace the waiting. It is in these moments of uncertainty that our faith is tested and our character is shaped.

In a world driven by instant gratification and swift outcomes, waiting often feels alien and exasperating. We are accustomed to dictating terms, making swift decisions, and receiving swift results. Yet, upon realization, we recognize that these were often the days of our fiercest trials. We inhabit an era where everything lies at our fingertips, accessible with a mere click. However, when it comes to God's timing, we must acknowledge His operation on a different timetable.

Like a master painter meticulously layers hues onto a canvas, God intricately weaves the fabric of our lives. He discerns the perfect moment to manifest the fulfillment of His promises. Though we may struggle to understand the delay or endure prolonged seasons of waiting, we can trust in God's covert workings, meticulously orchestrating every detail for our ultimate welfare. It is a time to exercise patience and permit God's plan to unfold.

The waiting period serves as a time of refining our character and strengthening our relationship with God. It's during this season that we learn to lean on Him and find solace in His presence. We discover the beauty of relinquishing our desires and expectations, fully assured that His plans far exceed our own.

It is essential to recognize that God's timing is never wasted. Every delay, setback, and moment of uncertainty plays a role in shaping us. Like a sculptor carefully carving a block of marble, God uses the waiting to shape us and draw us closer to Him. It is in the crucible of waiting that our faith is teste, and our perseverance is strengthened.

Consider the instances when a delay, seemingly inconvenient at the time, led to avoiding a tragic accident or unforeseen danger. These are not mere coincidences but manifestations of God's plan. Trusting in God's timing demands unwavering belief in His goodness and faithfulness. Though doubts and fears may arise during the waiting period, we must surrender them to Him, knowing He sees the bigger picture and has a perfect plan for our lives.

Even when time seems fleeting, and our dreams appear distant. We must grasp the truth that God's timing is impeccable. He is never late; He is always on time. We can have confidence that when He says, "It is time," everything will fall into place beyond our wildest imaginations.

Amidst the waiting, let us encourage one another in steadfast trust in God's timing and His plan. Let us remind ourselves and those around us of His faithfulness to His promises, assuring that our waiting is not in vain but rather part of His greater plan for us.

As we eagerly anticipate the fulfillment of God's promises, let us continue seeking Him, relying solely on Him, and fixing our gaze on His unwavering faithfulness. For in the waiting, we are being prepared for His divine appointments and blessings. And when the time is right, we will rejoice and give thanks for the faithfulness of our God, who guides us with unwavering love and wisdom.

The journey of trusting in God's timing may pose challenges, but it leads us to a deeper understanding of His love and unshakable faith in His perfect plans. So, let us preserve with patience, hope, and an unwavering trust in the One who holds our future in His hands.

The Faithful Journey: Cultivating A Perspective Of Purpose

In our life's journey, understanding the power of positive thinking and its impact on our faith is paramount. Cultivating a perspective imbued with faith enables us to confront challenges and uncertainties with courage and hope, embracing a mindset that trusts in God's goodness and His guiding hand in every step we take.

As adults, we often find ourselves weighed down by life's responsibilities and intricacies. The ceaseless flow of deadlines, expectations, and setbacks can cast a shadow over our faith, leaving us disheartened. However, adopting a faith-filled perspective can serve as a catalyst, reshaping our outlook and bestowing a sense of purpose and confidence.

Positive thinking is not about denying the existence of hardships or feigning perfection. Rather, it is a deliberate choice to focus on possibilities, silver linings, and the reservoir of strength within us. By redirecting our attention towards the positive aspects of life, we unlock the door to a deeper belief in ourselves and in God's providence.

A foundational step in nurturing a faith-filled perspective is through practicing gratitude. By acknowledging and cherishing both the significant and seemingly insignificant blessings in our lives, we cultivate a heart brimming with thankfulness. Gratitude allows us to transcend our circumstances and discern the hand of God actively at work in our lives, fostering a deep-seated trust that His guidance, evident in our past experiences, will continue to lead us into the future.

Additionally, maintaining a belief in the purpose inherent in every season of life is essential for fostering a faith-filled mindset. When confronted with challenges, viewing them as opportunities for personal growth and transformation shifts our perspective from one of resentment or frustration to a mindset characterized by perseverance and hope. Even amidst life's darkest moments, we hold firm to the understanding that God has a meticulously crafted plan and is working all things together for our ultimate good.

Irrespective of one's beliefs, the concept of finding meaning and purpose amid life's trials serves as a potent source of hope and resilience. It inspires people to seek positive outcomes, draw strength from adversity, and extend compassion and support to others. Ultimately, whether or not one adheres to the belief in divine intervention, the conviction that life's challenges hold inherent significance can serve as a guiding principle for navigating life's complexities.

Moreover, a faith-filled perspective beckons us to surrender our fears and worries to God's care. It serves as a poignant reminder that we need not bear life's burdens alone. As we surrender our anxieties, we create room for God's peace to permeate our beings—a peace that transcends human understanding, affirming our steadfast embrace by a loving and faithful God.

Throughout the annals of history, numerous individuals have exemplified the transformative power of a faith-filled perspective. Confronted with seemingly insurmountable odds and challenges, their unwavering trust in God's guidance propelled them to extraordinary achievements. Their narrative stands as beacons of inspiration, instilling within us the courage to develop our own faith-filled mindset.

Yet, in our quest to nurture such a faith-filled perspective, we may grapple with doubt, uncertainty, and moments of weakness. However, it is precisely in these junctures that our faith in God is tested and refined. We must continually reaffirm our trust in His timing, His provision, and His purpose for our lives. With each stride forward, our faith deepens as we recognize that our challenges serve as opportunities for God to demonstrate His unwavering faithfulness.

As we delve deeper into the potency of positive thinking and a faith-filled mindset, let us remain anchored in the assurance of God's unwavering love and guidance. His promises stand steadfast, and by nurturing this perspective, we position ourselves up to encounter His goodness in extraordinary ways.

Therefore, let us embrace this journey, allowing the foundation of a faith-filled mindset to underpin a life brimming with hope, courage, and trust. With our faith firmly rooted, we embark on a path of discovery and growth, prepared to confront the challenges that await us. As we progress through this book, we delve deeper into the practices that fortify our faith and draw us nearer to God.

Central to cultivating a faith-filled perspective is the transformative power of prayer. Far beyond a mere religious ritual or a monologue, prayer embodies a sacred conversation with our Heavenly Father. It is about fostering a deep relationship with God and approaching Him in our moments of need and vulnerability. Prayer enables us to pour out our hearts, express gratitude, seek divine guidance, and find solace in His presence. Through establishing a consistent prayer life, we create a space for God to communicate His will and reveal His plans for our lives. It is through prayer that our relationship with Him flourishes, fostering trust and intimacy.

In moments of jubilation or sorrow, ambiguity or clarity, turning to God in prayer and entrusting Him serves as an unwavering anchor amidst life's turbulent seas. It transcends mere utterances, fostering a deep and profound connection with the divine and affirming our unwavering belief in His boundless love and omniscience. Prayer emerges as a powerful way to deepen our faith and trust in God's unwavering guidance and wisdom. It provides a platform to express our hopes, fears, and gratitude while seeking solace and divine direction.

Furthermore, immersing ourselves in a community of believers significantly enriches our journey of faith. We are not meant to traverse this life in isolation; rather, God intricately designed us for fellowship and companionship. Engaging with kindred spirits who share our beliefs provides a reservoir of encouragement, accountability, and solidarity. Together, we uplift, challenge, and inspire one another, nurturing an environment that fosters a faith-filled perspective.

Another aspect of cultivating a faith-filled mindset involves intentionally saturating our minds with truth. In a world filled with negativity, doubt, and distractions, safeguarding our thoughts becomes imperative. By delving into the words of God, we equip ourselves with the reservoir of knowledge and wisdom necessary to navigate life's challenges. Through daily study and meditation on God's word, we allow His eternal truth to shape our perspectives, transforming our minds and revitalizing our spirits. As we steep ourselves in His promises and teachings, we discover the strength and confidence to confront any obstacle that crosses our path.

Furthermore, a faith-filled perspective draws its strength from a profound comprehension of God's character. Understanding His unchanging nature, unwavering faithfulness, and boundless love, we find solace in the knowledge that He continually works for our benefit. We acknowledge that His ways often diverge from our own, and His response may not always align with our expectations. Yet, in entrusting ourselves to God's plans and purpose, we unearth a tranquility that transcends uncertainty. By aligning our hearts with His, we understand the constancy of His guidance and provision, recognizing His orchestration of all things for our ultimate welfare.

Embracing a faith-filled perspective entails deliberate practices that shape our hearts, minds, and interactions with God and others. Through prayer, community, immersion in God's word, and a profound understanding of His character, we fortify our faith and embark on the journey with unwavering confidence and courage.

I fervently pray that you continue embracing a faith-filled mindset, allowing its transformative influence to permeate every aspect of your life. Amidst the complexities and uncertainties of this world, may you find solace and strength in the steadfast love and guidance of our Heavenly Father. Place your trust in Him, for His plans transcend our comprehension, and His faithfulness knows no bounds. Let your faith shine as a beacon of hope and inspiration to those in your midst. Persist on this journey of nurturing a faith-filled perspective, assured that God walks beside you every step of the way.

Finding Peace In Surrender: Trusting God's Will

Surrendering to God's will is not always an easy task. It demands trust, humility, and a profound acknowledgment that His plans eclipse our own. Yet, when we relinquish ourselves to His guidance, extraordinary transformations unfold. We tap into a wellspring of wisdom and resilience that surpasses our finite perspectives. Comfort envelops us as we recognize that we are not alone in navigating life's challenges; God accompanies us unwaveringly, through every twist and turn.

In a world where self-reliance and control are often celebrated, the concept of surrender may appear paradoxical. Society ingrains in us the notion that success and fulfillment stem solely from our own efforts as if we hold the reins of our destinies. However, the truth is that we are merely vessels in God's grand plan. Surrendering to His will entails recognizing Him as the true architect of our lives and acknowledging His omniscience even when our own vision falters.

In surrender, we relinquish the burden of navigating life's complexities independently. We liberate ourselves from the ceaseless striving and fretting, opting instead to place our faith in God's divine guidance. Far from a mark of fragility, surrender embodies an emblem of strength—a testament to our acknowledgment that we are not designed to shoulder the world's burdens alone. Rather, we are called to lean on God for support and direction.

Moreover, surrendering paves the path for a deeper communion with God. When we relinquish control and allow Him to guide our decisions, we invite His divine presence to permeate every facet of our existence. We metamorphose into co-creators with Him, partnering in the unfolding of His divine plan. With each surrendered stride, we draw nearer to aligning our lives with His intended purpose.

It is crucial to understand that surrendering is not synonymous with passive resignation; it is not about abandoning our dreams or ambitions. Instead, surrender entails aligning our desires with God's will, seeking His guidance, and allowing Him to shape our path. It means being open to His redirection, trusting that His plans surpass our own, even if they differ from our initial intentions.

As we surrender to God's will, we relinquish control, but in return, we gain so much more. We discover a profound peace that transcends understanding, experiencing a sense of freedom in the knowledge that we are not alone in life's journey. Through surrender, we find strength in vulnerability and hope in adversity, fostering a deep and unwavering trust in God's faithfulness.

Therefore, as we persist on this journey of surrendering to God's will, let us recognize it as a daily commitment rather than a one-time decision. It is an ongoing process of letting go, trusting, and seeking His guidance in every aspect of our lives. And in this surrender, may we find the courage to embrace the unknown, assured that God's plans for us exceeds our imagination.

In the subsequent chapters, we will delve deeper into practical steps to surrendering to God's will and allowing Him to direct our decisions. It is not a one-time resolution but a daily practice demanding intentionality and dedication.

One vital aspect of surrendering to God's will is cultivating a posture of humility. Acknowledging our limited understanding enables us to release our agendas and be receptive to God's divine wisdom, making room for His voice amidst life's clamor.

Prayer serves as a vital tool in surrendering to God's will. Consistent prayers invites God into our decision-making process, aligning our desires with His guidance. By praying for His will to be done, we create space for His intervention and align our lives with His plans.

Scripture plays a significant role in surrendering to God's will. Immersing ourselves in the Bible offers insight into God's character, promises, and desires for us. This equips us to discern His will and align our decisions with His truth.

Moreover, surrendering often entails stepping out in faith and embracing paths diverging from our desires or societal norms. Yet, trusting in God's faithfulness and obeying His purposes lead to the abundant life He promises, witnessing His provision and guidance along the journey.

However, surrendering does not imply passivity; it involves active partnership with God in His work. It is about surrendering our will and desires while actively pursuing His purposes, which may involve seizing new opportunities, making tough decisions, or relinquishing what no longer serves His plan.

Community is another important aspect of surrendering. Surrounding ourselves with believers sharing a similar commitment to surrendering to God's will provides support, encouragement, and accountability, reminding us that we are not alone in this journey.

Finally, surrendering entails letting go of our timelines and trusting in His perfect timing. Though we often crave immediate answers and results, God's ways surpass ours. Surrendering control and embracing His timing allows us to experience the fullness of His plans for us.

In our surrendering practice, let us remember it is a lifelong journey. Each day presents new opportunities to surrender and trust in His guidance, inviting God to mold us into His intended beings and discovering the abundance of life aligned with His will.

May you find the courage and strength to surrender to God's will daily, knowing His plans for you surpass imagination. Embrace the peace, freedom, and fulfillment from surrendering to His guidance, trusting in His faithfulness. May you be encouraged on this surrendering journey, assured of God's constant presence every step of the way.

Peace In The Storm: Trusting God's Presence Amid Uncertainty

In life, we often encounter uncertainty and the unknown, which can be daunting, leaving us feeling lost and fearful. However, amidst the chaos, we must remember that we are not alone. Trusting God's guidance can provide solace and direction in navigating these challenging times.

Trusting in God does not guarantee immediate answers or a journey free from obstacles. On the contrary, uncertainty tests our faith, revealing its depth and strength. It is a humbling experience that requires acknowledging our limitations as human beings.

Acknowledging our limitations is a critical aspect of trusting God amidst uncertainty. As humans, we often crave control and predictability, desiring to know the outcome of every decision we make. However, life does not always unfold according to our plans.

In times of uncertainty, surrendering our need for control becomes essential. Embracing humility and accepting our limitations allow us to recognize that God's ways surpass our understanding. It is through this surrender that we can find peace amidst chaos and trust in the divine guidance always available to us.

Trusting God also entails releasing our grip on fear. Fear, a powerful emotion, can paralyze us, hindering our progress. While feeling afraid in uncertain times is natural, we must not let fear dictate our actions and decisions. Instead, we can nurture trust in God's goodness and faithfulness.

Amidst uncertainty, we find solace in knowing that God is ever-present. He remains our steadfast companion, guiding us even through the darkest moments. By entrusting ourselves to Him, we welcome His wisdom and direction into our lives.

Furthermore, trusting God demands patience. Often, we seek immediate answers and swift resolutions. However, God's timing does not always align with ours. His plans unfold gradually, sometimes in mysterious ways. In such times, we must patiently await, anchoring by unwavering faith in His perfect timing.

Trusting God amidst uncertainty is not easy, but it is a journey worth undertaking. It necessitates surrendering control, relinquishing fear, and exercise patience. It is in these acts of surrender that we discover a peace that transcends all understanding.

As we further explore this topic, we will delve into practical steps for strengthening our trust in God during uncertain times. We will uncover stories of individuals who, despite immense uncertainty found solace and guidance through unwavering faith. In the following pages, we will learn how to trust in God's divine guidance, even amidst profound uncertainty.

It is crucial to recognize that trust is not a one-time decision but a continuous process—a daily commitment to rely on God's guidance and surrender our worries and fears to him. Here, we will explore practical steps to reinforce our trust in God amidst uncertainty.

First and foremost, prayer serves as an invaluable tool in strengthening our trust in God. Through establishing a consistent and genuine prayer life, we create a direct line of communication with our Heavenly Father. In prayer, we have the opportunity to pour out our anxieties, seek His guidance, and listen for His gentle voice in the amidst life's distractions.

God graciously welcomes us to bring all our worries and concerns before Him; in doing so, we humbly acknowledge our reliance on His wisdom and power. As we engage in prayer, we can earnestly ask for His guidance, clarity, and peace, knowing that every word we utter is heard by Him. Through the practice of prayer, we align our hearts with God's will, fostering a deep trust in His unwavering love and sovereignty.

Another practical step in nurturing trust in God amidst uncertainty is immersing ourselves in His word. The Bible serves as a treasure trove of wisdom, comfort, and guidance. Through scripture, God reveals His character and His promises to us. As we devote time to reading and reflecting on His word, we find solace in His faithfulness and deepen our understanding of His loving nature.

During times of uncertainty, anchoring ourselves in the unchanging truth of scripture is vital. By saturating our minds and hearts with its wisdom, we gain a fresh perspective on our circumstances. Scripture serves as a reminder of God's provision, His faithfulness in the past, and His promises for the future. This knowledge forms a firm foundation for our trust in Him, even amidst the most uncertain times.

Additionally, seeking support from fellow believers can prove immensely beneficial. Surrounding ourselves with a community of like-minded individuals who comprehend the journey of entrusting God amidst uncertainty can provide encouragement and solidarity. Sharing our struggles, doubts, and victories with others can serve as a reminder to us that we are not journeying alone.

Through fellowship, we have the opportunity to glean wisdom from those who have weathered storms of uncertainty and emerged stronger in their faith. Their stories serve as beacons of hope, reinforcing the truth of God's faithfulness and His ability to guide us through any trial or tribulation.

Finally, maintaining an attitude of gratitude can profoundly transform our perspective amidst uncertainty. Gratitude redirects our focus from what we lack to acknowledging the blessings and goodness of God in our lives. Cultivating a thankful heart enables us to recognize God's presence and provision, even amidst the unknown.

When we intentionally seek out and appreciate God's faithfulness, both in the past and present, our trust in Him deepens. Gratitude serves as a reminder of His unwavering love, constant guidance, and perfect timing. It fills our hearts with peace and joy, even when circumstances remain uncertain.

Trusting God amidst uncertainty demands active nurturing and strengthening of our faith. Through prayer, immersing ourselves in His word, seeking support from fellow believers, and cultivating gratitude, we can reinforce our trust in God's guidance and provision.

As we embark on this journey of trust, let us remember that we are never alone. God accompanies us every step of the way, guiding us through the turbulent seas of uncertainty and leading us toward a future brimming with hope and purpose. So, let us persist in trusting, allowing God to lead us with unwavering faith on this beautiful adventure we call life.

The Power Of Trust: Embracing Faith In Action

In life's journey, numerous uncertainties often lead us to doubt ourselves, question our decisions, and ponder our direction. Yet, it precisely during these uncertain moments that our trust in God's guidance and our unwavering faith become paramount. Through trust and faith, we discover the strength, tranquility, and bravery to navigate life's twists and turns with unwavering resolve.

Living a life grounded in trust in God's guidance entails surrendering our doubts and fears and entrusting ourselves to a higher authority. It involves acknowledging that we cannot control every outcome and understanding that God's plans for us may diverge from our own. This act of surrender is not a display of weakness but rather a demonstration of strength, acknowledging a greater wisdom beyond our limited understanding.

When we place our trust in God, we align ourselves with His divine plan for our lives. We gain a sense of purpose and direction that empowers us to take risks, step out of our comfort zones, and embrace the unknown. No longer constrained by the limitations of our own thinking, we are driven forward by the belief that God will lead us toward our true and fullest potential.

Furthermore, nurturing a life of trust and faith involves cultivating a deep and intimate relationship with God. Through our ongoing connection with Him, characterized by prayer, meditation, and reflection, we open ourselves to His presence and guidance. In these moments of communion, we find solace, clarity, and the assurance that we are not alone in our struggles.

Understanding that God accompanies us in our challenges is paramount. This realization underscores the idea that during difficult times, individuals can find solace in their faith, trusting in a higher power's presence and provision of support, guidance, and strength. Such belief offers comfort and hope, empowering people to persevere through adversity with the conviction that they are not abandoned. It reflects a profound trust in divine providence and the belief that challenges can lead to personal growth and spiritual transformation.

However, it is essential to recognize that trust and faith are not passive states. They demand action on our part. Trusting in God entails actively seeking His will and being prepared to follow the path He lays before us, even when it appears daunting or unfamiliar. It involves embracing the lessons and opportunities presented to us and acknowledging that they are integral parts of the overarching plan unfolding in our lives.

Living a life imbued with trust and faith entails anchoring ourselves in gratitude. By expressing appreciation for the blessings we receive, whether grand or mundane, we nurture a spirit of contentment and thankfulness. This attitude of gratitude enables us to discern the presence of God in everyday occurrences, instilling within us a profound sense of awe and wonder.

As we traverse the journey of life, trust and faith emerge as steadfast anchors amidst tumultuous storms. They furnish us with the resilience and strength to confront adversity head-on and to overcome any obstacles that confront us. When we wholeheartedly entrust ourselves to God's guidance and embrace unwavering faith, we tap into a wellspring of boundless power and grace that sustains us through the deepest valleys and propels us to the highest peaks.

I encourage you to pause and contemplate your own journey. Are you leading a life characterized by trust and faith? Are you relinquishing your doubts and fears to a higher authority? Trust that God is guiding you, even in moments of uncertainty. Have faith that He has chartered a course for you, one that is filled with purpose and joy. Embrace this existence of trust and faith, and you will embark on a transformative journey that unveils the extraordinary miracles that await you.

In our pursuit of a life grounded in trust and faith, we must acknowledge that challenges and trials are inevitable. These moments serve as litmus tests for our conviction and commitment to maintaining steadfast trust in God's guidance. As we persist in seeking His will, let us also remember the importance of perseverance and resilience.

Amid adversity, it is natural for doubt and fear to surface, tempting us to question the very foundation of our trust. Yet, it is precisely in these moments that we must steadfastly cling even to our faith, assured that God has promised never to abandon us. We must remember that His plans for us transcend any obstacle we encounter.

In times of uncertainty, the temptation to take matters into our own hands often looms large, enticing us with promises of quick solutions and temporary relief. However, I urge you to resist this temptation. Instead, take a moment and reflect on past instances where you witnessed the guiding hand of God and experienced His miraculous interventions in your life. Trust that He will continue to work wonders, even amidst your current struggles.

During moments of doubt, find solace in prayer and meditation. Turn to God's presence, knowing that He listens attentively to your every cry, understands your every need, and collects each tear you shed. Allow His words of comfort and wisdom to envelop you, rejuvenating your spirit and soothing your weary heart.

Living a life characterized by trust and faith also entails embracing a spirit of surrender. It involves relinquishing our desire for control and placing our complete trust in the belief that God's plans far surpass our own limited imaginations. Surrendering to God necessitates releasing our personal agendas and wholeheartedly submitting to His guidance, even when it diverges from our own desires.

As we progress on this transformative journey, it is vital to recognize that trust and faith are not one-time decisions but rather ongoing practices. Each day presents us with the opportunity to strengthen our trust in God and to delve deeper into our faith in His goodness. Through this daily commitment, we will gradually witness the myriad blessings and miracles unfolding before us.

Do not allow setbacks or delays to discourage you, for often, they are orchestrated by a divine hand for our growth and learning. Trust in the perfection of God's timing. Knowing that His plan for you is intricately woven together with purpose and intention.

Living a life of trust and faith is undoubtedly challenging, yet immensely rewarding. It necessitates a steadfast commitment to surrender our doubts, fears, and desires to a higher power. Root yourself in gratitude and actively seek God's will in every aspect of your life.

I encourage you to persist in embracing this life of trust and faith. Surrender your doubts and fears, confident that God is guiding you through every twist and turn. Remain steadfast in your commitment to follow His path, even when it feels unfamiliar or daunting. Above all, recognize the power of a life fully surrendered to God's guidance and sustained by unwavering faith.

In the embrace of trust and faith, you will discover a life filled with purpose, joy, and incredible miracles. Trust in God's guidance as you embark on this transformative journey with confidence and hope.

Trusting in God's plan requires a profound shift in how we perceive life's circumstances. It entails intentionally redirecting our focus away from human impulses of control, worry, and temporal thinking towards an outlook anchored in divine confidence, peace, and an eternal perspective.

While the decision to trust is ours to make, the ability to genuinely do so is a grace bestowed upon us by our benevolent Father. It is a supernatural work that enables us to see present realities through the transcendent lens of God's boundless wisdom and sovereignty.

Fully embracing this way of life involves a transformation from fear to faith, from striving to surrender, and from darkness to light. Yet, it is a journey of progress, not perfection. Even the most steadfast believers may encounter seasons where their trust is shaken by doubts, suffering, or unanswered prayers. In those moments, we must choose to be still and know that He is God (Psalm 46:10). We find solace in His unfailing love, trusting in His good heart, and clinging to the promises of His unchanging Word and character. The God who authored this intricately designed universe can certainly be trusted with every detail of our lives.

So may we have the courage to walk by faith and not by sight (2 Corinthians 5:7). May we fully embrace the profound truth that our sovereign God has ordained every step of our journey according to His higher wisdom and divine purposes - orchestrating all things for His ultimate glory and our supreme good.

As we surrender to this way of living, we unlock profound peace, unyielding hope, and the exhilarating adventure of resting in the perfect plan of our Heavenly Father. Indeed, the path is abundantly blessed for those who place their unwavering trust in the Lord.

CHAPTER 2
"Embracing the Way, the Truth, and the Life"

The Journey Within: Exploring The Depths Of Meaning

Deep within every human heart lies a longing for purpose and significance. We all yearn to unravel the mystery of our existence, to find our rightful place in this vast universe. From ancient philosophers pondering the meaning of life to modern seekers searching for answers, this timeless pursuit has captivated the minds and souls of countless generations.

We embark on a journey, a quest to unravel the enigma of our lives and unearth fulfillment. We crave validation, seeking assurance that our actions and endeavors transcend mere survival. Yet, amidst the complexities and uncertainties of the world, how do we discover a path that leads us to the true essence of our existence?

It our quest for meaning, Jesus offers a profound solution. His teachings resonate deeply with the human soul, providing timeless wisdom that reverberates through the ages. Jesus, often hailed as the Way, the Truth, and the Life, beckons us to embark on a journey that transcends earthly desires and pursuits.

The world often dictates that happiness is found in accomplishments, wealth, or external validation. We tirelessly chase success, hoping that it will fill the void within, only to find it leaves us feeling empty. Despite accumulating wealth, gaining recognition, and fulfilling worldly desires, a sense of emptiness remains. It is in these moments of disillusionment that we come face to face with the limitations of our human striving.

Jesus presents a different perspective, challenging our preconceptions and urging us to delve into the depths of our true purpose. He teaches that the search for meaning must commence with an inner transformation, independent of external circumstances. It is in the profound connection with Jesus, in knowing and being known by Him, that we unearth our ultimate purpose.

Through His life and teachings, Jesus illuminates the importance of love, compassion, and selflessness. He exemplifies a life propelled by mission and purpose, demonstrating that true significance comes from serving others and aligning with the divine. In Him, we encounter the perfect example of purpose, the example of a life brimming with meaning.

Jesus walked the path of self-sacrifice, pouring out boundless love and compassion for humanity. His life serves as a roadmap for finding meaning and fulfillment in our own journey. As we meditate on the teachings of Jesus, and delve into their depths, we begin to peel aways the layers of our own desires and ambitions. We are beckoned to let go of our self-centered pursuits and embrace a higher purpose.

In aligning ourselves with Jesus, we access a wellspring of significance that surpasses the transient trends of the world. This innate quest for purpose and significance finds its ultimate fulfillment in the person of Jesus. As we rediscover ourselves with His teachings and follow in His footsteps, we uncover a truth that resonates deeply within our souls.

Here, we embark on journey into the human quest for meaning and significance, laying the groundwork for a profound exploration of Jesus' transformative message. Subsequently, we delve into the tangible ways in which

Jesus illuminates a path to fulfillment and purpose. Stay steadfast in faith as we embark on this extraordinary journey, poised to challenge your perspectives, ignite your spirit, and lead you to encounter Jesus in a truly transformative way.

During His earthly sojourn, Jesus not only imparted words of wisdom and truth but also exemplified the depth and beauty of his teachings through His actions. Each of His deeds and interactions pointed toward a higher calling, one rooted in love, compassion, and selflessness. In Jesus, we witness the embodiment of a life fully embraced, offering a roadmap for discovering meaning and fulfillment in our own existence.

Jesus emphasized that true significance comes from serving others and aligning ourselves with the divine. He illustrated the importance of self-sacrifice, pouring out boundless love and compassion for all humanity. Through His life, He underscored that the essence of purpose lies in dedicating ourselves to a cause greater than our individual selves.

As we reflect on the extraordinary life of Jesus, we are prompted to peel back the layers of our own desires and ambitions. We are called to let go our self-centered pursuits and embrace a higher calling. Jesus urges us to relinquish our selfishness and embark on a journey characterized by selflessness and love.

This transformation is not instantaneous; it necessitates change of heart, a surrender of our own will to the divine will. By aligning ourselves with Jesus, we access a wellspring of significance that surpasses the transient trends of the world. It is through this alignment that we find discover true fulfillment and purpose.

Jesus extends an invitation for us to lead lives marked by intentionality and purpose, guiding us to make decisions that mirror His love and compassion. From the simplest acts of kindness to the grand gestures of sacrifices, every action becomes an opportunity to infuse meaning and significance into the world around us.

When we emulate Jesus's love and service, we become conduits of divine compassion in a fractured world. Our existence takes on renewed significance and direction as we collaborate with Him to foster healing, restoration, and transformation wherever we tread.

Rediscovering Jesus transcends mere intellectual pursuit or the accumulation of knowledge. It beckons us to embark on an extraordinary journey of self-discovery and personal transformation. Jesus extends this invitation with an open heart, inviting us to surrender ourselves to His guidance.

As we delve deeper into the teachings of Jesus and emulate His footsteps, we will uncover a truth that resonates deeply within us. We will bear witness to the transformative power of His love and experience the profound impact that a life lived in His service can have on the world around us.

As you immerse yourself in the chapters outlined in this book, I urge you to open your heart and mind to the possibilities that await. Allow Jesus to speak to you in moments of quiet reflection, to challenge your thoughts and actions, and to lead you on a journey of rediscovering your true purpose and significance.

Prepare yourself for your perceptions to be challenged and your spirit to be ignited. The path ahead may not always be smooth, but it is a journey worth embarking upon. For in the search for meaning and fulfillment, we uncover the ultimate truth: that Jesus is the Way, the Truth, and the Life, and in Him, we find the essence of our existence.

Journey Through Faith: A Story Of Jesus Christ

Throughout history, countless remarkable individuals have left an enduring legacy on the world. Their deeds, teachings, and legacies have resonated across generations, shaping the trajectory of human civilization. Among these towering figures, few can rival the enduring impact of Jesus Christ. The historical evidence supporting His existence and the profound imprint He left on humanity is nothing short of astonishing.

Upon scrutinizing the historical records, it becomes evident that Jesus Christ was not merely a mythical or fictional character. Rather, He was a real person who lived during the 1st century AD in the ancient region of Judea. The existence of Jesus is corroborated not only in biblical accounts but also in a wealth of external sources.

In exploring historical evidence, we encounter the Jewish historian Flavius Josephus, a contemporary of Jesus. Josephus mentions Jesus twice in his works, portraying Him as a wise teacher who performed remarkable deeds, garnered a significant following, and was unjustly crucified under the reign of Pontius Pilate. This historical account provides valuable insights attesting to Jesus' existence and the profound impact He had on His disciples and the wider community.

Furthermore, Roman historians like Tacitus and Suetonius also make references to Jesus Christ, corroborating key aspects of His life, including His crucifixion and the emergence of a religious movement following His death. These non-Christian sources enhance the credibility of Jesus' historical existence, affirming His significance as a figure in ancient times.

The influence of Jesus on the world is profound and enduring. His teachings and principles have shaped the moral and ethical framework of Western civilization for more than two thousand years. From the idea of love, forgiveness, and compassion to the principles of justice, equality, and charity, Jesus' message continues to inspire millions across the globe.

The growth and spread of Christianity, from its humble beginnings with a small group of followers to becoming the world's largest religion, underscore the profound impact of Jesus' life and teachings. The enduring legacy of Christianity has left an unmistakable imprint on art, literature, politics, education, and even the legal systems of numerous nations, shaping human history in profound ways.

Furthermore, the influence of Jesus transcends religious boundaries. He championed the cause of the marginalized, confronted hypocrisy and discrimination, and advocated for the equal dignity of all individuals. His radical teachings challenged prevailing societal norms, sparking numerous movements for justice and human rights over the centuries.

As we explore the life and impact of Jesus Christ more deeply, we come to grasp the magnitude of his historical importance. Beyond his religious significance, the evidence firmly establishes him as a pivotal historical figure whose teachings and deeds have left an enduring mark on the world we inhabit today.

Here, we will delve into the transformative influence of Jesus' teachings and the lasting legacy he bestowed upon humanity. From exploring his message of love and redemption to tracing the establishment of Christianity as a worldwide faith, we will unravel the remarkable story of Jesus and its enduring relevance in our modern world.

The journey into the life of Jesus Christ is just beginning, promising revelations that will captivate and inspire you. Here, we embark on our exploration, poised to uncover the depths of historical evidence and the enduring impact of this extraordinary figure. We delve deeper into the transformative influence of Jesus' teachings and the lasting legacy He left behind. As we further explore His message of love and redemption, we reveal the remarkable story of Jesus and its ongoing relevance in our modern world.

Jesus' teachings revolved around the radical concept of love, challenging the prevailing norms of His time. He advocated for love not only toward family and friends but also toward strangers, enemies, and the marginalized. His message emphasizes compassion, forgiveness, and acceptance of all individuals, regardless of their background or circumstances. Through His actions, Jesus demonstrated that love knows no bounds, extending even to outcasts and sinners, as seen in his interactions with tax collectors and his outreach to the oppressed and downtrodden.

This radical concept of love continues to resonate with millions today, transcending religious boundaries and inspiring countless individuals and organizations to engage in acts of kindness, charity, and social justice. Jesus' teachings have influenced movements for equality, human rights, and compassionate practices, shaping a better world for generations to come.

Moreover, Jesus' legacy is intricately intertwined with the establishment and growth of Christianity as a global faith. From a small group of disciples, His message spread rapidly, igniting hearts and minds across diverse cultures. Despite facing persecution and oppression, early Christian communities remained steadfast in their belief in Jesus' teachings. These early followers bore witness to His life, death, and resurrection, and their unwavering conviction in His message laid the foundation for the Church.

Over the centuries, the Church emerged as a formidable influence, shaping the moral, social, and political landscapes of societies. Christianity is intricately intertwined with diverse cultures, influencing and being influenced by them, thereby leaving an indelible mark on history. It became a cornerstone of education, art, science, and literature, perpetuating values of compassion, service, and the pursuit of truth.

Despite the criticisms and challenges Christianity has weathered throughout history, Jesus' teachings persist in inspiring and comforting countless individuals. His words, miracles, and exemplary life continue to serve as a beacon of hope, guidance, and transformation to millions of believers worldwide.

The transformative influence of Jesus' teachings transcends time and place, remaining as pertinent today as they were two thousand years ago. In a world rife with conflict, division, and suffering, Jesus' message of love impels us to pursue reconciliation, understanding, and empathy. It compels us to confront injustice, oppression, and inequality, urging us to champion the cause of the marginalized, to feed the hungry, and to care for the sick.

As we contemplate Jesus' historical importance and His enduring impact on the world, we are reminded that His story is not merely a relic of the past but a living testament that beckons us toward a brighter tomorrow. It calls upon us to embrace the values He espoused - love, compassion, forgiveness, and justice - and to embody them in our daily endeavors.

So, let's embark on this journey together, delving into the profound teachings of Jesus Christ with a shared aim to understand, internalize, and embody them. Through this exploration, we can uncover the transformative power of love and its immense impact on our lives and the world around us. The story of Jesus is timeless, and its lessons will endure, guiding us as we navigate life's complexities and endeavor to make a positive difference.

The Way, The Truth, And The Life: Understanding Jesus' Teachings

Embark on a journey into the profound wisdom and timeless teachings of Jesus as recorded in the Gospels. As we delve into His teaching, let us open ourselves to a transformative experience that challenges our perspectives and enriches our hearts with deeper understanding.

Jesus, often hailed as one of history's most influential figures, has left behind a legacy of teachings that continue to resonate with people today. His words, spoken over two thousand years ago, still reverberate with profound relevance, offering timeless guidance for navigating the complexities of life.

Central to Jesus' teachings is the theme of love. He imparted a message of love that transcended societal norms, urging for a radical transformation of hearts. Jesus advocated for a love that extended beyond the confines of familial bonds to encompass neighbors, strangers, and even adversaries. He challenged us to embrace unconditional love, mirroring the divine love upon us.

Forgiveness also held a prominent place in Jesus' teachings. In a world often characterized by grudges and revenge, He taught that forgiveness is a path to healing and liberation. Jesus' teachings on forgiveness encouraged individuals to relinquish the weight of resentment in favor of reconciliation. Through his own actions, Jesus exemplified the transformative nature of forgiveness, extending it even to those who crucified Him.

Another profound teaching of Jesus centered on the concept of humility. In a culture that esteemed pride and self-promotion, Jesus elevated humility as a virtue. He exemplified this by humbly washing the feet of his disciples, a task typically reserved for servants. Jesus urged his followers to regard others as more significant than themselves and to live lives marked by selflessly.

Jesus' teachings also emphasized the importance of compassion and empathy. Renowned for his ability to perceive beyond appearances, he reached out to the marginalized and forgotten. Through his parables, Jesus conveyed messages of compassion towards the poor, the sick, and the outcasts. He called upon his followers to extend a helping hand, demonstrating compassion towards those in need.

Beyond these foundational teachings, Jesus addressed a myriad of subjects, ranging from wealth and possessions to faith and prayer. His teachings disrupted societal norms, presenting a radical departure from the status quo. Jesus underscored the importance of a heart-transformed heart by a genuine connection with God, emphasizing authentic spiritual engagement over mere adherence to religious rituals and traditions.

In contemplating Jesus' teachings, we encounter timeless truths that resonate with the core of our being. His words persist in challenging and motivating us, prompting a life characterized by love, forgiveness, humility, and compassion.

In the first half of this chapter, we have merely skimmed the surface of Jesus' teachings. His teachings beckon us to embark on a transformative journey, one that can lead us to the abundant life he promised. Let us embrace these teachings with open hearts and minds, poised to uncover the profound truths that await us. Here, we delve deeper into the specific teachings of Jesus, exploring their implications for our lives today. As we progress on our journey, let us open ourselves to these profound truths that possess the power to inwardly transform us.

Among the teachings emphasized by Jesus was the importance of faith. He urged His followers to place their trust in God's provision and to maintain unwavering faith, even amidst adversity. Jesus employed vivid imagery to depict faith capable of moving mountains, reminding us that with faith, all things are achievable. Through His teachings, Jesus invites us to nurture a profound trust in God, knowing that He is ever-present, guiding, and providing for us.

Jesus also cautioned against the dangers of materialism and the relentless pursuit of worldly possessions. He warned against the allure of wealth, recognizing its potential to corrupt our hearts and divert us from what truly matters. Instead, Jesus implored us to prioritize eternal treasures and to invest in the kingdom of God. His teachings serve as a poignant reminder that true wealth resides in the richness of our relationships, in acts of kindness and generosity, and in the eternal promises of God.

Additionally, Jesus imparted a profound teaching on the importance of living harmoniously with one another. He underscored the value of unity, urging us to resolve conflicts, reconcile disputes, and actively seek peace in our relationships. Jesus emphasized our role as peacemakers, advocating for forgiveness and the pursuit of reconciliation. In a world often fraught with division and animosity, His teachings stand as a powerful testament to the transformative power of love, forgiveness, and unity.

Jesus also emphasized the significance of prayer, demonstrating its vital role in connecting us with God. He instructed his disciples to pray with humility and sincerity, urging them to align their own desires with God's will. Furthermore, Jesus also modeled the practice of regular solitude and communion with God, setting an example for us to prioritize our relationship with Him through prayer and reflection.

As we reflect on the entirety of Jesus' teachings, we are presented with a radical summons to lead lives characterized by love, forgiveness, humility, compassion, faith, and unity. These teachings transcend mere philosophical concepts; they serve as practical guidance for navigating the complexities of our daily lives.

Let us pause for a moment to ponder how these teachings resonate with us individually. How can we apply these timeless truths within our families, workplaces, and our communities? How can we embody the love and compassion of Jesus in our interactions with others?

May we carry with us the wisdom gleaned from this journey through Jesus's teachings. Let us embrace the call to undergo internal transformation, opening our hearts to the abundant and fulfilling life promised by Jesus.

May these teachings persist in challenging and inspiring us, guiding us toward a deeper understanding of ourselves and our purpose. Let us venture forth with renewed determination, living out the teachings of Jesus in our everyday lives and spreading His message of love, forgiveness, humility, and compassion to a world in need.

While this chapter and book will delve into the life and ministry of Jesus, exploring the miracles, parables, and encounters that shaped his earthly journey, let us take this moment to immerse ourselves in the profundity of His teachings, allowing them to steer and reshape us at every step.

Miracles Unveiled: Witnessing The Power Of Jesus

Experience the extraordinary acts of healing and supernatural occurrences performed by Jesus, unveiling His divine nature. Throughout His earthly ministry, Jesus showcased his power and compassion through a series of remarkable miracles. These miraculous interventions not only served as evidence of His divine identity but also brought hope and restoration to those in dire need.

In a world besieged by suffering and despair, Jesus emerged as a radiant beacon of light, offering a glimpse into the depths of God's love and mercy. Wherever he transverse, throngs of people gathered to behold His extraordinary deeds, yearning for a glimpse of the miraculous. And Jesus, in His boundless grace, never turned them away.

One of Jesus's most remarkable miracles unfolded on the shores of the Sea of Galilee. As He addressed a vast crowd, many had journeyed there, hungering for both spiritual and physical nourishment. Sensing their need, Jesus performed a breathtaking miracle. With just a few loaves and fish, He miraculously fed thousands. As each person received their portion, the crowd stood in awe of the abundance that defied human comprehension. In that moment, Jesus not only satisfied their physical hunger but also revealed His divine authority over creation.

Yet, Jesus' miraculous works extended far beyond multiplying food. His power encompassed healing the sick and afflicted. From restoring sight to the blind to enabling the lame to walk anew, Jesus displayed an incredible ability to bring restoration where hope seemed lost. In a remarkable encounter, a man incapacitated for 38 years lay beside the pool of Bethesda. Jesus approached him and, with a simple command, restored his strength and mobility. The once-paralyzed man stood in awe at the miraculous transformation before him. Through these acts of healing, Jesus showcased His capacity to restore wholeness to both body and spirit.

Moreover, Jesus demonstrated authority over the spiritual realm. Countless individuals tormented by unclean spirits found deliverance at the mere mention of His name. Whether it was the demon-possessed man in the region of the Gerasene or the afflicted woman in the synagogue, Jesus rebuked these spiritual oppressors and liberated the captives. His power and authority over the demonic realm were indisputable, leaving witnesses astounded and instilling renewed hope in the face of spiritual warfare.

The miracles of Jesus transcended mere displays of power and authority; they were profound expressions of His boundless compassion for humanity. At the wedding feast in Cana, Jesus transformed water into the finest wine, ensuring the joy and celebration of the newlyweds. Amidst a tempest, He stilled the raging waves and rescued His disciples from imminent peril, revealing His unwavering presence and care even amidst life's tumultuous storms.

These miracles left an indelible impact on all who bore witness to them, pointing towards something greater, beyond the realms of ordinary human experience. Through these miraculous acts, Jesus unveiled His heavenly purpose - to bring salvation and eternal life to all who would believe in Him. As we delve deeper into the astonishing miracles performed by Jesus, we will continue to unravel the truth of His identity and the transformative potency of His love.

While we will explore further miraculous events showcasing the divinity of our Savior, let us pause to appreciate the profound impact these initial miracles have had on our comprehension of Jesus and His extraordinary mission. As we journey onward, we will delve deeper into the extraordinary miracles performed by Jesus, unearthing the truth of His identity and the life-altering power of his love. These miracles not only affirmed His divine nature but also provided solace and assurance to those seeking hope and restoration.

One remarkable miracle that vividly showcased Jesus' compassion and authority was the healing of the woman with the issue of blood. For twelve agonizing years, she endured both physical agony and social isolation due to her condition. Despite her plight, she clung to a glimmer of hope, believing that a mere touch of Jesus' garments would bring about her healing. Amidst a thronging crowd, Jesus made His way, and the woman, summoning her courage, reached out and brushed the edge of His robe. Instantly, she felt her body restored to full health, her years of suffering evaporating. Sensing the power that had emanated from Him, Jesus turned and asked who had touched Him. Trembling, the woman fell before Him, sharing her story. With compassion and warmth, Jesus assured her that her faith had made her well. This miracle not only brought physical restoration but also reinstated her dignity and sense of belonging.

Another awe-inspiring event showcasing Jesus' unwavering authority was the raising of Lazarus from the dead. Upon arriving at his dear friend Lazarus's tomb, Jesus encountered a scene of profound grief and lamentation. Tears streaming down his face, he uttered with a commanding voice, "Lazarus, come forth!" To the astonishment of all present, Lazarus, who had been dead for four days, emerged from the tomb, still wrapped in burial garments. Jesus' compassion for His friends and His authority over death was unmistakable in this extraordinary moment. This miraculous resurrection bolstered the faith of many, compelling them to marvel at Jesus' power to triumph over death itself.

In addition to these profound miracles, Jesus continually revealed His divine nature through his teachings. His parables captivated the hearts and minds of His audience, unveiling profound spiritual truths in simple yet profound ways. Through stories like the parable of the prodigal son and the parable of the lost sheep, Jesus conveyed the boundless love and forgiveness of God, inviting all to experience true restoration and reconciliation with their heavenly Father.

Jesus' miracles transcended mere displays of power; they were transformative encounters that brought hope, healing, and freedom to those yearning for a touch from God. Whether it was restoring sight to the blind, expelling demons, or calming storms, each miracle showcased Jesus' incredible love, compassion, and authority over creation. They provided glimpses into the depths of his divinity and affirmed his mission to bestow salvation and eternal life upon all.

As we contemplate the miracles of Jesus, both in this book and within the Gospels, we are reminded that He is the way, the truth, and the life. Through His miraculous acts of healing and supernatural events, He unveiled His divine nature and exemplified the boundless love and mercy of God. Let us persist in seeking and rediscovering Jesus, allowing His miracles to fortify our faith and lead us toward a deeper understanding of His transformative power and eternal purpose. May His love and compassion serve as an inspiration for us to live lives that reflect his extraordinary mission, offering hope and restoration to a world in desperate need.

The Heart Of Sacrifice: Understanding The Power Of Love

In a world often marred by self-interest and scarcity of love, it becomes imperative to revisit the extraordinary example set by Jesus Christ. By delving into his sacrificial love, we gain profound insights into the boundless capacity of the human heart and are spurred to live lives marked by compassion and empathy.

At the core of Jesus' sacrificial love lies his unwavering devotion to humanity. His entire earthly journey was driven by a profound desire to heal, restore, and redeem. From the onset of His ministry, He selflessly dedicated His time and energy to be with the afflicted, the marginalized, and the downtrodden.

At every turn, Jesus embodied love in its purest essence. He embraced the outcasts, shared meals with sinners, and extended forgiveness to the seemingly unforgivable. He taught us that love transcends limits, boundaries, and conditions. It is a force that urges us to reach out, to care, and to uplift, irrespective of our differences or shortcomings.

Yet, it was upon the cross that Jesus unveiled the depth of His sacrificial love. As he bore the weight of our sins and the anguish of the world, he exemplified a love willing to endure unimaginable suffering for the sake of others. In that pivotal moment, He willingly surrendered His own life so that we might find salvation.

Through this supreme act of selflessness, Jesus transcended our limited understanding of love. He demonstrated that love is not merely an emotion or an abstract concept; it is a tangible force that necessitates action. It is the conscious decision to prioritize others, to shoulder their burdens, and to give without expecting anything in return.

As we contemplate Jesus' sacrifice, we are confronted with the profound truth that our lives are intertwined with His. His love permeates every facet of our existence. It serves as a reminder that we, too, can embrace sacrificial love in our daily lives, whether through a kind word, a helping hand, or a moment of forgiveness.

In rediscovering Jesus and His sacrificial love, we unearth the key to unlocking a deeper sense of purpose and fulfillment. Through His example, we are spurred to defy the selfish inclinations of our hearts and to embrace a life centered on love and service. It is a call to break free from the confines of our own desires and extend ourselves for the betterment of others.

As we journey through the chapters, we will delve deeper into the profound implications of Jesus' sacrificial love. We will explore how this love holds the power to transform lives, mend broken relationships, and kindle hope in the darkest of times. Prepare to be inspired, for the depths of Jesus' love are immeasurable, and its impact on our lives surpasses our wildest imaginings.

Let's reflect on the profound love that Jesus demonstrated on the cross. Let it stir within our souls, awakening a desire to follow in His footsteps and embrace the sacrificial love that possesses the power to change the world.

Amidst the hustle of our daily lives, it is all too easy to lose sight of the transformative power of sacrificial love. We get caught up in our own worries, desires, and ambitions, often overlooking the profound impact our actions can have on others. But when we open our hearts to the examples set by Jesus, we are reminded of the immense potential within us to make a difference in our lives and in the lives of those around us.

Jesus' sacrificial love challenges us to break free from the chains of self-centeredness and embrace a life of service and compassion. He not only showed us the way through His words but also through His actions. Each encounter He had with those in need was an opportunity for him to pour out His love, leaving no one untouched by his grace.

In the radiant glow of his sacrificial love, Jesus beckons us to peer beyond mere appearances, urging us to delve into the depths of the human heart and respond with boundless compassion and understanding. His profound example teaches us that love transcends barriers, refusing to tally deeds or discriminate based on status. It is a pure, selfless act that stretches its arms wide, embracing all souls yearning for solace, acceptance, and forgiveness.

As we endeavor to mirror the magnificence of Jesus' love, we uncover its transformative potency in our own lives and in the tapestry of humanity. Extending a hand to life the downtrodden not only alleviates their anguish but also bestows upon us a sense of purpose and contentment unattainable through self-serving pursuits.

Furthermore, sacrificial love possesses the remarkable ability to mend fractured bonds and restore harmony. It serves as a beacon of forgiveness, beckoning us to release the burdens of resentment and embrace the healing power of empathy. Choosing to love sacrificially opens the floodgates of reconciliation, paving a path toward healing and revitalized connections.

In the depths of despair, Jesus' sacrificial love emerges as a beacon of hope, illuminating even the darkest corners of our lives. It serves as a reminder that amidst our trials, a radiant light persists, offering solace and strength to weather the storm.

Yet, embracing sacrificial love is not without its trails. It challenges us to transcend our comfort zones, to confront our prejudices, and to prioritize the needs of others over our own. It demands humility, courage, and a willingness to relinquish our own desires.

In embracing the ethos of Jesus' love, we unearth boundless rewards. We experience a profound sense of fulfillment, surpassing the fleeting allure of worldly success. Witnessing lives transformed, hearts healed, and communities knit together in love and compassion becomes our greatest joy.

Let us steadfastly cling to the example set by Jesus and his sacrificial love. Let it permeate every aspect of our existence, guiding our thoughts, words, and actions as we endeavor to make a positive impact in the lives of those around us.

May we never underestimate the transformative power of sacrificial love, for within it lies the potential to heal, restore, and transform our world. Let it be the cornerstone of our interactions, the bedrock of our relationships, and the guiding star of our journey.

As we rediscover the essence of Jesus and His sacrificial love, we not only uncover a deeper sense of purpose and fulfillment but also become catalysts for change in a world yearning for transformations. So, let us march forward, emboldened by His example, and let love illuminate our path.

Risen: Exploring The Power Of The Resurrection

The Resurrection of Jesus Christ stands as a monumental event, forever etched in the annals of human history. Its significance transcends mere temporal occurrences, weaving a tapestry of faith, hope, and redemption. In this chapter, we shall delve into the evidence surrounding Jesus' resurrection and ponder its profound implications for our lives today.

As we delve into the evidence supporting the resurrection, we are met with a rich tapestry of eyewitness accounts. The Gospels offer meticulous testimonies from those who bore witness to the risen Christ, affirming the reality of this miraculous event. Among them stands Mary Magdalene, an unwavering disciple who beheld the empty tomb and encountered the resurrected Jesus. Her testimony, far from solitary, echoes the chorus of countless encounters during that transformative period.

The appearances of Jesus to his disciples after post-resurrection furnish yet another compelling testament. These encounters transcend mere wishful thinking or collective hallucination; they are authentic experiences of a risen Savior. Consider Thomas, initially skeptical, who later proclaimed, "My Lord and my God!" Such encounters catalyzed a metamorphosis among the disciples into bold and courageous witnesses, their doubt into unshakeable faith.

Moreover, the transformation of Saul of Tarsus serves as a poignant testimony to the reality of the resurrection. Once a fervent persecutor of early Christians, Saul underwent a dramatic encounter on the road to Damascus, encountering

Jesus and emerging as the Apostle Pual, a zealous advocate for the faith. His radical transformation underscores the seismic impact of the resurrection, reshaping not only his destiny but also igniting a global movement that reverberates through the corridors of time.

Beyond the compelling eyewitness accounts, the resonance of Jesus' resurrection reverberates in its implications for humanity. It stands as the ultimate validation of Jesus's divinity, affirming His identity as the Son of God and the long-awaited Messiah. Moreover, it serves as an unequivocal proclamation of victory over sin and death, extending a beacon of hope and eternal life to all who entrust themselves to Him. Through His sacrificial death and triumphant resurrection, Jesus shatters the chain of sin, forging a path to reconciliation between humanity and the Divine.

Furthermore, the resurrection bestows upon us the assurance of our future resurrection. Just as Christ emerged victorious over death, so too do we anticipate our resurrection and eternal communion with Him. This assurance carries a transformative potency, infusing our hearts with solace, hope, and the fortitude to navigate the vicissitudes of earthly existence.

As we ponder the evidence and ramifications of Jesus' resurrection, we are beckoned to a profound invitation. It invites us to scrutinize our own lives and acknowledge our inherent need for redemption and spiritual renewal in Christ. It beckons us to embrace the boundless hope and promise emanating from this pivotal event, offering each of us an intimate encounter with the risen Lord.

We stand on the brink of a profound journey, poised to delve into the enigma that is the resurrection. The story does not culminate here; rather, it beckons us to venture forth, uncovering the riches awaiting discovery, comprehension, and embrace. We are poised to unveil the profound implications of Jesus' resurrection and its transformative potency in our lives. Let us embark on this odyssey, ready to plumb the depths of this sacred mystery.

As we navigate the depths of Jesus' resurrection, we unfurl the myriad implications of this pivotal event and its transformative essence in our lives. Beyond merely offering hope and the promise of eternal life, the resurrection impels us to introspection, urging us to scrutinize our own narratives and embrace the prospect of redemption and spiritual renewal in Christ.

Foremost among these implications is the resolute assurance of our own resurrection. Just as Christ vanquished death, so too do we harbor the fervent hope of resurrection and eternal communion with him. This pledge serves as a beacon of solace and fortitude, assuring us that the trials and tribulations of this mortal coil are but a prelude to an eternity basking in the radiance of our Savior's love.

Moreover, the resurrection serves as an indelible testament to Jesus' divinity, vindicating his assertion as the Son of God and the long-awaited Messiah. It resounds as a triumphant proclamation of victory over sin and death itself. Through his sacrificial death and triumphant resurrection, Jesus liberates us from the shackles of sins, offering a pathway to reconciliation with the Divine. The resurrection stands as a resplendent affirmation that Jesus' sacrifice on the cross was not in vain but rather the ultimate manifestation of divine love, paving the way for our eternal redemption.

The resurrection wields transformative power in the tapestry of our daily lives, extending to us an invitation for a personal encounter with the risen Savior. When we truly embrace the reality of the resurrection, it kindles within us an ardent zeal to lead a life wholly surrendered to Christ. Much like the disciples, forever transfigured by their encounters with the resurrected Jesus, we, too, are beckoned to yield to the transformative might of His resurrection, permeating our very being.

This metamorphosis empowers us to emerge as intrepid ambassadors of our faith, mirroring the audacity displayed by the disciples post-encounter with the risen Christ. The resurrection emboldens us to share the good news of Jesus' victory over sin and death with those in our midst, proffering unto them the same wellspring of hope and transformative vigor that we ourselves have partaken of.

Furthermore, the resurrection serves as a poignant reminder of the intrinsic value and dignity inherent in every human life. In a world scarred by fractures and desolation, the resurrection resounds with the clarion call that each individual is fashioned in the divine likeness and harbors the potential for rebirth and renewal through unwavering faith in Jesus Christ. It impels us to extend unto others the same measure of love, grace, and compassion that Christ has so generously bestowed upon us.

The resurrection of Jesus transcends mere historical significance; it extends a profound invitation to each soul. It beckons us to introspect, to acknowledge our yearning for redemption and spiritual rejuvenation in Christ. It proffers unto us hope, assurance, and the transformative power to navigate life as jubilant and resolute heralds of our resurrected Savior. Embracing the veracity of Jesus' resurrection, we embark upon a journey suffused with purpose, significance, and enduring fulfillment.

Living The Way Of Christ: Nurturing A Christ-Centered Lifestyle

In our quest to reconnect with Jesus, one of the most impactful endeavors lies in translating his teachings into tangible actions that shape our everyday existence. Mere acknowledgment of his words or surface-level comprehension of his message falls short. To authentically lead a life centered on Christ, we must actively undergo a metamorphosis of our thoughts, attitudes, and behaviors, aligning them with the principles exemplified by Jesus.

Being Christ-centered necessitates striving to mirror his compassion, love, and selflessness in each interaction and decision we encounter. It involves acknowledging the potency inherent in our thoughts and recognizing that by anchoring our minds in the teachings of Jesus, we can catalyze positive transformation within ourselves and among those we encounter.

The inaugural step in integrating Jesus' teachings into our daily existence involves earnest scripture study. The Bible serves as our compass, furnishing us with profound insights into Jesus' life and ministry. Through immersion in his words, we glean the depth of his teachings and discern their relevance in our contemporary lives. Through reflective prayer, we know how best to apply these teachings to our circumstances.

Nevertheless, mere knowledge remains insufficient. Jesus underscored the imperative of translating his teachings into tangible deeds. He taught us to extend love to our neighbors as we do ourselves, to extend forgiveness to those who transgress against us, and to exhibit kindness and empathy to all within our orbit. Yet, how do we enact these lofty principles into palpable actions?

One practical approach to embodying a Christ-centered existence is nurturing a spirit of service. Jesus exemplified servanthood throughout his ministry, urging his disciples to emulate his example. Service mirrors the humility and love epitomized by Jesus and affords us a firsthand encounter with the transformative potency of selflessness. Whether through volunteering our time, assisting a neighbor in distress, or offering a sympathetic ear to a confidant, each act of service propels us closer to manifesting the life Jesus envisaged for us.

Another vital step in pursuing a Christ-centered life is embodying forgiveness. Jesus underscored the paramountcy of pardoning others, even when it may appear arduous or unwarranted. By unshackling ourselves from the burdens of resentment and hatred, we unfurl the pathway to healing and reconciliation. Forgiveness emancipates us from the shackles of anger, bestowing us the liberty to experience the boundless grace of God.

Leading a Christ-centered life also entails deliberately cultivating our thoughts and attitudes. Jesus imparted wisdom on the potency of positive thinking and its profound influence on our perspective. By embracing a mindset steeped in gratitude, faith, and hope, we transcend adversities and embrace a serenity that defies rationale. This transformative shift equips us to confront life's trials with resilience and an unwavering reliance on God's providence.

In our endeavor to internalize Jesus' teachings into the fabric of our daily existence, we embark on a voyage of personal evolution and metamorphosis. Through acts of service, forgiveness, and mindful contemplation, we propagate a wave of love and empathy that touches the souls of those in our midst.

Let us persist unwaveringly in our pursuit of a Christ-centered existence, aware that through this profound dedication, we authentically rediscover Jesus and experience the boundless joy that accompanies surrendering our lives to Him.

Leading a Christ-centered life also entails deliberately cultivating our thoughts and attitudes. Jesus imparted wisdom on the potency of positive thinking and its profound influence on our perspective. By embracing a mindset steeped in gratitude, faith, and hope, we transcend adversities and embrace a serenity that defies rationale. This transformative shift equips us to confront life's trials with resilience and an unwavering reliance on God's providence.

In our endeavor to internalize Jesus' teachings into the fabric of our daily existence, we embark on a journey of personal growth and transformation. Through acts of service, forgiveness, and mindful contemplation, we propagate a wave of love and empathy that touches the souls of those in our midst.

Let us persist unwaveringly in our pursuit of a Christ-centered existence, knowing that through this profound dedication, we authentically rediscover Jesus and experience the boundless joy that accompanies surrendering our lives to Him.

Living a Christ-centered life necessitates a steadfast dedication to continual growth and transformation. It's not merely a destination but an ongoing odyssey wherein we endeavor to harmonize our thoughts, attitudes, and deeds with Jesus' teachings. Here, we delve into additional practical strategies for nurturing a Christ-centered existence, enriching our connection with Jesus, and experiencing His love and grace.

A cornerstone of living a Christ-centered life is fostering a heart brimming with compassion and empathy. Jesus consistently exemplified empathy toward the downtrodden, marginalized, and needy. His directive to love our neighbors as ourselves extends to demonstrating compassion for all individuals, irrespective of their backgrounds, beliefs, or circumstances.

To cultivate compassion, we must actively seek avenues to connect with those in our midst. This entails stepping beyond our comfort zones, engaging in meaningful dialogue with individuals from diverse walks of life, and attentively listening to their narratives and trials. Through such endeavors, we gain genuine insight into the struggles faced by others while also affirming each person's inherent dignity and worth.

Embracing the potency of prayer constitutes another practical avenue for fostering a Christ-centered life. Prayer serves as a potent conduit for nurturing a deeper communion with God. Through prayer, we solicit guidance, derive solace amidst tribulations, and encounter the transformative presence of God in our lives.

Integrating prayer into our daily routines fosters a Christ-centered disposition and a reliance on God's wisdom and fortitude. Whether through structured prayer sessions or spontaneous dialogues with God throughout the day, prayer enables us to relinquish our anxieties, seek clarity in decision-making, and intercede on behalf of others.

Living a Christ-centered life encompasses heeding the call to emulate the holiness exhibited by Jesus. This pertains to both our outward conduct and our inner disposition. Jesus underscored the significance of integrity, truthfulness, and purity of heart. Living a Christ-centered life entails actively aligning our actions with these values.

This may entail establishing boundaries in our relationships, eschewing gossip and slander, and making decisions that mirror God's heart for justice and righteousness. It also entails assuming responsibility for our spiritual development by engaging in scripture study and meditation and fostering accountability and fellowship within a faith community.

Living a Christ-centered life demands perseverance and an unwavering commitment to ongoing discipleship. Just as Jesus summoned his disciples to follow him, we too are called to be lifelong learners, perpetually deepening our comprehension of Jesus' character and the demands of discipleship.

This may entail delving deeper into scripture, attending teachings or sermons that challenge and inspire us, and seeking guidance from mentors or spiritual counselors. By embracing an attitude of humility and receptivity, we create space for God to continue molding and refining us in the likeness of Christ.

In pursuing a Christ-centered life, let us not forget that we do not tread this path alone. We are all fellow travelers on this journey, offering support and encouragement to one another as we endeavor to integrate Jesus' teachings into our daily existence. May we draw strength from the knowledge that God's grace perpetually sustains us, empowering us to commit to a Christ-centered life.

We will further explore the concept of surrendering our will to God's will and the inherent transformative potency. Let us remain resolute in our resolve to live a Christ-centered life, trusting in God's guidance and love every step of the way.

Amidst The Storm: Seeking Solace And Serenity

Life is replete with unforeseen twists and turns, with challenges lurking at every bend. Amidst such turbulence, we often yearn for solace and tranquility. It is during these trying moments that the teachings of Jesus serve as a beacon of hope, guiding us toward serenity amidst the chaos.

In a world fraught with uncertainty, Jesus reminds us of the transformative power of faith. He encourages us to place our trust in a higher purpose that transcends our human comprehension. Through his own lived experiences, Jesus encountered countless trials yet remained unwavering in his steadfast belief. In doing so, he exemplified the importance of finding peace amidst adversity.

When adversity strikes, it's natural to question the purpose behind our struggles. Jesus offers us hope, assuring us that even in the darkest of times, there is profound meaning to be discovered. His teachings remind us that our challenges are not in vain but rather serve as opportunities for growth and enlightenment.

Jesus also provides us with a blueprint for cultivating peace in turbulent times through his teachings on forgiveness. During his earthly sojourn, he forgave those who wronged him, even amidst unimaginable suffering. His capacity for forgiveness empowers us to relinquish the burdens of resentment, paving the path toward inner peace.

In a world that often exalts competition and self-interest, Jesus calls us to embrace compassion and love. Through his teachings, he urges us to extend kindness to others, particularly during times of discord. By emulating his example, we foster an environment where peace can flourish, even amidst tumult.

Moreover, Jesus assures us that we are never alone in our struggles. He promises to walk alongside us, providing guidance and solace. In moments of despair, his presence brings comfort, reminding us that we are deeply loved and valued.

One of Jesus' most profound teachings is his call to surrender control. In a world fixated on certainty and control, this can be a daunting concept. Yet, when we relinquish our grip on the outcomes of our lives and surrender to a higher power, we discover a peace that transcends circumstances.

In tumultuous times, Jesus speaks to the depths of our souls, urging us to find solace in his presence. He offers us an inner sanctuary where we can retreat from the chaos and discover inner peace. This peace becomes our anchor, steadying us amidst life's storms.

As we navigate life's trials, the pursuit of peace may seem elusive. However, through Jesus' teachings, we are reminded that peace is not external but internal, a state of mind and heart that can be cultivated within us. It's a journey guided by his teachings as we seek tranquility amidst turmoil.

We'll delve into specific practices and principles that enable us to find peace in turbulent times. Together, we'll unearth the wisdom Jesus imparts and explore how to apply it to our lives. But for now, let's reflect on the foundational peace he offers, embracing the hope and reassurance they provide.

One crucial practice Jesus teaches us is the power of gratitude. Gratitude shifts our focus from scarcity to abundance, even amidst turmoil. Cultivating a grateful heart enables us to discern blessings amid adversity. Gratitude reminds us that even in darkness, there are reasons for thankfulness. Through this lens of appreciation, we find peace amidst storms.

Additionally, Jesus invites us to surrender our worries and anxieties to him. In a world inundated with stress, it's easy to feel overwhelmed. Jesus assures us that we need not bear these burdens alone. He beckons us to cast our cares upon him, finding relief and peace in his loving care.

Moreover, Jesus underscores the importance of self-care and rest. Amid the chaos, it's vital to pause, breathe, and replenish our energy. Jesus understood the significance of rest and invited us to follow suit. By nurturing ourselves physically, emotionally, and spiritually, we equip ourselves to face life's challenges with resilience.

Alongside self-care, Jesus teaches us the value of community and fellowship. In turbulent times, surrounding ourselves with a supportive community is essential. Connection and shared experiences provide comfort and strength. Together, we find solace in unity, knowing we're not alone.

Finally, Jesus emphasizes prayer and meditation. These practices facilitate communication with God and inner stillness. Through prayer, we pour out our hearts to God, finding peace in his presence. In meditation, we listen for divine guidance, receiving the peace that transcends understanding.

Let's carry these practices with us, infusing them into our daily lives. May we embrace Jesus' wisdom and embody peace amidst life's storms. By following his teachings, we navigate challenges with faith, gratitude, surrender, self-care, community, and connection with God.

Peace isn't a distant destination but a present reality awaiting our discovery. Open your heart to Jesus' teachings, and you'll find peace amidst turbulence. Trust in his guidance, and let his reassurance envelop you. You're not alone on this journey, for Jesus is the Way, the Truth, and the Life.

Heart-To-Heart: Building Authentic Connections

In a world increasingly dominated by virtual interactions, the value of authentic relationships cannot be overstated. We yearn for genuine connections that enrich our lives and remind us of our shared humanity. Who better to learn from than Jesus himself? His life and teachings offer invaluable lessons on cultivating meaningful connections with others and fostering love, compassion, and understanding.

Jesus' approach to relationships was founded on deep empathy and compassion. He genuinely cared for everyone he encountered, irrespective of social status or background. Jesus saw beyond superficial labels, recognizing the inherent worth and value in each person. His example teaches us to see and appreciate others for who they truly are—unique and precious individuals.

Furthermore, Jesus exemplified the power of active listening. He took the time to understand the thoughts, emotions, and experiences of those around him. Rather than offering quick fixes or empty advice, Jesus empathized with their struggles, offering compassionate words and a healing touch. He showed us that genuine relationships require us to be fully present, listening with our hearts and minds without judgment.

At the core of Jesus' relational model was unconditional love. He loved others without expecting anything in return, reaching out to the marginalized and the outcasts of society. By embracing them, Jesus broke down barriers and emphasized love as the foundation of authentic connection.

Jesus also emphasized forgiveness in nurturing relationships. He taught us that forgiveness is a profound act of strength and compassion, releasing us from resentment and fostering healing. Jesus' teachings on forgiveness mend broken bonds and cultivate understanding.

Moreover, Jesus stressed the importance of humility in our interactions. Despite his authority, Jesus served others with humility, washing his disciples' feet as a poignant example. He challenges us to set aside our egos and pride, approaching relationships with a servant's heart.

As we rediscover Jesus' approach to relationships, we find a blueprint for creating connections that transcend superficiality. Through empathy, active listening, unconditional love, forgiveness, and humility, we cultivate relationships that bring meaning and purpose into our lives.

We will delve deeper into practical steps and lessons from Jesus' teachings to help cultivate authentic relationships. As we embark on this journey together, we'll experience the transformative power of genuine connections and love.

First and foremost, building authentic relationships requires intentionality and effort. We must prioritize connections with others, investing time and energy into fostering them. Just as Jesus set aside time for his disciples, we, too, must make space for meaningful interactions.

One practical step is practicing active presence in our relationships. Let's put away distractions and engage fully with those around us. By actively listening and showing empathy, we demonstrate care and value for others.

We can also learn from Jesus' example of embracing diversity. Authentic connections often require us to step out of our comfort zones and connect with people from different backgrounds. By doing so, we expand our capacity for love and compassion.

Additionally, forgiveness plays a crucial role in nurturing relationships. By releasing grudges, we enable healing and reconciliation. Expressing gratitude also deepens connections, fostering a positive cycle of love and compassion.

As we practice empathy, active listening, diversity, forgiveness, and gratitude, our relationships will flourish. Let's take small steps each day toward meaningful connections guided by Jesus' teachings.

May we embrace Jesus' teachings as truths that guide us in our pursuit of authentic relationships. Let's nurture genuine connections with love, compassion, and understanding, transforming not only our relationships but also our lives.

A Path To Fulfillment: Embracing Way, Truth, And Life's Calling

In a world filled with distractions, it's easy to lose sight of what truly matters. We often search for meaning and purpose in the wrong places, yet deep within, there's a longing for something more profound beyond the mundane. It's a yearning to uncover the extraordinary, to embrace the way, the truth, and the life.

Jesus, the epitome of love and grace, extends an invitation to each of us—an invitation to journey with Him towards fulfillment and purpose. He calls us to embrace Him as the way, the truth, and the life, for in Him lies the path to ultimate fulfillment.

As we embark on this transformative journey, we're called to walk in Jesus' footsteps. It's not just a physical journey but a journey of the heart and mind. We must strive to understand His teachings, which have the power to ignite a spark within us and transform our lives.

Through His parables and teachings, Jesus reveals the way—the way to love, truth, and life. He teaches us to love our neighbors as ourselves, showing kindness and compassion to all we encounter. This love transcends boundaries and brings us closer to the essence of our humanity.

By embracing Jesus as the way, we embrace a life filled with purpose. No longer are we wandering aimlessly; we have a guiding star leading us towards a significant life. Jesus illuminates the path, unveiling the truth obscured by the noise of the world.

Truth is more than a collection of facts; it's a revelation of our purpose and identity. Jesus embodies this truth, being the epitome of love, mercy, and forgiveness. Through Him, we find freedom from the chains of sin and despair.

In Jesus, we find life in its fullest form—a life overflowing with joy, peace, and contentment. By embracing Him as the way, the truth, and the life, we tap into a wellspring of hope that sustains us amidst life's storms.

In this journey, we're not alone. Jesus extends His hand to guide us, to walk alongside us through every twist and turn. His presence offers comfort and assurance, inviting us to trust in His unfailing love as we navigate life's complexities.

As we embark on this journey, may we open our hearts and minds to the transformative power of Jesus. Embracing Him as the way, the truth, and the life leads us to a life of fulfillment and purpose. Let's set aside distractions, letting go of trivial pursuits, and open ourselves to the profound truths that await us.

This journey is just the beginning; there's more to unveil, more wisdom to ponder. With each step, we draw closer to the magnificence of embracing Jesus as the way, the truth, and the life. As we delve deeper into the journey of embracing Jesus as the way, the truth, and the life, we realize that this path isn't without its challenges. Life's trials and tribulations can shake our faith and cause doubts. However, it's crucial to remember the unwavering love and faithfulness of our Savior.

Jesus, who experienced profound human suffering, understands our pain and walks beside us through every storm. His presence anchors us, providing the strength and courage to persevere. Even when our faith wavers, Jesus remains constant, holding us close and reminding us of His promises.

Moreover, as we continue this transformative journey, we must confront barriers hindering our relationship with Christ. It's essential to acknowledge and address doubts, fears, and sins that separate us from God's love. By surrendering these barriers to Him, we allow Jesus to enter the deepest corners of our hearts and cleanse all hindrances to our spiritual growth.

Embracing Jesus as the way, the truth, and the life also entails discovering the power of surrender. Surrendering to Jesus means releasing our need for control and placing full trust in Him. It aligns our will with His and surrenders desires, plans, and ambitions to His divine purpose. This surrender grants us the freedom to align our lives with God's perfect will, leading to ultimate fulfillment, joy, and peace. Trusting in Jesus' guidance and surrendering to Him transforms our brokenness into beauty, weaving every aspect of our existence into a masterpiece that glorifies God.

Furthermore, embracing Jesus compels us to live with intentionality and purpose, reflecting the love and grace we've received. It means loving neighbors like ourselves, extending kindness and compassion, and standing up for justice and righteousness.

In doing so, we become agents of change in a world yearning for hope. Our lives testify to Jesus' transformative power, shining His light into darkness and leading others to discover the Way, the Truth, and the Life. As we answer the call to share Jesus' good news, we become vessels of His love, bringing meaning and fulfillment to those around us.

Reflect on the incredible invitation Jesus extends to each of us. Embrace Him as the way, the truth, and the life, allowing His love to guide your steps and illuminate your path. In doing so, you'll uncover a life filled with purpose, meaning, and eternal significance.

Continue onward in your journey, drawing closer to the magnificence of embracing Jesus as the Way, the Truth, and the Life. May His love overflow in your heart, transforming everything you do, and may you find fulfillment in the arms of the One who created you and knows you intimately. Trust in Jesus, and let Him lead you into a life that surpasses all expectations.

CHAPTER 3
"Put God First"

Guided By Grace: Understanding Divine Priorities

In our hasty and often chaotic lives, it's always easy to lose sight of what truly matters. We are constantly balancing multiple responsibilities, chasing after worldly achievements, and seeking immediate gratification. In the midst of it all, we often overlook the fundamental aspect of our existence - our spiritual priorities. Recognizing and harmonizing our priorities with God's will is a profound journey that leads to a fulfilled and purposeful life.

At the core of recognizing divine priorities is acknowledging the existence of a higher power. We must understand that we are not the sole architects of our destiny, but rather part of a greater plan. When we open our hearts to this truth, we allow ourselves to be guided by a wisdom beyond our own understanding. It is through this surrender that we begin to unravel the divine priorities that have been veiled by the distractions of the world pursuits.

Disposing of our priorities with God's will requires a sincere evaluation of our current way of life. We must be willing to scrutinize our motives, actions, and the things that consume our attention and efforts. Often, we discover ourselves chasing after fleeting pursuits that ultimately leave us feeling empty and unsatisfied. It is crucial to pause and reflect on whether our decisions resonate with the values and principles that God desires for us.

Embracing divine priorities calls for a shift in mindset. It entails not the accumulation of material possessions or attaining status but rather about seeking righteousness and serving others. As we focus on attaining our purpose within the framework of God's divine plan, we discover a deep sense of contentment and inner peace that transcends any worldly achievement. Every decision we make, whether big or small, becomes an opportunity to honor God and serve His greater plan.

Acknowledging divine priorities also demands us to shed the layers of self-centeredness and selfishness. We inhabit a culture that frequently promotes self-interest over consideration for others. Yet, as we align our priorities with God's will, we come to understand that true fulfillment lies in selflessness. It is through loving and serving others that we find true joy and purpose. When purposefully prioritize kindness, compassion, and empathy, we become vessels of God's love and reflect His divine character.

As we embark on this journey of discerning divine priorities, we may encounter challenges and resistance. The world around may exert us in different directions, tempting us to stray from God's intended path. However, when we root ourselves in faith and seek guidance through prayer and meditation, we can remain steadfast in our pursuit of divine priorities.

Recognizing and aligning our priorities with God's will stand as a pivotal step toward leading lives imbued with fulfillment and purpose. It requires a shift in our mindset from worldly pursuits to seeking righteousness and serving others. This transformative journey urges us to relinquish self-centeredness, embrace selflessness, and surrender to a divine plan greater than our own. As we delve into the second part of this chapter, we will explore deeper into practical ways to implement and nurture this divine alignment in our everyday existence. As we continue on the journey of recognizing divine priorities, we are met with the realization that this path requires a genuine commitment to living a life of integrity and authenticity. It is insufficient to simply acknowledge the existence of a higher power; we must actively seek to align our thoughts, words, and actions with the teachings and values imparted by God.

A practical way to infuse this divine alignment in our daily lives is through the practice of prayer. Prayer serves as a direct line of communication with God, a sacred opportunity to express our innermost desires, concerns, and gratitude. By engaging in prayer, we can seek guidance and clarity in discerning God's will for us. When we earnestly seek His direction, we invite His wisdom and strength to steer us towards choices that align with His divine priorities.

In addition to prayer, nurturing a relationship with God requires a dedication to studying His word. The Bible serves as a roadmap for the journey of recognizing and embracing divine priorities. Through studying Scripture, we attain insight into the character of God and the principles by which He desires us to live. The wisdom and guidance contained within its pages furnish us with a solid foundation upon which we can build a life that is pleasing to Him.

Recognizing divine priorities also involves cultivating a spirit of gratitude. When we consciously acknowledge and appreciate the blessings and gifts bestowed upon us by God, our outlook transitions from entitlement to humility and thankfulness. Gratitude fuels our desire to serve God and others, as we recognize that all we possess is ultimately a gift from Him. By expressing gratitude, we open ourselves up to the transformative power of God's love and experience the joy derived from selflessly giving and serving.

Furthermore, embracing divine priorities necessitates an ongoing commitment to self-reflection and evaluation. We must consistently assess our motives, actions, and desires to ensure that they align with God's will. This process of self-examination may reveal areas of our lives that require growth and change. It may prompt us to let go of certain attitudes, habits, or associations that impede our spiritual advancement. It is through these instances of introspection and surrender that we open ourselves up to God's transformative influence within us.

As we learn and grow on recognizing divine priorities, it is important to remember that this is not a one-time accomplishment but an ongoing endeavor. It is a lifelong voyage of striving to align ourselves with God's will, buoyed by His wisdom and grace. Each day unfolds fresh opportunities for us to embrace divine priorities, small choices that collectively shape the course of our all lives.

By recognizing and aligning our priorities with God's will, we embark on a transformative path toward a life filled with fulfillment, purpose, and profound connection with our Creator. This path beckons us to release our self-centeredness and embrace selflessness, to abandon worldly pursuits in favor of righteousness. It invites us to stand firm in our faith in the face of challenges and resistance, reassured by the support of a power far greater than our own.

As we embrace the profound impact of divine priorities in our lives, we are drawn into a closer, more intimate connection with God. Our deeds manifest His love, while our existence stands as a testament to His grace. May we persist in seeking His counsel, upholding His will, and extending kindness and empathy to others with humility and compassion. In doing so, we fulfill our purpose and find true fulfillment and joy in the embrace of divine priorities.

Beyond The Noise: Finding Peace By Letting Go

In our fast-paced world, we are constantly bombarded with worldly distractions that draw our focus away and consume our valuable time. These distractions can manifest in diverse forms, including social media, material possessions, and the pursuit of worldly ambitions. While they may appear innocuous initially, they can have detrimental effects on our spiritual growth and obstruct our ability to serve God with undivided devotion.

Examining the detrimental effects of worldly distractions is crucial for understanding the necessity of detaching from them. One of the primary consequences of being consumed by worldly distractions is the fragmentation of our focus. We find ourselves easily overwhelmed and unable to devote our full attention to the things that truly matter. Instead of channeling our energy toward serving God and nurturing and deepening our relationship with Him, we become preoccupied with trivial matters that are devoid of eternal significance.

Moreover, worldly distractions can distort our perception of success and contentment. Society frequently equates success solely with material wealth, status, and external achievements. However, this narrow definition of success overlooks the deeper, spiritual dimensions of our existence. Our attachment to worldly endeavors can blind us to the true essence of life, leading us down a path of endless striving and dissatisfaction.

Detaching from worldly distractions is not an easy task, but it is an essential one if we are to embrace divine priorities. Fortunately, there are practical ways to regain focus and redirect our attention towards what truly matters. Firstly, we must cultivate self-awareness regarding our habits and behaviors. Take a moment to evaluate your daily activities and identify those that contribute to worldly distractions. Are you spending excessive amounts of time scrolling through social media? Are you incessantly chasing after the latest trends and material possessions? Recognizing these patterns is a vital step towards transformation.

Next, we can actively opt to prioritize God in our daily lives. This involves consciously making time for prayer, meditation, and reciting scripture. By carving out dedicated moments for these spiritual practices, we open our hearts and minds to God presence, fostering a deeper, and more meaningful connection with the Divine. Furthermore, participating in acts of kindness and compassion towards others can further strengthen our devotion to God. When we extend our love and support to those in need, we detach ourselves from self-centered desires and align ourselves with the higher calling of service.

In the journey away from worldly distractions, it is important to acknowledge that progress takes time and that setbacks are inevitable. Be patient with yourself and cultivate a mindset of self-compassion. As you gradually detach from worldly distractions, you will begin to a newfound sense of freedom and clarity. The grip that these distractions once had over you will gradually weaken, enabling you to channel your energy towards serving God with a revitalized zeal.

This marks just the commencement of your journey towards letting go of worldly distractions. Here, we will delve deeper into practical strategies for overcoming specific distractions and share personal anecdotes of individuals who have successfully embraced divine priorities. Stay with me as we unveil the obscured pathway leading to wholehearted service to God.

Now that we have established the groundwork for comprehending the detrimental effects of worldly distractions, it is time to delve further into practical strategies aimed at overcoming specific distractions in our lives. Throughout this expedition, it is imperative to bear in mind that detaching from worldly distractions is a gradual process that requires patience and self-compassion.

One prevalent distraction we often encounter is the excessive use of social media. While social platforms can be valuable tools for connection and communication, they can also foster a perpetual cycle of comparison and dissatisfaction. To combat this, consider implementing a mindful approach to your social media usage. Establish specific time limits for scrolling and strive to engage in meaningful interactions rather than mindless scrolling. By doing so, you can reclaim the time once lost to these distractions and redirect it towards serving God and enriching your spiritual life.

Material possessions can likewise entangle us and divert us from our divine priorities. It is important to cultivate a mindset of contentment and gratitude for what we already have, rather than constantly chasing after the next latest trend or possession. Redirect your focus to appreciating the blessings in your life and explore ways in which you can simplify and declutter. Embracing a minimalist lifestyle can liberate both physical and mental space, enabling you to concentrate on what truly matters.

Another prevalent distraction is the pursuit of worldly ambitions. While there is nothing inherently wrong with setting goals and working towards success, it is important to frequently assess your motivations and intentions. Ask yourself if your ambitions align with your true purpose and if they contribute to your spiritual growth. Remember that true success stems from aligning our lives with God's will and serving Him with sincerity and devotion.

As we progress along the path of detachment, it is crucial to draw inspiration in the narratives of those who have successfully embraced divine priorities. These personal testimonies serve as reminders that the journey toward detachment is both attainable and fulfilling. Seek out mentors, spiritual mentors, or like-minded seekers who can impart their experiences and offer guidance along the way. Surrounding yourself with individuals who share your divine priorities can offer the support and encouragement needed to steadfast on track.

Furthermore, incorporate regular self-reflection into your routine. Take moments of solitude to evaluate your advancement and center your focus. These instances of introspection enable you to identify areas where distractions may be creeping back into your life and facilitate necessary adjustments. Consider keeping a journal to record your thoughts, insights, and reflections on your journey towards detachment.

Remember, serving God wholeheartedly demands continual commitment and devotion. There will be moments of vulnerability and setbacks along the way. During these times, extend gentleness to yourself, embracing self-compassion and understanding. Remind yourself that progress is not measured by perfection but by your determination to persist and continue striving for divine priorities relentlessly.

As we approach the conclusion of this exploration, I trust you have acquired valuable insights and practical techniques to embrace divine priorities and let go of worldly distractions. Detachment is a transformative process that liberates us from the shackles of worldly attachments, ushering us into a richer and more profound connection with God. Therefore, take the first step and let your voyage towards wholeheartedly serving God commence. You possess the capability, and with each minor victory along this path, you bring yourself nearer to experiencing the profound joy and fulfillment that accompany living a life in harmony with your divine purpose.

In God's Hands: Seeking Divine Guidance for Decision Making

In our journey through life, we encounter numerous decisions, both big and small. Whether choosing a career path or deciding where to invest our time and resources, our choices sculpt our future. But how can we ascertain that our decisions resonate with God's will? How can we seek His guidance in our decision-making process?

Seeking God's guidance entails an understanding of His character and a willingness to surrender our own desires. It involves embracing divine priorities as we navigate the complexities of life. When we devote ourselves to seeking His wisdom, we can discover clarity, peace, and confidence to make sound decisions.

First and foremost, seeking God's guidance begins with fostering a personal relationship with Him. We must cultivate a heart of intimacy and devotion to our Heavenly Father. As we spend time in prayer, reading His word, and engaging in worship, our hearts become aligned with His, enabling us to comprehend His desires for our lives.

The Bible serves as a compass for our decision-making and our relationship with God. It serves as a treasure trove of wisdom and guidance that illuminates the path we ought to follow. Through the scriptures, we gain insight into God's character, His promises, and His commands. As we meditate upon His word, we cultivate discernment and develop a deeper understanding of His will.

Prayer is our lifeline to God, and it is through prayer with Him, that we actively seek His guidance. In our decision-making process, we should never underestimate the potency of prayer. As we bring our concerns and desires before him, we invite Him into every facet of our lives. Prayer is not just a one-way conversation; it is an opportunity to listen to God's voice and open our hearts to His Direction.

God communicates with us in diverse ways, and His guidance manifests through the gentle whisper of the Holy Spirit. In our decision-making, we should pay heed to those nudges, those subtle promptings deep within our spirits. The Holy Spirit serves as our counselor and guide, directing us toward God's flawless will. When we learn to listen and follow His leading, we unlock a profound source of wisdom and direction.

Seeking God's guidance also involves seeking wise counsel. Proverbs 15:22 says, "Without counsel, plans fail, but with many advisers, they succeed." No one can perceive all aspects of a situation alone; we need to gain the perspective of others. God places people in our lives who can provide guidance and wisdom derived from their own experiences and understanding of His word. Surrounding ourselves with trusted mentors, and fellow believers can help us gain clarity and perspective when making important decisions.

As we pursue God's guidance, we must remember that His ways surpass our ways, and His thoughts transcend our thoughts (Isaiah 55:9). At times, His guidance may not coincide with our initial desires or expectations. It requires faith and trust to surrender our plans and embrace God's will.

In our journey of seeking God's guidance in decision-making, we can rest assured that He is with us every step of the way. He remains faithful to lead us, even in the face of uncertainty. As we persist to explore the power of seeking His guidance, we will discover a deeper understanding of His will and a strengthened faith that can withstand any circumstance.

So, as we engage in the decision-making process, let us fix our eyes on the One who possesses all wisdom and knowledge. Let us earnestly seek His guidance through prayer, reliance on His word, and the counsel of trusted companions. Together, let us embrace God's priorities and yield to His shaping of our thoughts, desires, and decisions.

On our journey of seeking God's guidance in decision-making, we must also learn to recognize His signs and confirmations. As we align ourselves with His will and invite him into each aspect of our lives, He will guide us by opening doors and closing others.

Often, God speaks to us through circumstances, sending signals that lead us in the right direction. These signs can be subtle or blatant, but they are always purposeful. It could be a sudden opportunity that aligns perfectly with our desires and abilities, or it could be a closed door that forces us to reassess our path. As we prayerfully navigate through these moments, we can trust that God is orchestrating all things for our good.

Additionally, seeking God's guidance demands patience and tranquility. In our fast-paced world, it is easy to rush into decisions without pausing to listen and await His timing. God's timetable may not always synchronize with ours, but His timing is invariably flawless. As we nurture patience and trust in Him, we will find that waiting on His guidance yields greater blessings and fulfillment.

Another essential aspect of seeking God's guidance is discernment. The road ahead may be fraught with multiple options and possibilities, making it challenging to discern which path to take. However, as we deepen our relationship with God and mature in our faith, He equips us with discernment to recognize His voice amidst the clamor.

Discernment does not solely rely on our own understanding; it involves surrendering to the direction of the Holy Spirit. It encompasses seeking wisdom from God and diligently seeking His counsel. It may require seeking advice from Godly mentors, consulting His Word, and remaining open to correction. By embracing humility, we position ourselves to receive God's guidance and make sound decisions.

Seeking God's guidance means surrendering our own desires and submitting to His will. In our humanity, we often cling to our plans, dreams, and aspirations, longing to maintain control. However, when we release our grip and trust in God's sovereignty, we permit Him to lead us according to His perfect plan.

Surrendering to God's will requires courage and faith. It necessitates fostering a relationship with Him, laying down our own ambitions, and aligning our desires with His desires for us. As we yield to His guidance, we find the peace and contentment that can only arise from being in harmony with His purpose for our lives.

Finally, seeking God's guidance is an ongoing process. It is not an immediate reaction, nor is it a one-time decision, but rather a continual reliance on His wisdom and direction. As we integrate this practice as a consistent part of our lives, it becomes easier to discern His voice and align our choices with His will.

In conclusion, seeking God's guidance in decision-making is a journey of intimacy and surrender. Through prayer, meditation on His Word, seeking wise counsel, and exercising discernment, we can navigate life's complexities with confidence and assurance. As we trust in His wisdom and align our desires with His, we discover a peace that surpasses all understanding. Let us, therefore, continue to seek God's guidance, embracing His priorities and allowing Him to shape our thoughts, desires, and decisions. In doing so, we will experience the abundant life that comes from following His will alone, knowing that He is faithful to guide us every step of the way.

Let Go, Let God: Surrendering Control And Finding Peace

Life, with all its twists and turns, has a tendency to pull us in multiple directions, making it challenging to maintain a steady sense of control. We often find ourselves attempting to manipulate circumstances or desperately trying to steer our lives towards our desired outcomes. We try everything to gain control, or maintain control of our lives. However, what if surrendering control was the key to finding true peace and fulfillment?

In a world where self-reliance is celebrated, the notion of surrendering control to something greater can appear counterintuitive. Yet, as paradoxical as it may seem, surrendering control becomes an act of liberation. It is an acknowledgment of our limited perspective and an admission that there is an all-knowing, all-loving being whose plans far surpass our own.

When we surrender control to God, we tap into a power beyond our own understanding. We acknowledge that our desires and plans are not always aligned with God's will. This realization demands a profound shift in our mindset, one that necessitates letting go of our ego, our fear of uncertainty, and our relentless need for control.

Trusting God and His plans for us is not always easy, especially when life presents challenges that test our faith. However, as we reflect on the significance of surrendering control and trusting in God's plan, we begin to discern the purpose behind these trials. They serve as opportunities for growth, resilience, and deepening our connection with God.

Trusting God means embracing the belief that He has a grander vision for our lives, even if we cannot comprehend it in the present moment. It means having the courage to release our grip on the steering wheel, allowing God to navigate us through life's uncharted territories. It is in this surrender that we discover a peace that surpasses all human understanding.

Surrendering control to God and trusting Him doesn't mean that we become passive observers to our lives. Instead, it invites us to actively participate in the unfolding of His divine plan. As we surrender, we align our efforts, intentions, and actions with God's will, enabling him to work through us in miraculous ways.

Trusting God also entails fostering deeper connection with Him. It beckons us to solicit His guidance through prayer, meditation, and the study of His teachings. In these moments of solitude and reflection we cultivate a bond that fortifies our trust, empowering us to confront life's trails with unwavering faith.

Consider surrendering control and trusting in God as embarking on an adventurous journey. It requires us to let go of the map we drew for ourselves and to trust in a superior guiding force. Just as a ship surrenders itself to the ocean's currents, we surrender ourselves to God and His divine will, knowing that He will lead us towards our ultimate destination.

Trusting in God's plan and surrendering to it is a journey of faith and acceptance. It's about relinquishing control and entrusting your trust to a higher power, knowing that there is a divine purpose and direction for your life. Surrendering doesn't mean giving up; rather, it's about letting go of resistance and opening yourself to guidance and blessings that accompany with God's will. It's a mindset of letting go of your worries, fears, and desires, and instead embracing a deep sense of peace, knowing that God's plan surpasses our own. Through surrender, we find strength, resilience, and a profound sense of peace amidst life's challenges and uncertainties.

Amidst our chaos and uncertainty, there's solace in trusting God's plan and surrendering to His will. It's a narrative interwoven with strands of faith and acceptance, where every twist and turn forms part of a grand design beyond our comprehension. Surrendering isn't a sign of weakness but a testament to our conviction in something greater than ourselves.

In surrendering, we unearth freedom from the weight of attempting to control every outcome, releasing our hold on the steering wheel and allowing God to guide us on our journey with him. Through this surrender of control, we encounter a peace that transcends understanding, assured that we are cradled in the loving hands of our God.

Through the highs and lows, the victories and struggles, we discover resilience in surrendering to God's plan, trusting that each step we take is steered by His wisdom and love. And in this surrender, we find the courage to embrace whatever may come, knowing that we are not alone on this journey.

As we delve further into the exploration of surrendering control and trusting God, it is important to recognize that our journey is fraught with challenges. Doubts and fears may surface, tempting us to stray from fully embracing God's priorities. However, it is during those moments of vulnerability that we have the opportunity to deepen our trust and cultivate unwavering faith.

To surrender control and trust in God requires a level of surrender that goes beyond mere surrendering of external circumstances. It demands surrendering our very selves, including our ego, and desires. This surrender embodies humility, acknowledging that our understanding is limited, and that there is a higher wisdom at work in the tapestry of our lives.

To deepen our trust in God, it is imperative to turn inward and examine the depths of our hearts. We must squarely face our doubts and fears, acknowledging that they stem from a place of separation from God. By shedding light on these doubts and seeking God's guidance, we create space for transformation and spiritual growth.

A practical approach to surrender control and strengthening our trust is through prayer. Prayer enables us to lay our concerns before God, confident that He will provide guidance and support. It is through prayer that we invite God's presence into our lives, letting him to work miracles in ways we cannot fathom.

Another powerful method for surrendering control is the practice of meditation. By calming our minds and diving into the depths of stillness, we cultivate a space for God's wisdom to blossom within us. In this sacred sanctuary, we harmonize our intentions with God's will, empowering us to navigate life's trail with poise and a sense of deep connection.

Furthermore, studying God's word is paramount in fortifying our trust. The scriptures furnish us guidance and insight, providing a blueprint for living a purposeful and fulfilling life with God. By immersing ourselves in the teachings of God, we develop a stronger sense of trust and understanding, empowering us to face any adversity that may arise in future.

As we surrender control and place our trust in God, we must also acknowledge the power of surrender in our relationships with others. Letting go of control means relinquishing the need to manipulate or enforce our will upon others. It means honoring individual journeys and trusting that God is at work in their lives just as He is in ours. By honoring the autonomy and agency of others, we create an atmosphere of love, empathy, and compassion.

Surrendering control and trusting God is a lifelong journey, one that profoundly transforms our lives in countless ways. It requires a commitment to give up our desires and submit to a higher power. It is a transformative process that empowers us to negotiate life's challenges with resolute faith. As we submit, we find liberation and peace, knowing that we are being led towards our ultimate destination. So, let us persist on this adventure, striving to deepen our trust and surrender with every step, knowing that God's divine plan unfolds in ways far greater than we could ever imagine.

Purposeful Living: Embracing Service As A Way Of Life

In a world that glorifies individual accomplishments and personal success, it's simple to overlook the incredible joy and fulfillment found in selflessly serving others. However, as believers in a higher power, we are summoned to adopt a life of service and to follow in the footsteps of our compassionate God. In doing so, we unlock our hearts to a new level of purpose and fulfillment that cannot be achieved through any other means.

Assisting those in need, is an expression of love, an act that goes beyond ourselves and extends a helping hand to those who in need. When we selflessly serve others, we tap to a deeper part of our own humanity, discovering the true value of compassion and empathy. It is through service that we can witness the transformative power of God's love in the lives of those we touch, as well as our own lives.

Inspired by God's endless love and grace, we are moved to action and recognize that we have been blessed with gifts and talents, which are not solely meant for our personal gain but to be bestowed upon others. We become conduits of God's love, the instruments through which He works to bring kindness, healing, and hope to a broken world.

As we embrace a life dedicated to serving others, we learn to see beyond ourselves and our concerns. We begin to recognize the struggles, the suffering, and the isolation that often plague our fellow human beings. In those instances that we are called to respond, to step out of our comfort zones, and to extend a helping hand. Whether it involves volunteering at a local shelter, lending a listening ear to a friend in distress, or even offering a kind smile to a stranger, every act of service matters.

This experience inevitably brings about a transformation with a person, regardless of how someone perceives it. I was at a local home improvement store, purchasing some supplies one day. It was a busy Saturday afternoon and the store was packed with people doing their weekly shopping, due to this store clerks were busy. Though this task would not have been difficult under normal circumstances, due to an injury I sustained, it only made it this more difficult for me.

As I was retrieving supplies, a stranger approach me and asks if he could help me, I thanked him and said yes. He helped me to retrieve the items from high above and place them onto my cart, and asked if there was anything else I needed. Once I was done loading my cart, we had a brief conversation and went on our way. Later, I shared this with my wife and told her, "Can you imagine if the whole world operated in such a compassionate manner?"

You see, serving others is not a chore, but a privilege. In a world that could sometimes be harsh and indifferent, this stranger who assisted me, determined to be a force of goodness, spreading hope wherever his path led. Though the needs are great, if we understood that each person who commits to service in this way, together they could make the world a bit brighter.

This is precisely why service to others holds such immense importance. Service enables us to forge authentic connections with others, acknowledging their worth and inherent dignity. In serving, we humanize one another, recognizing that we are all part of a larger tapestry of life woven together by a divine thread. Through service, we break down the barriers that divide us, fostering a sense of unity and solidarity. It is in serving others that we reveal our true selves and gain deeper insight into our own identity.

Moreover, service acts as a poignant reminder of our own blessings and the gratitude we should cultivate in our hearts. Through engaging in acts of service, we heighten our awareness of the abundance in our lives and the privilege we enjoy. We realize our duty to responsibly steward these blessings, utilizing them to create a positive impact in the lives of others.

The beauty of service lies in its accessibility - it is not limited to grand gestures or extravagant gestures. It can be found in the simplest acts of kindness, in the everyday choices we make to prioritize others over ourselves. Service evolves into a way of life, a mindset that permeates our thoughts, attitudes, and actions. It is not something we do only when we have spare time or during designated service projects but rather a constant way of existence.

As we progress in our journey to embrace a life of service, let us remember that it is not solely our duty but also our privilege to serve others. Let us be encouraged by the countless examples throughout history of ordinary individuals who turned their hearts towards service and left a lasting impact on the world. As we continue to explore the depth of joy and fulfillment found in selflessly serving others, may we be inspired by God's love and grace, continuing to live out our divine priorities.

As we continue on our path of embracing a life of service, we must not overlook the potency of small acts of kindness and the ripple effect they can initiate. At times, it's tempting to believe that our efforts are insignificant in the grand scheme of things, but every act of service holds weight and carries the potential to create a positive change. Just like the aforementioned example, even seemingly minor gestures can yield significant impact.

In this fast-paced world, where everyone is constantly rushing from one task to another, it's essential to pause and take a moment to slow down. By doing so, we can truly observe the individuals around us who may be in need of a helping hand or a sympathetic ear. It's often the small things that can make a big difference in someone's day, like offering a genuine compliment, holding the door open, or simply asking how someone is doing and attentively listening to their response.

Service encompasses more than just the physical or material support we provide; it's also about the emotional and spiritual support we offer. Sometimes, all it takes is a kind word or a compassionate gesture to uplift someone's spirit and remind them that they are seen and valued. We possess the incredible opportunity to be instruments of healing and hope, spreading kindness wherever we go. We have a great opportunity to not only help others but make positive changes through the service we offer others.

However, it's important to remember that embracing a life of service doesn't entail neglecting our own well-being. On the contrary, when we take care of ourselves, we are better equipped to serve others effectively. It's akin to the safety instructions given on airplanes; we must secure our own oxygen masks first before assisting others. Similarly, we need to prioritize our own physical, emotional, and spiritual health, striving for balance in our lives to ensure we can wholeheartedly continue our services to others.

As we immerse ourselves further into a life of service, it's inevitable that obstacles and challenges will arise. There may be times when we feel discouraged or burdened. But in those moments, let us remember our divine calling - to serve selflessly, mirroring the unconditional compassion of our gracious God towards us unconditionally. It is inevitable that the service we offer others will have a positive effect on that of others and their lives.

We can find strength and inspiration by seeking guidance from scripture and the examples set by those who have gone before us. Countless individuals throughout history have selflessly dedicated their lives to serving others. They have shown us that it is possible to make a difference, even in the face of adversity.

So, let us never underestimate the potential impact of our acts of service. While we may never fully see or understand the extent of their influence, we can trust that they ripple out into the world, touching lives and sowing seeds of love and compassion.

Embracing a life of service is not just an obligation but a privilege. As we continue to serve others with joy and humility, we not only transform their lives but our own as well. Let us remember that we are part of a larger tapestry of interconnectedness, where every act of kindness and service draw us nearer together.

May you be encouraged and inspired to embrace a life of service. As you go about your day, may you extend love, compassion, and grace to those around you. May you experience the beauty and fulfillment that comes from selflessly serving others, guided by the endless love and grace of our divine Creator.

The Soul's Compass: Navigating Towards Spiritual Growth

Understanding the importance of focusing on our spiritual growth through prayer, study, and fellowship leads to a stronger relationship with God and a transformed life.

In today's fast-paced world, it's easy to get swept up in the chaos and lose sight of what truly matters. We find ourselves juggling countless responsibilities, often neglecting the most vital aspect of our lives: our spiritual well-being. However, by prioritizing God's intentions and deliberately investing in our connection with Him, we tap into a deep well of strength, guidance, and fulfillment.

At the core of prioritizing our spiritual growth lies the practice of prayer. Through prayer, we establish a direct line of communication with our Creator, allowing us to open our hearts, share our joys, express our sorrows, and seek guidance. In these moments of connection with God, we find inner peace and take comfort in knowing that we are never alone, regardless of the challenges we face.

Moreover, prayer acts as a catalyst for change. As we consistently seek God's presence, we invite transformation into our lives. Our desires align with His will, and we become vessels for His purposes. Through prayer, we learn to surrender our own plans and trust in a greater plan. It's through this surrender that we experience the profound joy of being part of something much bigger than ourselves.

In addition to prayer, we must recognize the profound significance of study. When we delve into the sacred texts of the Bible, we discover a treasure trove of timeless wisdom, guidance, and revelation. By immersing ourselves in these teachings, we nurture our minds, broaden our perspectives, and deepen our comprehension of God's purpose for us.

Studying the scriptures equips us with invaluable tools to navigate life's complexities. Within its pages, we encounter tales of faith, resilience, and redemption, serving as beacons of hope even in our darkest moments. As we reflect on these narratives, our spiritual resolve is fortified, empowering us to surmount obstacles and mature into the individuals that God envisions us to become.

Furthermore, alongside prayer and study, fellowship holds a pivotal role in our spiritual journey. Surrounding ourselves with kindred spirits who share our faith walk fosters a sense of accountability, encouragement, and collective advancement. Through meaningful connections with fellow believers, we discover solace, inspiration, and the fortitude to persevere through life's trials.

Fellowship is a chance for us to glean wisdom from one another's stories, exchange testimonies, and uplift each other through shared worship and service. When we join together with a common goal, we magnify the impact of our individual spiritual paths, fostering an environment ripe for growth and change.

As we explore the many blessings that come with prioritizing our spiritual journey, we must remember that this isn't merely a task to cross off our lists. It's a lifelong dedication to nurturing a relationship with God, one that demands deliberate time, effort, and dedication.

By embracing God's priorities and carving out space for prayer, study, and fellowship, we set ourselves up for a profound transformation. We shift our gaze from the fleeting distractions of the world to the eternal truths that hold the power to shape our lives and redefine our purpose. Let's embark on this journey together, hearts open, minds eager, and spirits primed for renewal.

Within the realm of spiritual growth, fellowship acts as a catalyst for change, providing us with invaluable connections that nurture our faith. When we surround ourselves with kindred spirits who share our journey, we create a space of accountability, support, and collective progress.

In fellowship, we discover the richness of learning from each other's life journeys. Each person's path is a tapestry of trials, victories, and moments of revelation. Sharing our stories brings insight and understanding, reminding us that our struggles are shared and that wisdom can be found in the diverse paths we tread.

Coming together in fellowship, we uplift one another through shared worship and service. As we join our hearts, hands, and voices in praise, we create a collective expression of worship that resonates deeply within us. In these moments, we feel the transformative presence of God among us, filling us with His love and grace.

Furthermore, serving together allows us to put our faith into action. Through acts of kindness, compassion, and selflessness, we reflect the character of our Creator. By reaching out to the vulnerable, caring for the sick, and extending a helping hand to those in need, we embody God's love in tangible ways, both within our community and beyond.

Within the fellowship, we find the strength to persevere and move forward. The journey of spiritual growth has its challenges, and there are times when our faith wavers or the path ahead seems unclear. Yet, surrounded by fellow believers, we are reminded of the power of collective faith. Their unwavering support, prayers, and words of wisdom guide us back to the path aligned with divine priorities.

As we journey through life, let's remember that prioritizing spiritual growth isn't just another item to tick off a list. It's a lifelong commitment to nurturing a deep, meaningful relationship with God. It calls for intentional time, effort, and devotion to prayer, study, and fellowship. It requires vulnerability, humility, and a willingness to align our desires with our Creator's will.

So, as you ponder the importance of placing spiritual growth at the forefront, remember it's a journey to embrace and relish. It's a path of self-discovery, transformation, and divine connection. It's a journey that shapes your life, refines your purpose, and equips you to tackle the challenges ahead.

Guard this sacred commitment with determination, steering clear of worldly distractions. And as you invest in spiritual growth through prayer, study, and fellowship, take comfort in knowing you're not alone. God walks beside you, guiding, supporting, and molding you into the person He intended.

Step forward with hope, an open mind, and a spirit ready for change. Your journey toward spiritual growth is a treasure, unveiling new wonders each day. Embrace this opportunity, letting God's plan steer you toward a life filled with purpose, joy, and steadfast faith.

In embracing God's priorities, we discover true strength, and the chaos of the world fades away. Prioritizing spiritual growth connects us to something greater, immersing us in eternal truths that shape our lives and transform our souls.

Walking With God: Deepening Your Relationship Daily

As we traverse through life, one truth becomes evident: our relationship with God is the foundation from which everything else flows. It is the source of guidance, strength, and love that bolsters us through both the trials and triumphs we encounter. Yet, cultivating a deep and intimate relationship with God demands intentionality and dedication. It mandates prioritizing our time, creating space for communion, and earnestly seeking a genuine connection with God.

The initial step in nurturing our relationship with God is to prioritize regular communion. Similarly to any relationship, consistent communication is essential for building intimacy. We need to set aside dedicated time each day to connect with God through prayer, meditation, and reflection. This deliberate practice allows us to immerse ourselves in His presence, listen to His voice, and share our hopes, fears, and dreams. It is through this communion that we cultivate a deeper understanding of His will for our lives and allow His guidance to shape our decisions and actions.

Establishing a sturdy foundation for our life journey also involves seeking spiritual nourishment. Just as our physical bodies require sustenance to thrive, our souls need the nourishment of God's word to grow. Scripture is a reservoir of wisdom and truth, providing us with guidance, comfort, and inspiration. By immersing ourselves in scripture, we open our hearts and minds to the transformative power of God's message. Through reading, studying, and meditating on His word, we cultivate a deeper understanding of His character and purpose, allowing His truth to shape our perspectives and actions.

However, our relationship with God extends beyond our personal devotion and study. It also thrives within the context of community. Surrounding ourselves with like-minded believers helps us grow and gain new insights through fellowship and shared experiences. Engaging in discussions, attending worship services, and participating in small groups enable us to learn from one another and witness the diverse ways God interacts with His children. Being part of a faith community encourages us, challenges us, and strengthens our connection to God as we walk this spiritual journey together.

Lastly, nurturing our relationship with God includes surrendering control and relying on His guidance. Often, we try to navigate life's complexities entirely on our own, relying on our own understanding and limited perspective. Nonetheless, true intimacy with God comes when we acknowledge our need for His wisdom and let go of our personal agenda. Surrendering control allows us to trust in His plans, even when they differ from our own. It requires a demeanor of humility, acknowledging that His ways are higher than ours and His timing is perfect.

We have explored the fundamental aspects of nurturing our relationship with God. We have seen the importance of regular communion, the value of spiritual nourishment, the importance of community, and the power of surrender. By prioritizing these aspects in our lives, we establish a robust foundation upon which our relationship with God can flourish.

As we continue our exploration, we will delve deeper into practical ways to implement these principles into our daily routines. We will explore specific practices and habits that can help us cultivate a profound and transformative connection with God, where we will discover actionable steps to deepen our relationship with God. Here, we will explore practical ways to implement the fundamental aspects of nurturing our relationship with God into our daily lives. These actionable steps can assist us in cultivating a profound and transformative connection with God.

One practical approach to deepening our relationship with God is through practicing gratitude. Allocating time each day to express gratitude for the blessings in our lives redirects our focus from what we lack to what we have been given. Gratitude opens our hearts to recognize God's abundant love and provision, fostering a sense of contentment and joy. We can start by keeping a gratitude journal, wherein we jot down moments, experiences, or people for which we are truly grateful. This simple practice reminds us of God's faithfulness and aligns our hearts with His goodness.

Another essential practice is that of embracing silence and solitude. Amidst the hustle and bustle of life, finding moments of stillness can be challenging, but they are crucial for nurturing our relationship with God. Carving out intentional time for silence and solitude provides space for us to listen to His gentle whisper, to reflect on His presence in our lives, and to discern His guidance. Whether it is a few minutes in the morning or a longer period of retreat, these moments of solitude enable us to quiet our minds and open our hearts to God's voice.

Serving others with love is an integral part of our spiritual journey. When we serve selflessly, we mirror Christ's example of love and compassion. It is through serving others that we experience the unconditional love of God flowing through us. Whether it's volunteering at a local charity, helping a neighbor in need, or using our skills to make a positive impact in our community, service becomes an expression of our love for God and others.

Additionally, cultivating a spirit of forgiveness is vital for deepening our relationship with God. Forgiveness is not solely an act we bestow on others but also a gift we receive from God. When we forgive those who have wronged us, we release the burden of bitterness and resentment, creating space for healing and reconciliation. Just as God forgives us, we are called to forgive others, allowing the transformative power of His love to restore relationships and bring about inner peace.

Nurturing our relationship with God involves maintaining a posture of humility and perpetual learning. Recognizing that we are always students of God's wisdom keeps us open to growth and transformation. We can engage in regular spiritual practices such as reading, enriching literature, attending conferences or retreats, or seeking guidance from wise mentors and spiritual leaders. These opportunities enable us to deepen our understanding of God's love and broaden our horizons.

As we contemplate these practical steps, let us remember that our relationship with God is an ongoing journey. It is not about achieving perfection but rather about continually seeking and growing closer to Him. By integrating these practices into our daily lives, we can foster a deep and intimate connection with God, finding guidance, strength, and love in our relationship with him.

Nurturing our relationship with God demands intentionality and commitment. By prioritizing regular communion, seeking spiritual nourishment, participating in a faith community, surrendering control, practicing gratitude, embracing silence and solitude, serving others, cultivating forgiveness, and maintaining a posture of humility, we lay a solid foundation for our relationship with God to flourish. These practical steps pave the way for a profound and transformative connection with God, equipping us to navigate life's journey with grace and love. May we embrace these practices eagerly and wholeheartedly, for in doing so, we deepen our relationship with God and experience the abundant life He has promised.

Hope In The Storm: Navigating Life's Challenges With Faith

Examining how our faith equips us to overcome various challenges and adversities allows us to grow spiritually and experience God's faithfulness.

Life is a beautiful journey brimming with ups and downs, joys and sorrows. It is during the difficult moments, the times when we confront adversity head-on, that our faith truly comes into play. When we encounter obstacles that seem insurmountable, it is our steadfast belief in a higher power that allows us to persevere and overcome.

Faith is often depicted as a source of strength, a light that illuminates our path and provides us with the courage to face any challenge that comes our way. It is through faith that we discover solace and comfort in the face of adversity, knowing that we are not alone in our struggles. As we traverse life's trials, our faith becomes a stronghold, a refuge where we can find serenity and optimism.

One of the most remarkable facets of faith is its ability to transform our mindset. When we encounter challenges, it is easy to succumb to despair and doubt. However, when we choose to embrace faith, we shift our focus from the problem itself to the belief that there is a purpose behind it. We understand that challenges are not meant to shatter us but rather to strengthen us and mold us into the individuals we are destined to become.

Faith teaches us to view challenges as avenues for growth and evolution. It reminds us that even in the midst of adversity, there is always a lesson to be learned, a chance for both personal and spiritual growth. When we face challenges with faith, we open ourselves up to the possibility of transformation, allowing God to work through us and refine us into improved iterations of ourselves.

Faith grants us the assurance that we are never alone. During trials, it's common to feel isolated, as if no one understands or cares about our struggles. But faith reminds us that God is with us, walking beside us every step of the way. When we confront challenges with faith, we can draw strength from the knowledge that we are upheld and loved by God's presence, far greater than ourselves.

In the midst of challenges, it is important to remember that faith doesn't promise a life devoid of difficulties. Instead, it equips us with the tools necessary to surmount them. Faith empowers us to face adversity head-on, knowing that we are not defined by our circumstances but rather by how we choose to respond to them. Faith gives us the strength to persevere, even when the odds seem stacked against us.

As we journey through life, encountering various challenges along the way, let us hold to our faith with unwavering determination. May we remember that challenges are not roadblocks but stepping stones toward personal growth and spiritual enlightenment. With faith as our guide, we can surmount any obstacle, confident in the knowledge that God's faithfulness knows no bounds.

As we continue our exploration of faith and its profound role in overcoming challenges, let us delve deeper into the intricacies of this remarkable journey. Throughout our lives, we will hear stories of individuals who have witnessed the transformative power of faith in their own lives. Be prepared to be inspired and uplifted as these stories unfold. Through their experiences, I hope your spirit is also inspired and uplifted, reaffirming the belief that faith can truly overcome any challenge.

Let us begin with the story of someone I will name as Rosa, a single mother who found herself grappling with financial hardships. Despite working tirelessly, she struggled to make ends meet and provide for her children. In the midst of her despair, Rosa turned to her faith, seeking solace and guidance. With unwavering determination, she clung to her belief that God would provide for her family's needs. Through a series of unexpected events and connections, Rosa miraculously received a job opportunity that surpassed her expectations, enabling her to not only support her children but also find a sense of stability in her life. Her story serves as a reminder that even in our darkest moments, faith can bring forth miracles and open doors we never thought possible.

Another remarkable story is that of Mark, who was diagnosed with a life-threatening illness. Faced with the uncertainty of His health, Mark chose to face His challenges with faith. Instead of succumbing to fear and despair, He relied on His steadfast belief that God had a purpose for His life. Throughout His journey, Mark unearthed a profound sense of inner peace and strength that carried him through the most difficult times. His story stands as a testament to the power of faith to provide comfort and courage, even when faced with seemingly insurmountable obstacles.

Finally, we have the story of Elsa, a survivor of domestic abuse who found the strength to break free from an abusive relationship. In her darkest moments, Elsa turned to her faith in pursuit of liberation and healing. Relying on her belief in a higher power, she gradually gained the courage and self-worth needed to escape her abusive situation. Through her journey, Elsa discovered that faith not only empowers us to overcome external challenges but also enables us to find the inner strength necessary to reclaim our lives and reconstruct after enduring trauma.

These stories of resilience and triumph illustrate the remarkable capacity of faith to empower individuals to overcome adversity. As you read through their narratives, may you find encouragement and inspiration to face your own challenges with unwavering faith. Remember that regardless of the nature or magnitude of the obstacles you encounter, your faith can provide the foundation for transformation and growth.

Faith empowers us to overcome challenges by instilling in us a sense of purpose, granting us the resilience to persevere, and reminding us that we are never alone. Through faith, we can view challenges as opportunities for personal and spiritual growth, allowing God to work through us and mold us into improved versions of ourselves. Therefore, as you traverse your unique journeys and face your own trials, may you hold onto your faith with unwavering determination and experience the transformative power it holds. May you continue to find solace, hope, and the unending love of God amidst the challenges that come your way.

Spiritual Harmony: Embracing God's Priorities In Love

In our journey of embracing God's priorities, we come to the aspect that affects every single one of us—relationships. The bonds we form with others are fundamental to our lives and shape who we are as individuals. When we invite God's priorities into our relationships, we witness a profound transformation that fills our lives with love, forgiveness, empathy, and harmony.

Love becomes the driving force that steers our interactions. The divine love bestowed upon us by the higher power flows through us and radiates outwards, impacting the lives of those around us. It is a love that transcends limitations, embraces differences, and seeks to uplift and inspire. When we prioritize serving God first, our relationships become an avenue to exemplify this extraordinary love.

Forgiveness, often a difficult trait to cultivate, assumes a new meaning when God's priorities are at the forefront. As we acknowledge the inherent worth of each individual, we become more willing to let go of past hurts and grudges. The divine perspective reminds us that we are all imperfect beings seeking growth, and extending forgiveness becomes an act of compassion and restoration. It opens the door to reconciliation and allows relationships to flourish in ways we could never have imagined.

Empathy blossoms as we prioritize God in our relationships. Viewing others through the lens of shared humanity, we develop a deep understanding and compassion for others. We are able to put ourselves in their shoes, allowing empathy to guide our words, actions, and decisions. This empathetic bond strengthens our relationships, fostering an environment of kindness, support, and understanding.

Embracing God's priorities, we also discover the beauty of harmony within our relationships. By aligning our intentions with those of a higher power, we create a space where differences can coexist peacefully. Recognizing that every individual has a unique contribution to make, we learn to appreciate diverse perspectives and opinions. Instead of succumbing to conflict or division, we prioritize unity, working together towards a common purpose and creating a harmonious bond that strengthens the fabric of our relationships.

As we reflect on the influence of embracing God's plan and priorities in our relationships, we are reminded of the boundless potential inherent that lies within each connection we forge. There is immense power in recognizing that serving God first invites a divine presence into our interactions, infusing them with unconditional love, forgiveness, empathy, and harmony.

Incorporating divine priorities into our relationships is a conscious choice, one that requires us to consistently shift our focus away from ourselves and towards a higher purpose. It is through this selfless commitment to prioritize God that we truly find ourselves, as well as the strength to build meaningful and fulfilling relationships.

But what transpires when challenges emerge? How do we traverse the complexities of relationships while keeping God's priorities at the forefront? Join us in the second part of this chapter as we explore practical strategies and insights to overcome obstacles and enhance our adherence to God's priorities in relationships.

In our journey of embracing God's priorities in relationships, we are bound to confront challenges that test our commitment and resolve. These obstacles may manifest as misunderstandings, conflicts, or divergent perspectives. However, it is precisely in these moments that we have the opportunity to enhance our understanding and practice of God's plan and priorities in our lives.

One crucial aspect of fostering God's priorities in our relationships is developing effective communication. Clear and empathetic communication serves as a potent tool for building bridges of understanding and resolving conflicts. By actively listening to others with an open heart and mind, we can genuinely strive to understand their point of view and find common ground. Through compassionate communication, we can address differences with respect and grace, allowing our relationships to grow and blossom.

Another vital practice in embracing God's priorities is exercising patience and forgiveness. As imperfect beings, we are prone to making mistakes and inadvertently hurt those around us. It is in these moments that God reminds us of the need for forgiveness. By embodying forgiveness, we acknowledge our own fallibility and extend compassion to others, enabling healing and reconciliation to take place. In doing so, we create room for growth and transformation in our relationships.

While prioritizing God's perspectives, it is also essential to set healthy boundaries. Boundaries help safeguard not only our own well-being but also the integrity of the relationships we value. By clearly articulating our needs, expectations, and limits, we create an environment of respect and understanding. This enables each individual to express themselves authentically while maintaining a sense of safety and mutual support.

Moreover, embracing God's priorities calls us to practice empathy and understanding even when confronted with difficult people or challenging circumstances. It is important to recognize that everyone is on their own unique journey, and they cannot fully comprehend the burdens they may be carrying. By empathizing with their experiences and perspective, we cultivate a genuine empathy that fosters compassion, connection, and meaningful growth in our relationships.

In our quest to prioritize God's intentions within relationships, self-reflection plays a crucial role. Taking the time to examine our own thoughts, attitudes, and behaviors grant us to identify areas for personal growth and transformation. Through introspection, we gain clarity and insight into how we can better align ourselves with His priorities, allowing our relationships to thrive.

Ultimately, embracing His priorities in relationships demands a commitment to ongoing growth and self-improvement. It is a continuous practice that invites us to be mindful of our intentions, words, and actions. By prioritizing God, we invite a deep-seated transformation that enriches not only our relationships but also our own lives.

As we conclude this exploration of embracing God's priorities in relationships, let us remember that the journey toward His connection and fulfillment is ongoing. It requires patience, perseverance, and a deep commitment to serving God first in all our interactions. By embracing His priorities in our relationships, we can transcend the limitations of our human nature and experience the true joy and fulfillment that arise from building loving, forgiving, empathetic, and harmonious connections.

I pray that this chapter serves as a reminder and guide on your journey toward embracing God's plans for us in all your relationships. May the transformative power of God's love continue to flow through you, touching the lives of those around you. And as you navigate the complexities of relationships, may you find solace and strength knowing that His priorities are not a distant concept but a profound reality that can be lived and embodied each day.

Walking In Grace: Embracing God's Plan For Us Every Day

In a world brimming with competing agendas and endless distractions, it is easy to lose sight of what holds significance. As individuals striving to serve God first, it becomes crucial to integrate God's priorities into our daily routines. By doing so, we not only harmonize our lives with God's purpose but also become vessels through which God's light can shine, impacting the world around us.

Embracing God's priorities commences with a steadfast understanding of what they entail. It goes beyond mere religious rituals or acts of service; it involves a sincere commitment to living out God's love, grace, and truth in every aspect of our lives. It requires a deliberate choice to prioritize God's will over our own desires and to seek His guidance in all decisions.

The initial step in integrating His plans into our daily routines is to cultivate a vibrant and consistent connection with God through prayer and reflection. God longs to converse with us and reveal His will, and it is through prayer that we can forge a deep and personal relationship with him. By carving out time each day to commune with God, we invite His presence into our lives, opening ourselves up to receive divine guidance, wisdom, and strength.

Building upon this foundation, we can begin to navigate our daily routines with a renewed perspective. Every action, no matter how mundane, can present an opportunity to shine God's light. Whether it is at work, in our relationships, or within our communities, our commitment to live out His priorities should be evident through our words, actions, and attitudes.

At work, we can exemplify integrity, honesty, and humility, seeking to glorify God in all that we do. By treating our colleagues with love, respect, and kindness, we create a positive environment wherein the radiance of Christ can shine forth. Embracing God's priorities in our work means placing excellence and diligence at the forefront, knowing that our efforts are ultimately a reflection of our dedication to serving God.

Similarly, in our relationships, we can prioritize forgiveness, reconciliation, and compassion. By extending grace to others, even when it is difficult, we exemplify the love and forgiveness God has shown us. We can perceive our interactions with others as God's assignments, opportunities to offer encouragement, hope, and healing into their lives. Our relationships become a platform to share God's love and truth with those around us, profoundly impacting their lives.

In our communities, we have the opportunity to serve as agents of change, echoing God's heart for justice, mercy, and compassion. By actively participating in acts of service, extending help in need, and advocating for causes close to God's heart, we demonstrate our commitment to living out His priorities. Through small acts of kindness and intentional acts of generosity, we contribute to the transformation of our communities, one life at a time.

As we integrate God's priorities into our daily routines, we realize that serving God first is not a burden but an honor. In every situation, we have the opportunity to be a vessel through which God's love and grace flow. By aligning our lives with His priorities, we become beacons of hope, diffusing God's light and influencing the world around us.

In living out God's plans for us, we fulfill our ultimate purpose, glorifying God and drawing others closer to Him. This journey of embracing His plans is ongoing, and as we continue to seek God's guidance and grow in His love, we are constantly transformed into His likeness. It is a journey that requires persistence, faith, and unwavering commitment, but the rewards are immeasurable, both in this life and the next.

And so, as we embark on this journey, let us embrace His priorities with open hearts and minds, knowing that through our daily routines, we have the incredible opportunity to shine God's light and impact the world around us. With every step we take, let us remember that when we serve God first, everything else falls into place. Living out His priorities in everyday life requires perseverance, faith, and an unwavering commitment. As we progress on this journey, we must be prepared for the challenges and obstacles that may come our way. It is through these trials that our character is tested, and our faith strengthened.

One of the key aspects of living out God's priorities is the importance of self-reflection. Consistently dedicating the time to examine our thoughts, motives, and actions allows us to ensure that we are aligned with God's will. Self-reflection helps us identify areas where we may have strayed from His priorities and offers an opportunity for growth and course correction. By humbling ourselves before God, acknowledging our flaws, and seeking His forgiveness and guidance, we can continue to walk in His ways.

In our pursuit of God's priorities, we must also need to be mindful of the power of our words. Our words have the ability to build up or tear down, to bring comfort or cause pain. When we speak with kindness, love, and respect, we reflect the character of God. It is important to remember that our words can have a substantial impact on those around us, and by speaking life-giving words, we can be instruments of healing, encouragement, and hope.

Living out God's priorities also entails adopting a mindset of gratitude. Gratitude shifts our focus from what we lack to what we have been blessed with. It is a catalyst for contentment and joy. When we cultivate an attitude of gratitude, we become aware of God's hand at work in our lives and recognize His faithfulness and provision. Gratitude not only transforms our own hearts but also permeates the atmosphere in which we live, infusing it with optimism and thankfulness.

Furthermore, living out God's priorities requires us to extend grace to ourselves and others. As imperfect beings, we are bound to make mistakes and fall short. It is in these moments that we must remember that God's grace is abundant and His love is unconditional. By demonstrating patience, forgiveness, and understanding to ourselves and those around us, we exemplify the grace and love that God has shown us.

In the midst of our daily routines, we may encounter situations that test our commitment to His priorities. It is in these moments that we must stand firm in our faith and trust that God's wisdom and guidance will lead us through. By seeking His counsel and relying on Him, we can navigate the complexities of life with confidence and discernment.

Let us be reminded that living out God's priorities is not a one-time event but a lifelong journey. It is a daily choice we make, a commitment to put God first in all areas of our lives. By doing so, we not only experience the joy and peace that come from aligning with His will but also become agents of transformation in the world around us.

May this journey of embracing His priorities continue to shape and mold us into the image of Christ. Let us embrace the trials and triumphs, knowing that through our daily routines, we have the incredible opportunity to shine God's light and impact the world. By serving God first, we become instruments of His love, grace, and truth, bringing glory to His name and drawing others closer to Him.

And so, as we step forward in faith, may we find solace in perseverance, knowing that we are not alone. God is with us every stride of the way, guiding and empowering us to live out His plans in our everyday lives. Through him, we can make a significant and lasting impact on the world around us.

CHAPTER 4
"The Power Of Forgiveness"

Forgiveness: The Key To Empowerment And Inner Peace

Deep within us lies the profound ability to heal and grow, a power capable of liberating us from pain and resentment. This extraordinary force is forgiveness. Through forgiveness, we open the door to a life of freedom, peace, and genuine liberation.

Forgiveness transcends mere pardon; it's a transformative journey that starts from within. It's a deliberate decision to release the weight of anger, hurt, and resentment, freeing our hearts and minds from the chains anchoring us to our past.

Embracing forgiveness lays the groundwork for personal growth and healing. It empowers us to reshape our perspectives and rewrite our narratives. Forgiveness offers us the chance to retell our stories, shifting the focus from pain and suffering to resilience and triumph. It enables us to reclaim our agency and take charge of our emotional well-being.

Through forgiveness, we nurture compassion, both for others and ourselves. It's a compassionate acknowledgment of our shared humanity, recognizing that we're all imperfect beings capable of causing harm, whether knowingly or unknowingly. By extending forgiveness, we embrace the reality that we've all made mistakes and seek mercy.

Moreover, forgiveness holds the profound ability to liberate us from the past's grasp. It's through forgiveness that we find freedom from the burdens of grudges and the heaviness of resentment. When we opt for forgiveness, we seize back our control and break free from the cycles of pain that bind us. We carve out space within ourselves for healing, growth, and, ultimately, peace.

Forgiveness isn't a sign of weakness but an act of strength. It takes immense courage and vulnerability to embrace forgiveness fully. It demands that we confront our pain directly and embark on a journey of self-discovery and self-compassion. Through forgiveness, we break down the barriers of bitterness and open ourselves to the vast array of opportunities that await us.

The power of forgiveness transcends the past; it reaches into the present and future alike. By choosing forgiveness, we pave the way for meaningful connections and relationships. We create room for love, empathy, and understanding to thrive. Our willingness to forgive becomes a guiding light, drawing positivity and fostering harmony within our lives and communities.

In embracing the transformative potential of forgiveness, we set out on a path of healing and growth. We enter a realm where compassion, understanding, and peace reign supreme. As we let go of resentments and shed the chains of our past, we unlock a future where freedom and joy become our constant companions.

The journey of forgiveness calls to us, urging us to embrace its profound potential for transformation. Will you courageously take that pivotal first step toward freedom and healing? Will you unlock the profound power of forgiveness and set out on a path toward inner peace? Remember, the decision rests with you.

In our quest for forgiveness, we must navigate the intricate labyrinth of our emotions and confront the lingering pains within. This journey is no easy feat, yet its rewards are immeasurable. As we embark upon this exploration of forgiveness's potency, let us delve into the rich tapestry of transformation awaiting us.

Forgiveness is not merely a singular event; it is an ongoing process demanding patience and self-compassion. It often commences with the acknowledgment of our own wounds, allowing ourselves to intimately experience the pain inflicted upon us. Through the recognition and validation of our emotions, we open ourselves to the prospect of genuine healing.

Through forgiveness, we challenge the narratives that have ensnared us, breaking free from the shackles of victimhood to reclaim our personal power. It is through forgiveness that we unearth our inner strength and resilience, transcending the constraints of our past. Forgiveness empowers us to ascend beyond our circumstances, forging a future grounded in love, compassion, and growth.

On our journey towards forgiveness, it's vital to understand that it doesn't equate to forgetting or excusing others' actions. Forgiveness doesn't entail erasing pain or downplaying its impact on our lives. Instead, it's an act of self-compassion and preservation—a pledge to our own well-being and a refusal to let past wounds dictate our present.

In the pursuit of forgiveness, we discover the art of setting healthy boundaries and shielding ourselves from further harm. We acknowledge that forgiveness doesn't demand reconciliation or an invitation for our transgressors to re-enter our lives. Sometimes, forgiveness is a solitary act—a liberation from emotional bonds that enables us to advance unburdened by resentment.

As we navigate the complexities of forgiveness, practicing self-compassion becomes paramount. We must extend patience to ourselves as we undergo healing, respecting our individual journeys and timelines. Forgiveness isn't a linear path; rather, it's a fluid, evolving process unique to each of us. Along the way, we may encounter setbacks and moments of uncertainty, yet with each stride forward, we emerge stronger and more resilient.

In our quest for forgiveness, we're also called to extend compassion and forgiveness to ourselves. Recognizing our own imperfections and past mistakes, we embrace self-forgiveness, liberating ourselves from the weight of guilt and shame. Through this act of self-compassion, we affirm our inherent worthiness of love and acceptance.

As we progress through this chapter, let's keep in mind that forgiveness isn't a final destination but a continual practice. It demands courage and offers liberation, unlocking the door to a life brimming with freedom, peace, and joy. The journey of forgiveness beckons us to release the grip of the past, freeing ourselves from the chains of resentment and embracing a future overflowing with boundless potential.

So, I invite you to take a deep breath, summon your courage, and embark on this transformative voyage toward forgiveness. It's a selfless act that promises to alter your life indefinitely. Embrace the profound healing it offers and trust in its ability to profoundly impact your existence. Know that within you lies the strength to heal, to forgive, and to cultivate a life enriched with compassion, empathy, and serenity.

The choice is yours. Will you choose forgiveness?

The Heart Of Forgiveness: Embracing Understanding And Compassion

Forgiveness entails releasing feelings of resentment and the urge for retaliation. Clinging to these negative emotions only prolongs our suffering and impedes our ability to heal.

It's a nuanced and deeply personal journey involving letting go of resentment, anger, and the desire for revenge toward those who've wronged us. Forgiveness doesn't equate to condoning or excusing their actions, nor does it mean forgetting the past. Instead, it's a deliberate choice to relinquish negative emotions and embrace peace and understanding as we move forward.

Forgiveness is a multifaceted concept brimming with transformative power. It serves as a liberation from the chains of anger, resentment, and pain. In the following exploration, we'll delve into the many facets of forgiveness—clarifying its definition, dispelling common misconceptions, and uncovering the profound benefits it bestows upon both the forgiver and the forgiven.

To grasp the essence of forgiveness, we must first define it clearly. Forgiveness isn't about excusing or justifying others' actions, nor does it signal weakness. Rather, it's a deliberate choice to release negative emotions, granting ourselves the chance to heal and progress. It's a voluntary surrender, allowing the scars of the past to evolve into personal growth and inner tranquility.

Yet, forgiveness often faces misconceptions that breed hesitancy or resistance. One prevalent myth suggests that forgiveness entails forgetting or denying the pain inflicted upon us. However, true forgiveness doesn't erase the memory of hurt; instead, it acknowledges it while refusing to let it dictate our future. Recollecting our pain can spur growth, guiding us toward wiser choices.

Another misconception is that forgiveness hinges on receiving an apology or witnessing justice served. While an apology can facilitate healing, it isn't a prerequisite for forgiveness. Waiting for an apology may trap us in bitterness and resentment, hindering our own happiness. True forgiveness transcends external actions, empowering us to safeguard our emotional well-being.

The journey of forgiveness is transformative, benefiting both the forgiver and the forgiven. By embracing forgiveness, we shed the heavy burden weighing on our hearts and minds. We break free from the cycle of negativity, finding solace and fulfillment within. Forgiveness allows us to rewrite our story, redirecting our focus toward personal growth and nurturing healthier relationships.

Furthermore, forgiveness generates a ripple effect that extends beyond ourselves. It offers the forgiven a chance at redemption, reclaiming their humanity, and fostering personal development. It fosters empathy and understanding, creating an atmosphere conducive to change and healing.

Studies underscore the myriad physical, mental, and emotional benefits of forgiveness. Releasing grudges in favor of forgiveness has been linked to reduced stress, anxiety, and depression, along with improved heart health. It bolsters our immune system, enhances self-esteem, and elevates overall well-being. Forgiveness serves as a catalyst for restoration and renewal, illuminating a path toward a brighter, more enriching life.

Understanding forgiveness is pivotal in unlocking its transformative power. By delving into its dimensions, dispelling myths, and acknowledging its benefits, we set the stage for profound change. Though the path to forgiveness may be arduous, its rewards are immeasurable. As we embark on this collective journey, let's open ourselves to the profound potential of forgiveness.

Forgiveness, across time, has been revered as a force capable of repairing fractured relationships, healing deep wounds, and instilling inner peace. As we delve deeper into its essence, let's explore its significance and practical strategies for fostering forgiveness in our lives.

Central to forgiveness is recognizing our shared humanity and fallibility. Just as we seek empathy and understanding of our own shortcomings, extending the same to others becomes imperative. This doesn't mean excusing harm or subjecting ourselves to repeated hurt, but rather, embracing empathy and acknowledging our shared imperfections. Through forgiveness, we affirm our interconnectedness and the inherent capacity for growth in every individual.

To fully embrace forgiveness, we must confront our emotions head-on and actively process the pain inflicted upon us. While anger, hurt, and betrayal are natural responses to wrongdoing, holding onto them only prolongs our suffering. By allowing ourselves to experience these emotions, acknowledging their presence, and seeking healthy outlets for expression, we can gradually loosen their grip on our hearts.

Self-reflection is indispensable on the path to forgiveness. Taking time to understand our triggers, vulnerabilities, and behavioral patterns fosters compassion for ourselves and others. It unveils that often, others' actions stem from their own struggles and pain. This compassionate understanding paves the way for forgiveness, shifting our focus from blame and resentment to empathy and healing.

Another effective method for nurturing forgiveness is through the practice of gratitude. Despite the sting of betrayal or hurt, expressing gratitude may initially feel counterintuitive. However, consciously seeking gratitude redirects our focus from negativity toward the blessings and lessons within the experience. This shift in perspective enables us to find purpose and meaning in our pain, creating space for forgiveness to take root in our hearts.

It's crucial to understand that forgiveness isn't a one-time event but an ongoing journey. It may entail revisiting painful memories, confronting fears, and extending forgiveness repeatedly as healing unfolds. Each act of forgiveness serves as a catalyst for personal growth, both individually and within our relationships.

As we ponder over this chapter on understanding forgiveness, let's contemplate the profound transformative potential it holds. Embracing forgiveness liberates us from the burdens of the past, allowing us to fully embrace the present and shape a future steeped in love, compassion, and empathy.

In choosing forgiveness, we reclaim our agency. We relinquish the role of the victim and emerge as active agents in our own healing process. By releasing resentment and embracing forgiveness, we break free from the chains that bind us, bestowing upon ourselves the invaluable gifts of inner peace and emotional liberation.

So, I urge you to embark on this potent journey towards forgiveness. Whether you seek forgiveness or extend it to others, remember that forgiveness is a gift that catalyzes boundless healing and growth, enriching not only your life but also the lives of those around you. Embrace the transformative power of forgiveness, liberate yourself from the grip of anger and pain, and embrace the myriad possibilities that await—a life adorned with love, joy, and the liberty to journey forward with an open heart.

Freeing Yourself: Unpacking Emotional Baggage For A Lighter Journey

As humans, we inevitably encounter events and experiences that leave indelible marks on our lives. These encounters, whether uplifting or challenging, shape our outlooks, define our connections, and ultimately sculpt our identities. Yet, it's often the negative experiences that wield the most profound impact on our emotional well-being.

Unresolved anger, resentment, and pain act as burdensome emotional baggage, weighing down our spirits and impeding our quest for true liberation. Like a cumbersome load we carry on our backs, this emotional baggage becomes a barrier to our happiness, stunting our personal growth and stifling our capacity for fulfillment.

Imagine yourself embarking on a journey, burdened by a backpack laden with stones. Each stone symbolizes a negative emotion—a lingering disagreement with a loved one, a betrayal by a trusted friend, feelings of regret, or the haunting echoes of past trauma. As you trudge forward, the weight of these stones drags you down, slowing your stride and dimming your spirit. Yet, amidst this struggle, you envision the possibility of shedding this weight, of liberating yourself from the burdens of the past.

Forgiveness serves as the key to unburdening ourselves from the weight of these emotions. It's not about excusing the wrongs done to us; rather, it's a potent act of self-liberation. Through forgiveness, we release ourselves from the grip of anger and resentment, making room in our hearts for healing and personal growth.

However, forgiveness is often misconstrued. It doesn't entail forgetting or excusing past actions that caused us pain. Instead, it's a deliberate decision to untether ourselves from the negative emotions tethered to those experiences, redirecting our focus towards a more positive trajectory. By forgiving, we empower ourselves to break free from the chains of the past and embark on a journey of healing.

Clutching onto unresolved anger and resentment relinquishes our power. It allows others' actions to govern our emotions and dictate our lives. Only through forgiveness do we reclaim that power, asserting mastery over our emotional well-being.

Letting go isn't effortless. It demands courage, introspection, and a willingness to confront our deepest wounds. Revisiting moments of profound hurt may be painful, yet it creates an avenue for healing and evolution. In this light, forgiveness becomes a transformative odyssey—a voyage toward self-discovery and emotional liberation.

As we journey down the path of forgiveness, we gradually shed the emotional burdens that have weighed us down for far too long. We come to realize that clinging to anger and resentment only prolongs our suffering, while forgiveness offers a gateway to peace and joy.

Throughout this chapter, we delve into practical steps to embrace forgiveness, providing guidance and insights to unlock our inner strength. But for now, take a moment to reflect on the emotional baggage you carry. Consider its impact on your life and envision the freedom forgiveness can bring. Remember, acknowledging the weight of our emotional baggage is the first step toward healing, opening the door to forgiveness's transformative power.

Forgiveness isn't a one-time act; it's an ongoing journey requiring patience, understanding, and self-compassion. To embark on this journey, cultivating empathy and compassion towards ourselves and others is crucial. Recognizing our shared humanity and inherent imperfections allows us to release the resentment and anger holding us captive.

Practicing mindfulness is a powerful tool for nurturing empathy and compassion. By immersing ourselves in the present moment and observing our thoughts and emotions without judgment, we gain deeper insights into our pain's root causes. Mindfulness grants us the space to acknowledge our emotional reactions without being consumed by them, empowering us to respond to challenging situations with kindness and forgiveness.

Moreover, gratitude serves as another potent ally in embracing forgiveness. By focusing on the positives in our lives and expressing gratitude for our blessings, we shift our perspective away from past grievances toward contentment and appreciation. Gratitude reminds us that despite the pain endured, there are countless reasons to be thankful and optimistic about the future.

Moreover, it's crucial to establish healthy boundaries in our relationships. Forgiveness doesn't equate to permitting others to mistreat us or neglect our needs. It entails recognizing our inherent worth and advocating for ourselves in a firm yet respectful manner. Setting boundaries not only safeguards our emotional well-being but also cultivates more genuine and fulfilling connections with others.

Another pivotal aspect of embracing forgiveness is extending it to ourselves. Often, we're our own toughest critics, harboring guilt and shame over past mistakes. Yet, it's essential to acknowledge our humanity and capacity for growth. By forgiving ourselves for past actions or choices, we grant ourselves the space to learn and evolve with greater self-compassion and acceptance.

Lastly, it's crucial to understand that forgiveness doesn't guarantee instant healing or the eradication of pain. Healing is a gradual process that demands time and patience, unique to each individual. While some wounds may heal swiftly, others may require ongoing effort and introspection. Embracing forgiveness entails being gentle with ourselves and recognizing that healing unfolds at its own pace.

I encourage you to ponder the practical steps we've explored and contemplate how you can integrate forgiveness into your life. Remember, forgiveness is a personal journey, and the timing and pace of your progress are entirely yours to determine. Be gentle with yourself, embrace the power of forgiveness, and have faith in its transformative potential. By unloading our emotional baggage and embracing healing, we open ourselves to a future brimming with joy, peace, and authentic connections. Trust in the potency of forgiveness to illuminate your path toward self-discovery and liberation.

Healing Begins From Within: Embracing Personal Responsibility

In our quest for healing, it's paramount to acknowledge and embrace the power of taking responsibility for our own healing journey. Our world is fraught with pain and suffering, tempting us to adopt the role of victim, attributing our anguish solely to others' actions. Yet, genuine healing demands a shift in perspective—a readiness to recognize our own role in the hurtful scenarios we encounter.

Taking responsibility doesn't entail assuming the blame for every misfortune in our lives. Rather, it involves owning up to our contributions to the pain, whether through our actions, choices, or emotional responses. By claiming agency over our experiences, we empower ourselves to progress and actively pursue the healing we desperately seek.

A crucial step in assuming responsibility for our healing is acknowledging the impact of our actions on others. Forgiveness hinges on understanding that we're all fallible and that our mistakes can inflict profound wounds on those around us. It requires courage and humility to confront the repercussions of our actions, yet doing so is integral to the healing journey.

When we confront the hurt we've caused, it paves the way for seeking forgiveness from those we've wronged. Requesting forgiveness isn't a display of weakness; rather, it signifies strength and a genuine commitment to rectification. It compels us to confront our flaws and actively endeavor to mend the harm we've inflicted.

Seeking forgiveness isn't solely about earning redemption in others' eyes; it's also about finding it within ourselves. It involves shedding the weight of guilt and shame that burdens us, granting ourselves the opportunity to heal and evolve. Genuine contrition opens the path to reconciliation and reconnection, both with others and with ourselves.

Moreover, taking responsibility for our healing journey entails examining our emotional responses to painful situations. Often, we react with anger, resentment, or withdrawal—a natural response. Yet, clinging to these emotions prolongs our suffering and impedes our healing.

By acknowledging our emotional responses, we delve into the deeper wounds beneath the surface. It's a moment of introspection, an opportunity to unravel the roots of our reactions and identify the patterns we may inadvertently perpetuate. This self-awareness propels us towards breaking free from negative cycles and discovering healthier ways to navigate pain.

Assuming responsibility for our own healing necessitates strength, courage, and a readiness to confront our vulnerabilities. It's an active, ongoing endeavor that demands honesty, introspection, and a sincere desire for reconciliation. By doing so, we unlock the transformative potential of forgiveness, laying the groundwork for a future brimming with healing, evolution, and fresh starts.

In our pursuit of healing, it's vital not only to acknowledge our own actions but also to extend forgiveness to those who've wronged us. Forgiveness isn't facile; it demands immense fortitude and bravery. Yet, in embracing forgiveness, we carve out space for healing and catalyze opportunities for growth.

Forgiveness doesn't entail condoning others' hurtful actions or forgetting the pain they've inflicted upon us. Rather, it's about liberating ourselves from the grip of resentment and bitterness. Through forgiveness, we unshackle ourselves from the negative emotions that bind us, enabling us to forge ahead and discover inner peace.

As we embark on our forgiveness journey, it's crucial to understand that forgiveness is a process, not a one-time occurrence. It requires time, patience, and self-compassion. Healing wounds is a gradual endeavor, and it's essential to afford ourselves the grace to heal at our own pace.

Forgiveness doesn't equate to forgetting; it signifies relinquishing the power the past holds over us. It involves freeing ourselves from the clutches of anger and opting to prioritize love, empathy, and personal development. Through forgiveness, we grant ourselves the chance to sever the chains of resentment and pave the way for a brighter tomorrow.

Extending forgiveness also entails cultivating empathy and understanding. It involves acknowledging that everyone is navigating their own unique journey, and at times, they may act out of their own pain and insecurities. Cultivating empathy fosters connection and compassion, rendering forgiveness more attainable.

Nevertheless, forgiveness isn't solely about others; it encompasses forgiving ourselves as well. Self-forgiveness is a profound act of self-love and self-acceptance. It necessitates acknowledging our imperfections, embracing our mistakes, and gleaning wisdom from them. Through self-forgiveness, we commence treating ourselves with kindness and empathy, fostering space for personal growth and metamorphosis.

In the journey of self-forgiveness, it's paramount to shed the weight of guilt and shame that burdens us. We're all fallible beings, prone to making mistakes. The crux lies in owning up to our actions, assimilating their lessons, and striving to evolve into improved versions of ourselves.

Self-forgiveness entails treating ourselves with gentleness and granting permission to heal. It encompasses acknowledging the emotions surging within us and affording ourselves the compassion and space we require. Through self-forgiveness, we relinquish the grip of the past, embrace the present, and carve out a future brimming with possibility.

Amidst the journey of healing and forgiveness, it's essential to surround ourselves with a supportive network that comprehends and nurtures our growth. These allies may include friends, family members, or professional counselors, offering guidance and a receptive ear. Sharing our trials and victories with others fosters solace and affirmation as we navigate the path toward healing.

As we draw to a close in this chapter of assuming responsibility for our healing, let's bear in mind that forgiveness isn't always facile, but it's eternally worthwhile. It enables us to mend once-consuming wounds, unburden ourselves from lingering weights, and embrace a life suffused with love, joy, and inner tranquility. May we persist in our journey, united in our dedication to healing and forgiveness, and may each stride propel us closer to a life replete with wholeness and contentment.

Shackles Of The Heart: Understanding And Releasing The Blocks To Forgiveness

Here, we embark on a profound exploration of the human experience—forgiveness. For many, forgiveness is not merely an act but a complex emotional landscape marked by pain, resentment, and, often, the inability to let go. Within these pages, we delve into the depths of the heart, seeking to understand the intricate web of emotions that bind us to our grievances and past hurts. We shine a light on the invisible shackles that keep us tethered to the pain of betrayal, injustice, and disappointment. But fear not, for this narrative is not one of despair but of hope and transformation. As we navigate the terrain of forgiveness, we will uncover powerful insights, personal anecdotes, and practical tools to help break free from the chains that bind us. Together, we will embark on a journey of self-discovery and healing—a journey towards understanding and releasing the blocks to forgiveness.

Forgiveness is not a simple act; it is a labyrinth of emotions, beliefs, and experiences that often hold us captive. We carry the weight of past hurts, betrayals, and injustices, unaware of the chains that bind us. Yet, in our quest for understanding, we uncover the power within to break free. In this chapter and throughout the book, we confront the shadows of resentment and pain, seeking to illuminate the path toward healing and reconciliation. Through introspection, empathy, and courage, we navigate the terrain of forgiveness, unraveling the knots of anger and bitterness that entangle our hearts. Join me as we explore the depths of forgiveness—the journey from bondage to liberation, from woundedness to wholeness. Together, let us unlock the shackles of the heart and embrace the transformative power of forgiveness.

One of the major roadblocks to forgiveness is pride. It whispers in our ears, convincing us that holding onto resentment and anger is a sign of strength. We believe that by refusing to forgive, we maintain control and protect ourselves from further harm. However, the truth is that holding onto grudges only weighs us down, trapping us in a cycle of negativity and preventing any chance for growth. To overcome this barrier, we must humbly acknowledge our own flaws and recognize that forgiveness is not a sign of weakness but rather an act of courage and self-empowerment.

Another significant obstacle standing in the way of forgiveness is fear. We fear being hurt again, betrayed, or taken advantage of. This fear paralyzes us, trapping us in a state of guardedness and preventing us from opening up to the possibility of healing. However, we must remember that forgiveness does not require us to forget or tolerate harmful behavior. It is a choice to let go of the negative emotions associated with the past and reclaim our personal power. By facing our fears head-on and allowing ourselves to be vulnerable, we can start the journey towards forgiveness.

A lack of empathy is yet another hurdle that obstructs our journey toward forgiveness. When we cling to resentment, it becomes difficult to empathize with others and understand their perspective. We get lost in our own pain, losing sight of the humanity in others. However, empathy is vital in the forgiveness process. It enables us to acknowledge that everyone makes mistakes and deserves compassion. By nurturing empathy through reflection and seeking to understand rather than judge, we can begin dismantling the barriers to forgiveness.

It's essential to understand that overcoming these obstacles takes time and effort. Forgiveness isn't a quick fix; it's a personal journey unique to each of us. Patience and self-compassion are crucial as we navigate our emotions' complexities. We might stumble along the way, but it's through these struggles that we learn and grow.

As we venture down this forgiveness path, let's remember it's for our benefit, not just the transgressors. Holding onto grudges binds us to the past, dictating our present and future. However, choosing forgiveness liberates us from these chains, opening up a world of possibilities.

We'll delve further into practical strategies for overcoming these obstacles to forgiveness. We'll explore cultivating humility, conquering fear, and nurturing empathy within ourselves. These tools empower us to break free from the shackles of resentment and embrace a life guided by forgiveness.

For now, let's reflect on these barriers and acknowledge their presence in our lives. In doing so, we take the first step toward unlocking forgiveness's power and embracing the healing it offers. The journey may be challenging, but the rewards are immeasurable. It's time to let go, forgive, and set ourselves free.

As we venture deeper into this chapter on the barriers to forgiveness, let's continue our exploration of practical strategies and insights to empower us in overcoming these hurdles. Through this journey, we can gradually unlock the transformative potential of forgiveness and embrace the healing it offers.

Cultivating humility stands as a pivotal step on our path to forgiveness. It beckons us to acknowledge our imperfections, relinquish the need to be right or seek vengeance. By accepting that no one is flawless, including ourselves, we open the door to empathy and understanding. Humility allows forgiveness to bloom from a place of compassion, recognizing our shared humanity and the possibility of redemption.

Self-reflection serves as a potent tool for nurturing humility. By examining our actions and motivations, we gain insight into the ripple effects of our choices. It's a process that prompts us to acknowledge moments where we've caused harm and moments where we've yearned for forgiveness. Through this self-awareness journey, empathy deepens for both ourselves and those we aim to forgive.

Confronting fear emerges as another critical aspect of the forgiveness odyssey. The dread of being wounded anew or betrayed can paralyze us, prompting the construction of emotional barriers. However, forgiveness doesn't mandate forgetting or tolerating harmful conduct. It's a deliberate decision to release the grip of negative emotions tethering us to the past and reclaim our autonomy.

To combat fear, we must learn to release resentment and embrace vulnerability. This calls for courage and self-assurance. We must trust in our ability to set healthy boundaries, shielding ourselves from harm while remaining open to the prospect of forgiveness. By confronting our fears and taking incremental steps toward healing, we gradually dismantle the chains fear has bound around our hearts.

Nurturing empathy within ourselves emerges as yet another potent tool for surmounting forgiveness roadblocks. Empathy enables us to recognize the humanity in others and grasp that everyone stumbles. It empowers us to transcend our pain and truly engage with the narratives and viewpoints of those who've wounded us. Through empathetic practice, we sow the seeds of compassion, laying fertile ground for forgiveness to flourish.

One method to foster empathy is by seeking understanding rather than passing judgment. We can strive to envision ourselves in the shoes of the individual who caused us pain, attempting to grasp the circumstances that influenced our actions. This approach doesn't justify or excuse their behavior but rather allows us to acknowledge their humanity, recognizing their potential for growth and change.

As we progress through this chapter on the barriers to forgiveness, let's keep in mind that the journey toward forgiveness is unique for each person. It demands time, dedication, and, above all, self-compassion. We might encounter setbacks along the way, and that's perfectly okay. In these moments of adversity, we're presented with opportunities to learn, evolve, and strengthen our resilience.

Therefore, I urge you to contemplate these insights and identify the obstacles impeding your own capacity to forgive. Embrace humility, confront your fears, and cultivate empathy within yourself. Remember, the path of forgiveness isn't effortless, but the benefits it bestows are profound and life-altering. By releasing, forgiving, and liberating ourselves, we unlock a life guided by healing, empathy, and personal growth.

The potential for forgiveness rests within your reach. With patience, determination, and self-assurance, you possess the fortitude to overcome any hindrance in your path. Embrace this transformative journey and step into a future illuminated by inner peace and boundless opportunities.

Compassionate Living: Empathy As The Key To Fulfillment

In a world often bustling with activity, where personal success and material wealth often dominate, the importance of empathy and compassionate living can sometimes fade into the background. Yet, amidst the hustle and bustle, there remains a profound truth: empathy is not just a virtue but also a pathway to fulfillment.

As we traverse the complexities of life, it becomes ever clearer that our own well-being is deeply intertwined with our capacity to comprehend, relate to, and uplift others. In this exploration of compassionate living, we will delve into the transformative potency of empathy, both towards others and ourselves.

In our quest for stronger connections and more resilient communities, empathy emerges as a guiding force, nurturing mental and emotional well-being along the way. By delving deeper into the experiences and emotions of those around us, we not only enrich their lives but also find greater purpose and satisfaction in our own.

Through narratives, insights, and actionable strategies, this exploration aims to shed light on the profound influence of empathy on personal growth and societal harmony. It calls upon us to reassess our priorities, embrace empathy as a cornerstone of our humanity, and embark on a journey toward a more compassionate way of life.

As we set forth on this path toward a world ruled by empathy, where fulfillment is not merely a destination but a way of existence, let us hold onto the transformative power of compassion and empathy.

In our pursuit of forgiveness and healing, it's crucial not to overlook the potent force of compassion and empathy. These virtues possess the remarkable ability to reshape not only our interactions with others but also, significantly, our relationship with ourselves. By nurturing compassion and empathy, we unlock doors to profound healing and set in motion ripples of change that extend far beyond our immediate circles.

Compassion, grounded in a deep sense of empathy and understanding for others' suffering, demands emotional attunement. When we authentically connect with others' struggles and pain, we transcend judgment and condemnation. Compassion empowers us to offer solace and support where it's most needed, fostering an environment of kindness and empathy.

Too often, we hold ourselves to unreachable standards, chastising ourselves for perceived failings or mistakes. However, by embracing self-compassion, we shift our internal dialogue from criticism to nurturing. We learn to acknowledge our own pain and challenges with gentleness and empathy, carving out space for healing and self-forgiveness to flourish within our hearts.

But how do we nurture compassion amidst the chaos of our daily lives? It begins with a willingness to slow down and truly listen. By tuning in to the experiences and emotions of others, we forge an authentic connection that transcends surface-level interactions. When we listen attentively, not just with our ears but also with our hearts, we gain invaluable insight into the emotions and vulnerabilities of those around us.

Empathy, the capacity to understand and share the feelings of another, complements compassion seamlessly. It serves as the bridge that links us on a deeper, emotional level. When we step into someone else's shoes, we gain profound insight into their pain, their aspirations, and their fears. In this process, our own ability to forgive deepens.

Through nurturing empathy, we come to realize the inherent interconnectedness of all human beings. We acknowledge that we're not alone in our struggles and that each individual carries their own burdens. This awareness prompts us to extend kindness and forgiveness to others, recognizing that their actions often stem from their own pain and suffering.

It's crucial to recognize that compassion and empathy are not finite resources. Rather, they're qualities that can be cultivated and expanded upon. The more we practice compassion and empathy, the more they become second nature, infusing every aspect of our lives. With each act of kindness and understanding, we contribute to a world in dire need of healing and forgiveness.

As we embark on the journey of nurturing compassion and empathy, we mustn't overlook their pivotal role in our own healing process. By embracing these qualities towards ourselves, we lay a firm foundation for forgiveness and transformation. We grant ourselves the grace to acknowledge our humanity, learn from our missteps, and evolve into the best versions of ourselves.

Here, we'll delve into practical steps and exercises to deepen our compassion and empathy, both towards others and ourselves. We'll explore the intricacies of forgiveness, recognizing its potential to heal and uplift. Through our continued exploration, we'll uncover the profound connection between compassion, empathy, and forgiveness. By actively integrating these practices into our lives, we can make significant progress on our journey of healing and forgiveness.

A potent method to deepen our compassion is through practicing loving-kindness meditation. This practice entails directing warm, positive intentions towards ourselves and others, even towards those whom we may find challenging to forgive. By silently repeating phrases such as "*May I be happy, may I be healthy, may I live with ease,*" we foster feelings of compassion and empathy within ourselves. As we extend these well-wishes to others, our capacity for forgiveness expands, revealing the universality of suffering and the shared desire for peace and happiness.

Another valuable exercise is perspective-taking. This practice enables us to step into the shoes of another person, gaining a deeper understanding of their experience. It involves imagining their thoughts, feelings, and motivations and reflecting on how these may have influenced their actions. By cultivating empathy through perspective-taking, we develop a greater ability to forgive, acknowledging that everyone, ourselves included, is capable of making mistakes and being influenced by their circumstances.

Additionally, engaging in everyday acts of kindness and empathy is vital. Small gestures such as offering a kind word, a listening ear, or a helping hand can profoundly impact others and ourselves. When we demonstrate compassion towards others, we create a ripple effect of positivity and healing that extends far beyond our immediate interactions. These acts of kindness not only promote forgiveness in others but also strengthen our own capacity for self-forgiveness and growth.

On our journey of cultivating compassion and empathy, prioritizing self-care and self-compassion is crucial. Taking time to nurture ourselves physically, mentally, and emotionally is essential for our well-being and our ability to extend compassion to others. This may involve engaging in activities that bring us joy, practicing self-compassionate self-talk, or seeking support from trusted loved ones or professionals. By prioritizing our own healing, we establish a solid foundation for forgiveness and transformation.

Reflecting on the profound connection between compassion, empathy, and forgiveness, we unlock the potential for deep healing and lasting transformation. By embracing compassion and empathy, we break free from the chains of anger, resentment, and hurt, opening our hearts to forgiveness and understanding.

Remember, forgiveness is not a linear process, and it often requires time and patience. However, by committing to the regular practice of compassion and empathy, we can gradually soften our hearts and create space for forgiveness to flourish. We possess the power to break the cycle of pain and transform ourselves and our relationships. This journey towards forgiveness and healing is a testament to our resilience and our capacity for growth and love.

As you continue on your personal path toward forgiveness and healing, carry these teachings with you. Cultivate compassion and empathy towards yourself and others, knowing that by doing so, you contribute to a world in desperate need of healing and forgiveness. Embrace the power of forgiveness, and let it guide you toward a future filled with peace, freedom, and love.

The Art Of Forgiveness: Techniques For Cultivating Peace And Freedom

Forgiveness holds immense power for both personal liberation and healing, not only for ourselves but also for others. In a world often fraught with conflict and hurt, mastering the art of forgiveness becomes essential for nurturing inner peace and fostering harmonious relationships. This guide is dedicated to exploring various techniques and strategies for embracing forgiveness and empowering individuals to break free from the shackles of anger and bitterness.

Throughout this chapter and the book, we will delve into the psychological, emotional, and spiritual dimensions of forgiveness, offering practical insights and exercises to support your journey toward greater inner freedom and compassion. Whether you're grappling with past traumas, navigating interpersonal conflicts, or seeking to release self-imposed burdens, the wisdom within these pages will serve as a guiding light.

From the power of empathy and understanding to the transformative potential of letting go, each chapter will illuminate different facets of forgiveness and provide actionable steps for integration into your daily life. By embarking on this journey of forgiveness, you set foot on a path toward personal empowerment, emotional resilience, and profound spiritual growth.

As we embark on this journey together, let's remember that forgiveness isn't about excusing wrongdoing or erasing past hurts. Instead, it's a courageous choice to rise above pain and embrace the potential for redemption and reconciliation.

By embracing forgiveness, we reclaim our power and create room for healing, compassion, and peace to thrive within ourselves and in the world around us.

I hope this book serves as a beacon of hope and inspiration on your path toward inner transformation and collective healing. Let's continue our exploration of the art of forgiveness, where peace and freedom await those willing to embrace its transformative power.

Forgiveness is a journey that demands courage, strength, and a willingness to release past hurts. While it may feel daunting, there are powerful tools and techniques available to assist you along the way. In this book, we'll explore various strategies to help you practice forgiveness, enabling you to embrace healing and move forward.

Self-reflection serves as the cornerstone of forgiveness. Taking the time to introspect and honestly evaluate our emotions, thoughts, and beliefs can be truly transformative. It allows us to gain insights into our own pain and triggers, helping us understand why forgiveness is crucial for our well-being. Engaging in self-reflection can be as simple as finding a quiet space to be alone with our thoughts, journaling, or seeking guidance from a therapist or counselor. By delving into our inner landscape, we create space for growth and forgiveness to flourish.

Another potent tool for practicing forgiveness is writing forgiveness letters. Putting our thoughts and feelings onto paper can be incredibly cathartic and therapeutic. Start by addressing the person you wish to forgive, expressing your emotions honestly and without judgment. Pour your heart onto the pages, leaving no stone unturned. This exercise allows you to release pent-up emotions that may hinder forgiveness. Remember, these letters are for your eyes only and don't need to be sent to the recipient. The act of writing itself is a cleansing process that opens the door to forgiveness.

Meditation is yet another valuable practice that can aid in the forgiveness journey. Find a quiet, comfortable space, close your eyes, and focus on your breath. As you inhale and exhale, allow thoughts and emotions to arise naturally, acknowledging them without judgment. Gradually shift your attention to the person you seek to forgive. Visualize them in your mind's eye and imagine releasing any resentment or anger toward them. As you continue to meditate, cultivate feelings of empathy and compassion, recognizing their humanity and imperfections. Through regular practice, meditation can help soften your heart and pave the way for forgiveness to take root.

Finally, seeking support from others becomes pivotal in the journey of forgiveness. Encircling yourself with empathetic and understanding souls can furnish solace, direction, and affirmation. Extend your hand to friends, family, or support networks where judgment holds no sway and where the shared narratives of forgiveness become a beacon of hope. Bonding with fellow travelers who have trodden similar paths can infuse you with strength and reassurance, reminding you that your odyssey toward forgiveness is not solitary.

As you traverse the terrain of forgiveness, keep in mind that it unfurls gradually, on its own cadence. Each method and stratagem discussed in this chapter acts as a stepping stone towards embracing restoration and progression. Cultivate patience and kindness towards yourself, recognizing that forgiveness is an individual expedition, nuanced and bespoke. Embrace these tools as companions, guiding you towards emancipation and a heart unburdened.

In the journey toward forgiveness, it's paramount to recognize the profound impact forgiveness holds. Forgiveness possesses the remarkable ability to not only reshape our connections with others but also to redefine our relationship with ourselves. It bestows upon us the liberating gift of releasing the heavy burdens of resentment, anger, and pain, granting us the freedom to reclaim our inner peace and joy.

A potent instrument in the practice of forgiveness lies in nurturing empathy and compassion. Walk a mile in the shoes of those who have caused you pain, endeavoring to grasp their perspective. Understand that we are all imperfect beings, prone to lapses in judgment. By embracing this truth, we begin to perceive that those who have wounded us are not solely defined by their actions but are complex individuals with their own vulnerabilities, anxieties, and battles.

Through the lens of empathy, we unlock our hearts to the shared humanity of others, transcending surface-level grievances. It's crucial to emphasize that empathy doesn't excuse or validate the wrongs committed against us; rather, it facilitates a profound comprehension and acceptance. This comprehension serves as a potent catalyst for the journey of forgiveness.

In tandem with empathy, nurturing self-compassion proves indispensable on the voyage toward forgiveness. Often, our clenched fists of anger and resentment towards others stem from an inability to extend forgiveness to ourselves for perceived failings or missteps. Acknowledge that self-forgiveness forms a vital thread in the tapestry of forgiveness, emancipating us from the shackles of self-imposed guilt and shame.

Embrace self-compassion by showering yourself with the same tenderness and empathy you would extend to a cherished confidant. Remind yourself that imperfection is the common thread binding humanity and that forgiveness is a birthright we all deserve. Traverse the labyrinth of forgiveness with gentleness towards yourself, carving out space for healing and evolution.

Another invaluable facet of the forgiveness mosaic lies in the practice of kindness and gratitude. Delve into acts of benevolence towards both those you seek forgiveness from and those untouched by the scenario. From genuine compliments to lending a helping hand or dispatching a heartfelt note, every gesture resonates with the melody of forgiveness. By channeling our energies into acts of kindness, we pivot away from the realm of pain and resentment, fashioning a sanctuary for healing and optimism.

The journey of forgiveness may initially seem daunting, shrouded in uncertainty and ambiguity. Yet, as the veil lifts, the profound potency of forgiveness reveals itself, illuminating the path towards self-redemption and reconciliation with others.

Practicing gratitude also emerges as a potent ally in the journey towards forgiveness. Dedicate a moment each day to reflect on the blessings amidst life's trials. By fostering a mindset of gratitude, we sow the seeds for positivity to take root, providing fertile ground for forgiveness to blossom.

As we navigate through the depths of this chapter, it's paramount to acknowledge that forgiveness is a deeply personal odyssey unique to each individual. There's no one-size-fits-all approach; what resonates with one may not with another. Thus, it's crucial to tread gently and with patience as we explore these tools and techniques.

Let's not forget that forgiveness doesn't entail sweeping past grievances under the rug or condoning hurtful actions. It's about unshackling ourselves from the grip of resentment and liberating our hearts to embrace healing and growth. By welcoming these tools into our lives, we embark on a journey toward openness, peace, and a newfound sense of completeness and joy.

Forgiveness stands as a profound act of closure, lifting the weight of resentment and anger from both the forgiver and the forgiven. It's a transformative journey that can mend wounds, mend relationships, and pave the path to inner peace and reconciliation. Through this exploration of closure through forgiveness, we've delved into its deep psychological and emotional impacts, its role in personal growth and healing, and practical strategies for nurturing forgiveness in our lives.

The voyage towards closure through forgiveness is one of great depth and significance. It calls for courage, empathy, and a readiness to release past grievances. By embracing forgiveness, we not only unshackle ourselves from the chains of resentment but also unlock doors to healing, reconciliation, and inner tranquility. As we ponder the transformative force of forgiveness, let's keep in mind that it's a gift we bestow upon ourselves as much as it is extended to others. Through forgiveness, we not only find closure but also create room for fresh beginnings and a brighter future. Let's continue nurturing forgiveness in our hearts, knowing it to be the path to true liberation and contentment.

It's essential to grasp that forgiveness is a journey of transformation, demanding courage, introspection, and a willingness to release the grip of past pain. Through practices like self-reflection, forgiveness letters, meditation, empathy, self-compassion, acts of kindness, and gratitude, we empower ourselves to embrace healing and progress. Remember, each stride towards forgiveness is a stride towards liberation and a more compassionate spirit. Stay steadfast on your journey, allowing the power of forgiveness to illuminate the path to a brighter and more fulfilling tomorrow.

Pathways To Forgiveness: Embarking On The Journey Of Healing

Understanding that forgiveness is a journey, not a destination, underscores the importance of patience, self-compassion, and perseverance as we navigate this transformative path.

When we contemplate forgiveness, we often envision it as a straightforward act—a singular moment where we release our anger, hurt, or resentment. Yet, in reality, forgiveness is much more intricate and profound. It's a journey, a process that unfolds over time, requiring patience, understanding, and self-care.

As we set out on the journey of forgiveness, it's vital to grasp that it's not a linear road. There's no clear starting point or definitive end marked by complete forgiveness. Instead, forgiveness unfurls gradually, like a delicate tapestry weaving its way through our hearts and minds.

One of the initial steps in this journey is acknowledging and embracing our pain. While it may seem counterintuitive, allowing ourselves to fully experience our emotions is essential for forgiveness to take root. It's through this acknowledgment that we gain insight into the impact of the wrongdoing, both on ourselves and those involved.

Patience plays a vital role in the journey toward forgiveness. It's tempting to rush through the process, craving instant relief from the heavy burden of resentment. Yet, genuine forgiveness demands that we honor our own healing pace. Each person's path is unique, with no fixed timetable for forgiveness.

During moments when we're confronted with the weight of inflicted pain, practicing self-compassion becomes essential. Forgiveness isn't solely about extending compassion to others; it also involves showing kindness inwardly to ourselves. We must recognize that making mistakes, stumbling, and grappling with forgiveness are all part of being human. Through this gentle self-compassion, we pave the way for authentic healing and growth.

Persistence serves as another crucial element in the forgiveness journey. It's not a one-time event but rather a series of daily choices. We might take steps forward only to stumble backward at times. It's in these setbacks that our dedication to forgiveness truly reveals itself. However, with persistence, we discover the resilience to continue along this transformative path, inching closer to the peace we yearn for.

As we navigate this journey of forgiveness, it's important to realize that it's not just for the benefit of the wrongdoer—it's for ourselves as well. Clinging to anger and resentment binds us to past pain, hindering us from fully embracing the present and future possibilities. Forgiveness releases us from these chains, granting us the freedom to move forward with newfound liberation and joy.

Here, we will explore practical strategies to cultivate patience, self-compassion, and persistence in our journey toward forgiveness. We will delve deeper into the transformative power of forgiveness, unveiling the tools and insights that will assist us in embracing healing and moving forward. But for now, let us continue to embrace the intricacies of forgiveness's process, knowing that each step we take brings us closer to its profound gifts.

Now, let's dive into practical strategies to nurture patience, self-compassion, and persistence in our journey toward forgiveness. These insights and tools will aid us as we embrace healing and stride forward.

A potent strategy to cultivate patience in the forgiveness process is through mindfulness. Mindfulness entails consciously and non-judgmentally observing our thoughts, emotions, and physical sensations in the present moment. By honing this awareness, we gain insight into the triggers and patterns that surface when faced with the pain caused by others. Mindfulness empowers us to create space between our initial emotional reactions and our subsequent responses, enabling us to opt for compassion and forgiveness rather than reacting impulsively from a place of anger or hurt.

Furthermore, nurturing self-compassion stands as a crucial facet of the forgiveness expedition. Self-compassion prompts us to extend kindness, understanding, and acceptance to ourselves, especially during moments of struggle with forgiveness. It entails recognizing our humanity and imperfections, akin to everyone else. Through self-compassion, we afford ourselves the same empathy and forgiveness we offer to others, establishing a bedrock of compassion that bolsters our personal healing.

Sustained dedication to forgiveness serves as yet another cornerstone of the journey. There will be occasions when discouragement creeps in, when forgiveness appears unattainable, or when old wounds resurface with heightened intensity. Amid these trying times, it becomes imperative to recall the motivations behind embarking on this expedition. We can revisit the potential for transformation that forgiveness holds, offering liberation from the weight of resentment and fostering our well-being. It's through these reflections that we unearth the resilience to persist, even amidst setbacks or resistance.

Additionally, immersing ourselves in a supportive community can significantly bolster our journey toward forgiveness. Sharing our emotions and experiences with trusted individuals who embody empathy and non-judgment can offer validation, encouragement, and a sense of belonging. Through this communal exchange, we may glean insights and perspectives that broaden our understanding of forgiveness and its intricacies. Seeking guidance from therapists, support groups, or spiritual leaders can also furnish invaluable tools and viewpoints to navigate the nuances of forgiveness, both its challenges and its rewards.

Throughout this endeavor, it's crucial to remember that forgiveness doesn't equate to forgetting or condoning the wrongdoing. It doesn't necessitate reconciliation or interaction with the individual who caused harm. Rather, forgiveness stands as a deeply personal and empowering choice that releases us from the grip of anger and resentment, enabling us to reclaim our emotional well-being and stride forward with heightened peace and joy.

Let's honor the courage and fortitude required to embark on the path of forgiveness. It's a transformative journey that demands patience, self-compassion, and unwavering persistence. With each step we take, we draw nearer to the profound gifts of forgiveness—liberation from the pain of yesteryears, full immersion in the present, and a vista of possibilities for the future.

May we continue to embrace the complexities of forgiveness, recognizing its transformative impact not only on the wrongdoer but also on ourselves. May we find solace in the knowledge that forgiveness lies within our grasp, empowering us to heal, evolve, and advance with hearts unshackled from the chains of resentment.

Embracing Grace: Forgiving Others, Forgiving Ourselves

In the journey of life, we inevitably encounter situations where we feel wronged or hurt by others. These experiences can inflict lasting wounds, casting shadows on our hearts and minds. Yet, as we navigate the intricacies of forgiveness, we realize that our capacity to forgive others is deeply intertwined with our ability to forgive ourselves. It's within this interconnectedness that we discover the power to embrace healing and progress.

When we cling to grudges and withhold forgiveness, we bear a heavy burden that weighs us down. Resentment and bitterness consume our thoughts and emotions, hindering us from experiencing genuine freedom and inner tranquility. We become ensnared in a cycle of negativity, replaying hurtful events endlessly. However, by opting for forgiveness, we can shatter these chains and unlock the gateway to personal growth and healing.

Forgiving others doesn't equate to condoning their actions or denying the pain they caused. Instead, it's a deliberate choice to liberate ourselves from the clutches of anger and resentment. It's an act of compassion and empathy, acknowledging that we all err and possess the potential for change. Through forgiveness, we cultivate empathy, shifting our perspective on the situation. We grant ourselves permission to release the past, creating space for new experiences and opportunities.

In extending forgiveness to others, we discover the art of forgiveness within ourselves. Often, our struggle to forgive others stems from our own challenges with self-forgiveness.

We harbor guilt and shame, meting out self-punishment for past actions or perceived shortcomings. However, self-forgiveness is vital for our personal growth and overall well-being. It entails embracing our imperfections and acknowledging that we are worthy of compassion, just like anyone else.

As we learn to forgive ourselves, we liberate ourselves from the shackles of self-judgment and self-criticism. We grant ourselves permission to heal, to glean lessons from our missteps, and to evolve into our best selves. Self-forgiveness fosters self-awareness and emboldens us to enact positive changes in our lives. It's a transformative journey that nurtures our self-worth and fosters healthier relationships with others.

As we intertwine the delicate threads of forgiving others and forgiving ourselves, we realize that forgiveness isn't a one-time event but an ongoing voyage. It demands patience, empathy, and a readiness to let go. It's a profound act of self-compassion driven by the yearning for personal growth and emotional liberation. Through embracing forgiveness, we carve out space for fresh beginnings and a brighter horizon.

Now, we will delve deeper into the practical steps for cultivating self-forgiveness and explore the profound impact it has on our relationships and overall well-being. We will uncover powerful strategies for breaking free from the chains of guilt and self-judgment, and we will discover the transformative effects that self-forgiveness can have on our lives. Prepare yourself for a journey of self-discovery and healing as we continue to explore the power of forgiveness.

One pivotal step in nurturing self-forgiveness is to acknowledge and accept our past mistakes or perceived failures. We cannot alter the past, but we can alter our perspective toward it. Recognize that these experiences do not define our worth or our essence as individuals. We all possess the capacity for growth, learning, and transformation. By embracing our imperfections, we grant ourselves the space to progress and evolve into the finest versions of ourselves.

Another potent strategy for self-forgiveness involves reframing our thoughts and challenging negative self-talk. Often, we are our own toughest critics, incessantly replaying past mistakes in our minds. This perpetual self-criticism only perpetuates the cycle of guilt and impedes our forward momentum. Instead, practice self-compassion and self-kindness. Extend to yourself the same understanding and forgiveness you would offer to a cherished friend. Remind yourself that everyone stumbles, and it is through these missteps that we glean invaluable lessons and mature.

Furthermore, cultivating gratitude can wield significant influence in the journey of self-forgiveness. Dedicate a moment each day to reflect on the positive facets of your life and the strides you have taken. Fostering gratitude redirects our focus from dwelling on our errors to appreciating our strengths and achievements. By recognizing and celebrating our progress, we cultivate a nurturing environment for self-forgiveness to blossom.

Moreover, seeking support from others can play a vital role in the journey of self-forgiveness. Share your feelings and experiences with a trusted friend, family member, or therapist who can offer a non-judgmental ear and guidance. At times, an outside perspective can challenge our self-perception and reinforce our inherent worthiness of forgiveness and healing.

As we embark on this path of self-forgiveness, remember that it's not a linear journey. There may be moments when the weight of guilt and self-judgment resurfaces, and that's perfectly normal. Self-forgiveness is an ongoing practice that demands patience and persistence. Be kind to yourself during these tough times and acknowledge the strides you've made.

Through embracing self-forgiveness, we not only unburden ourselves from the weight of the past but also enrich our relationships with others. When we learn to forgive ourselves, we cultivate greater empathy and understanding toward others' mistakes and imperfections. This newfound compassion nurtures healthier and more fulfilling connections with those around us, fostering a positive and supportive environment.

The potency of forgiving others and forgiving ourselves is deeply intertwined. Through self-forgiveness, we emancipate ourselves from guilt, shame, and self-judgment, paving the way for personal growth and healing. By implementing practical strategies such as acknowledging our imperfections, reshaping negative thoughts, fostering gratitude, and seeking support, we actively foster self-forgiveness in our lives.

Embrace the transformative power of self-forgiveness, and allow it to illuminate your path towards a future brimming with inner peace, joy, and expansion. Remember, you are worthy of forgiveness and the boundless opportunities it bestows.

The Path To Self-Forgiveness: Acknowledging And Embracing The Journey

In life, we often find ourselves entangled in a web of regrets, mistakes, and moments of self-blame. We carry the weight of our past actions, dragging them along our journey and impeding our progress. It is during these times that acknowledging the need for self-forgiveness becomes paramount.

Self-forgiveness is a potent tool; it can liberate us from the chains of guilt, shame, and self-condemnation. It enables us to heal wounds inflicted upon ourselves, paving a path toward self-love and inner peace. However, before embarking on this transformative journey, we must grasp why self-forgiveness holds such significance in our lives.

A vital aspect to recognize is our humanity. Imperfection is inherently woven into the fabric of our existence. We all make mistakes, take wrong turns, and stumble along our paths. Instead of clinging to these mistakes as an enduring identity, we must embrace our capacity for growth and change. Self-forgiveness acknowledges our fallibility, allowing us to progress with compassion for ourselves.

Moreover, clinging to grudges against ourselves burdens us emotionally, stifling our ability to live fully. The weight of self-blame can deplete our energy, trapping us in a cycle of negativity. By nurturing self-forgiveness, we shed this burden, freeing ourselves from self-imposed suffering. As we relinquish our past mistakes and learn to forgive ourselves, we create space for self-compassion to thrive.

Additionally, self-forgiveness is pivotal in fostering inner peace. When we harbor resentment towards ourselves, inner turmoil becomes a constant companion. We remain ensnared in perpetual self-judgment, unable to find solace or tranquility. By extending forgiveness to ourselves, we invite peace into our hearts. We grant ourselves permission to heal, grow, and find harmony within.

Furthermore, self-forgiveness is not an indulgence or complacency. It does not excuse or diminish the impact of our actions. Instead, it is an act of self-empowerment and growth. It enables us to acknowledge our mistakes, learn from them, and make amends if necessary. Self-forgiveness imbues us with the strength to evolve into better versions of ourselves, inspiring personal growth and transformation.

As we embrace the necessity of self-forgiveness and its profound impact on our lives, we begin to comprehend the true essence of self-love. Self-love is not a destination but a journey, and self-forgiveness is a vital component along the way. It is an act of compassion, acceptance, and unconditional love towards ourselves. Through self-forgiveness, we recognize our inherent worth and navigate the path to self-love.

As you embark on the journey of recognizing the need for self-forgiveness, remember the profound power it holds. Embrace your imperfections, release the burdens of guilt and regret, and allow self-compassion to usher in inner peace. Open your heart to forgiveness, both for yourself and others, and discover the transformative gift of self-love.

But the journey doesn't end here. There is much more to explore and unravel as we delve deeper into the realm of self-forgiveness. In this book, we will uncover practical techniques to foster self-forgiveness and delve into real-life stories that illustrate its incredible healing potential. So, the adventure continues, and the path to self-love awaits!

As we progress on the journey of recognizing the need for self-forgiveness, it's important to explore practical techniques that can nurture this transformative process. While self-forgiveness may seem daunting at times, with dedication and patience, it's possible to cultivate a profound sense of compassion towards ourselves.

One potent technique to foster self-forgiveness is through the practice of mindfulness. Mindfulness allows us to become aware of our thoughts and emotions without judgment or attachment. By observing our inner landscape with kindness and curiosity, we gain insights into the root causes of our self-blame and guilt.

In moments of self-forgiveness, it's essential to practice self-compassion. We must learn to treat ourselves with the same kindness and understanding we would offer to a close friend or loved one. Remind yourself that you deserve forgiveness, that you are worthy of love and acceptance. Treat yourself with gentle words and gestures, nurturing the seeds of self-forgiveness to bloom within.

Another valuable technique is the use of affirmations. Affirmations are positive statements that help reframe our thoughts and beliefs. By repeating affirmations such as "I am worthy of forgiveness" or "I release myself from past mistakes," we gradually rewire our minds to embrace self-forgiveness as a natural and necessary part of our growth.

Journaling remains a potent tool for self-forgiveness. Set aside dedicated time to pour out your thoughts, emotions, and experiences related to self-forgiveness onto paper. Delve into your inner landscape, unveiling any hidden beliefs or patterns that obstruct your ability to forgive yourself. Use the act of writing as a cathartic release, allowing forgiveness to flow from your pen onto the pages.

To further enrich your practice of self-forgiveness, seek guidance from a trusted mentor, therapist, or support group. At times, external guidance may be necessary to navigate the complexities of our emotions and experiences. These professionals can offer valuable insights, tools, and strategies to support your journey toward self-forgiveness.

Real-life stories of forgiveness stand as beacons of inspiration and motivation. While each journey is unique, hearing the tales of those who have embraced self-forgiveness can offer hope and encouragement. Seek out books, podcasts, or support groups that share these narratives. Listening to accounts of personal growth and transformation can remind us of our own capacity to heal and forgive.

Remember, self-forgiveness is an ongoing process. It may not occur overnight, and setbacks are inevitable. Be patient and gentle with yourself as you navigate the complexities of healing and growth. Celebrate the small victories along the way and never lose sight of the immense power self-forgiveness holds in unlocking inner peace and self-love.

As we journey through this exploration of self-forgiveness, it is my heartfelt wish that you continue on this path of self-discovery and self-compassion. I pray you embrace your imperfections, release the burdens of guilt and regret, and nurture a deep sense of self-love. Remember, you deserve forgiveness, and your trek toward self-forgiveness is nothing short of courage. Trust in the process, stay committed, and your heart will be unwaveringly guided towards inner peace and serenity.

With each stride you make towards self-forgiveness, may you behold the unfolding of a life adorned with love, compassion, and genuine inner healing. Embrace the splendor of self-forgiveness and let it serve as the foundation of your voyage towards self-love and inner peace.

Embracing Renewal: Healing And Moving Forward With Purpose

Life is a voyage marked by highs and lows, elations and sorrows, triumphs and setbacks. Along this path, we accumulate a tapestry of experiences, both uplifting and challenging, that sculpt our essence. In this segment of the chapter, we'll delve into the potency of forgiveness and explore how embracing healing and progression can draw us nearer to a life imbued with grace, fortitude, and purpose.

Embracing healing demands bravery, for it entails facing our pain head-on and allowing ourselves to authentically feel and process it. It's not about burying our anguish and feigning indifference; rather, it involves acknowledging the scars we bear and embracing them as integral parts of our narrative. Through this acknowledgment, we unlock a gateway to compassion, both for ourselves and others. It's through forgiveness that we can commence shedding the weight of our past, making space for healing and evolution.

However, forgiveness should not be misconstrued as forgetting or excusing the actions that inflicted pain upon us. Instead, it's a deliberate choice to relinquish the bitterness and resentment that ensnare us in a cycle of negativity. Forgiveness is a gift we bestow upon ourselves—a liberation from the shackles that impede our progress. It's an assertion of self-love and autonomy, empowering us to reclaim our serenity and reconstruct our lives on our terms.

As we advance on the journey towards embracing healing, it becomes paramount to extol the potency of forgiveness. Forgiveness is a formidable force capable of repairing fractured relationships, reinstating tranquility within our hearts, and endowing us with the freedom to embrace a future unencumbered by the past. It's not a display of frailty but a testament to our resilience and fortitude. Through forgiveness, we carve out space for comprehension, empathy, and maturation.

Moving forward with grace involves assimilating the wisdom gleaned from our experiences. It's a pledge to transcend our circumstances and embrace the potential for metamorphosis. Progressing forward doesn't entail eradicating the past; instead, it encompasses merging our past with our present and future selves, leveraging it as a cornerstone for personal development and constructive change.

Resilience serves as the bedrock of our voyage toward healing and advancement. It embodies the capacity to rebound from adversity, discover fortitude in moments of vulnerability, and foster a mindset of perseverance. Resilience empowers us to navigate the trials that cross our path with bravery and resolve, reminding us that setbacks are transient and serve as stepping stones toward our personal evolution.

For those who opt to embrace healing and forgiveness, a rejuvenated sense of purpose awaits. It's a purpose propelled by the aspiration to lead a life of genuineness, affection, and connection. As we relinquish our past grievances and embrace healing, we unlock a realm of opportunities. The scars that once ensnared us metamorphose into catalysts for personal development and a deeper comprehension of ourselves and others.

In this voyage of forgiving others and ourselves, embracing healing, and moving forward, I encourage you to embark on a journey of self-discovery, resilience, and forgiveness. As you reach the conclusion of this chapter, remember that healing commences from within. It's a choice we make, a dedication to ourselves, and a testament to our unyielding spirit. Embrace the potency of forgiveness and have faith that the path to healing will guide you to a future overflowing with joy, love, and purpose.

As we persist on our expedition of embracing healing and moving forward, it's vital to recognize that this path isn't always smooth. There may be moments of uncertainty, fear, and doubt, yet it's in these moments that our resilience truly illuminates.

Resilience isn't merely about rebounding; it's about propelling forward. It's about leveraging the lessons we've assimilated and using them as propulsion for growth and metamorphosis. It demands us to harness our inner fortitude and have confidence in our capability to surmount any obstacle that crosses our path.

In the midst of challenges, it's easy to dwell on negativity, letting anger and resentment consume us. But true resilience involves transcending these emotions and focusing on the positive aspects of our journey. It's about embracing gratitude for the lessons learned, the strength gained, and the growth experienced.

A potent tool for resilience is the practice of self-care. Tending to our physical and emotional needs lays a sturdy foundation for confronting any obstacles that come our way. It entails dedicating time to activities that bring us joy and peace, surrounding ourselves with positivity, and nurturing our well-being.

Embracing self-forgiveness is another pivotal aspect of moving forward gracefully. Just as we forgive others, it's crucial to extend that same forgiveness to ourselves. We're all human and prone to mistakes. While we may regret past choices, fixating on them only perpetuates our suffering. By forgiving ourselves, we create room for growth and learning, enabling us to progress with compassion and understanding.

Moving forward with grace also entails establishing healthy boundaries and relinquishing toxic relationships. Sometimes, to truly heal and welcome positive change, we must distance ourselves from those who introduce negativity into our lives. Though challenging, this step is necessary for fostering a healthier and more fulfilling future.

Lastly, as we traverse the path of embracing healing and progress, let's not overlook the importance of self-reflection and introspection. Carving out time to scrutinize our thoughts and beliefs grants us deeper insight into ourselves and any recurring patterns or tendencies that may hinder our growth. Through self-reflection, we can pinpoint areas in need of healing and begin making deliberate choices that propel us toward a future in alignment with our values and aspirations.

To all those who have journeyed alongside us in this exploration of forgiveness and healing, remember that you are not alone. We're united on this path, offering support and encouragement as we strive to embrace lives imbued with grace, resilience, and purpose. Regardless of where you find yourself in your journey, know that there is always hope for healing, growth, and renewal.

As we wrap up this chapter and contemplate the impact of forgiveness, let's remember that healing isn't a final stop; it's an ongoing journey. It's a pledge to ourselves and a lifelong pursuit of completeness. Embrace this journey, trusting that as you persist in healing and progressing, you're paving the way for a future brimming with love, joy, and boundless opportunities.

CHAPTER 5
"God's Unconditional Love"

God's Unconditional Love

Unconditional love surrounds us daily; we just need to recognize it, understand its essence, and, most importantly, feel its embrace. We witness unconditional love in various aspects of our lives, starting from our own childhood and upbringing, observing the bond between our parents and siblings as we mature. However, the most profound manifestation of unconditional love is often found between a parent and child. Picture a parent's unwavering love for their child, irrespective of the child's successes or failures, strengths or weaknesses. This love endures through life's highs and lows, offering unwavering support, guidance, and forgiveness without hesitation.

In the parent-child relationship, a parent's love transcends any conditions or expectations placed upon the child. It isn't based on the child's achievements or meeting certain standards but simply exists because the parent sees the inherent worth and dignity of their child.

Regardless of the mistakes a child makes or their shortcomings, the parent's love remains steadfast, providing comfort and security. It's a love that accepts the child for who they are, including their imperfections and encourages their growth and development in their own unique way.

This relationship beautifully illustrates the idea of unconditional love, demonstrating how it can deeply impact the most intimate and meaningful connections we have in life.

Similarly, across various cultures and religions, the concept of God's unconditional love serves as a source of hope and comfort for many individuals as they navigate life's challenges.

In Christianity, the idea of God's unconditional love holds a central place. It's seen as a foundation, something solid upon which believers build their spiritual lives. This love surpasses human understanding, embracing all individuals regardless of their imperfections.

But what exactly does it mean to talk about God's unconditional love? How does it show up in our lives, and what does it mean for our relationships, communities, and the world? Exploring these questions takes us deep into matters of faith, prompting us to think about love itself and how it changes us.

During this exploration, we'll dive into theological ideas, using scripture, tradition, and reason to shed light on the mysteries of God's love. We'll consider how it shapes our understanding of ourselves and others and how it influences our moral and ethical beliefs.

Our goal isn't just to gain knowledge but to feel a deeper connection—to God, to each other, and to the world. God's unconditional love isn't just comforting; it also challenges us to embody that love in our actions and to spread compassion and healing in a world that needs it.

So, let's embark on this journey together—a journey guided by the light of God's unconditional love, leading us closer to its endless embrace.

Embracing Imperfection: Finding Beauty in Brokenness

In our toughest times, when it feels like everything is falling apart, we might wonder if there's any point in our pain. We ask ourselves if our tears mean anything at all. It's in these moments of despair that we often search for answers and cling to hope. But even in the midst of chaos, God extends an invitation to us—an opportunity to find His unconditional love, even in our darkest hours.

Brokenness isn't easy to understand. It challenges what we believe and tests our faith. In a world that values success and strength, being vulnerable and broken can feel like weakness. We're pushed to wear masks, hiding our pain from others. But embracing our brokenness can lead to a deep encounter with God's love.

When everything seems beyond repair, we face a choice. We can fight against our brokenness, holding onto who we used to be, or we can embrace it, surrendering to a higher power that wants to rebuild us. By accepting our vulnerabilities and recognizing our brokenness, we open ourselves up to God's transformative love.

Letting go of pride and self-sufficiency isn't easy. Society often praises independence and self-reliance, making it hard to admit our brokenness. But it's in our brokenness that we discover our true selves. Like a sculptor molding clay into a masterpiece, God wants to shape us into vessels of love, compassion, and grace.

In our brokenness, it's important to remember that we're not alone. God is always there, waiting for us to turn to Him, to lay down our pain and sorrow. He meets us in our brokenness, holding us close and whispering words of comfort and healing. It's in our darkest moments that God's love shines the brightest.

Embracing brokenness takes courage—it means facing our fears and doubts head-on. It's not an easy journey, but it shows us the strength we never knew we had. As we confront our brokenness, we discover a resilience that comes from encountering God's unwavering love.

Brokenness reveals the beauty of redemption. Just like a mosaic is made from countless shattered pieces, our brokenness allows God to create a masterpiece from the fragments of our lives. We start to see that our struggles and pain shape who we are becoming.

This book has only scratched the surface of the connection between brokenness and God's love. As we journey together, let's hold onto hope. Embracing our brokenness is not the end but a new beginning. There's more to explore, discover, and experience—revealing the immense love waiting for us in life's darkest moments.

So, with open hearts and willing spirits, let's embrace God's love in our brokenness. We're on the edge of a profound shift in perception. We've explored the depths of brokenness and recognized its power to reveal God's unconditional love. In this chapter, we'll delve deeper into the transformative power within life's darkest moments.

Embracing brokenness means admitting we can't heal ourselves. We surrender to a force greater than ourselves, one that understands our pain and wants to bring restoration.

In surrender, we find the strength to let go of burdens we've carried for too long. We release shame, guilt, and self-condemnation, allowing God's love to fill the cracks in our shattered hearts.

As we journey through brokenness, transformation occurs within us. Our pain becomes a catalyst for growth, deepening our capacity for compassion and empathy. Like a broken vase painstakingly reassembled, we're pieced back together with care and intention. Through brokenness, we discover our true essence—the radiant light that shines through our flaws.

However, let's not equate brokenness with a life devoid of joy. Even in our darkest moments, we can find glimmers of hope and pockets of grace that carry us through the storm. Even when the path forward seems unclear, we can trust that God's guiding hand is there, gently leading us through our pain.

In embracing our brokenness, we welcome a newfound vulnerability that intersects with our inner strength. We realize that our struggles don't define us but refine us. We learn to let go of our need for control, understanding that true strength comes from surrendering to God's plan for our lives.

The journey of embracing brokenness isn't easy. We may stumble along the way, but even in our weakest moments, God's love remains constant. It's in these moments of weakness that we find our greatest strength and the ability to rely on God's unwavering love. As we release the burdens of our past, we're free to rise to new heights, unburdened by the weight of our brokenness.

Embracing our brokenness also means embracing the beauty of community. We realize that we're not alone in our struggles, finding comfort in shared experiences. Together, as a community, we can extend grace and compassion to those around us, reminding each other that our brokenness doesn't diminish our worth or capacity for love. Instead, it amplifies the power of God's redeeming love within and through us.

Let's hold onto the truth that our brokenness is just the beginning. It's the start of a journey toward healing, restoration, and encountering God's transforming love. So, my friends, let's embrace our vulnerabilities, release our pain, and allow God's love to shape us into vessels of light, for there's immense love waiting for us even in life's darkest moments.

With hearts wide open, let's step into the embrace of God's unconditional love, ready to embark on the next stage of our journey—a journey filled with hope, healing, and the profound joy found only in the arms of our loving Creator.

Embers Of The Soul: Confronting The Darkness Within

Within our own souls lie hidden depths of darkness. It's a darkness we often avoid acknowledging, as it reveals vulnerabilities and imperfections we strive to hide. Yet, it's within this darkness that our true struggle resides—a battle waged within our hearts, minds, and spirits.

The journey into this darkness isn't easy. It demands courage, vulnerability, and a readiness to confront the parts of ourselves we'd rather ignore. It's a journey peeling away the layers of masks we wear, revealing the complexities and contradictions that define our humanity.

At times, this darkness overwhelms us. We get lost in a maze of doubts, fears, and insecurities. In those moments, we question our worth and purpose, wondering if we deserve love, forgiveness, and redemption. Our shortcomings, failures, and mistakes cast shadows over our hearts, creating dissonance within our souls.

Yet, it's precisely in this darkness that we stand at a crossroads—a place where hope's flickering light casts its gentle glow. In these darkest moments, we can encounter God's unconditional love, a love that knows no bounds, no matter how deep our struggles.

God's love is like a beacon, illuminating our shadows and guiding us toward redemption. It reaches into our depths, embracing us with warmth and tenderness. It whispers reassurance, reminding us we're never alone and that even in our darkest moments, purpose and beauty await discovery.

This love doesn't ask for perfection; it embraces us in our brokenness. It meets us in our doubts, fears, and failures, offering healing and restoration. It shows us that our darkness doesn't define us but gives us a chance to grow and change.

As we face our own darkness, we see that our struggles aren't unique. We're part of a shared human experience, navigating life's complexities together. Our battles aren't isolated incidents; they're part of being human.

In our quest for redemption, we find we're not alone. We're embraced by a love that stands firm, bridging the gap between our darkness and the light that leads us forward. In this embrace, we find strength, hope, and the courage to keep going.

As we journey through our darkness, let's hold onto the promise of God's unconditional love. Let it brighten our hearts, heal our brokenness, and guide us toward redemption. Through this love, our darkest moments become opportunities for growth and self-discovery.

At the crossroads of our darkness, we long for hope's flickering light to lead us forward. In our darkest times, when doubts and fears loom large, we find comfort and strength in God's embrace.

As we continue our journey of self-discovery and redemption, let's remember that God's love has no limits. It reaches deep into our souls, easing our insecurities and reminding us that we're worthy of love, forgiveness, and redemption, no matter how deep our struggles may be.

Despite our flaws and mistakes, God's love stays strong. It doesn't expect perfection but meets us in our brokenness, offering healing and renewal. It shows us that our darkness doesn't define us—it's a chance to grow and change.

As we face the darkness within, we realize that our struggles are part of the human experience. We're not alone in our battles; we're connected, sharing life's journey together. Our stories intersect, and in seeking redemption, we find a sense of unity and empathy.

God's unconditional love bridges the gap between our inner darkness and the guiding light. It gives us the strength to confront our fears, hopes to overcome doubts, and the courage to move forward. This love empowers us to accept ourselves fully, with all our complexities.

In God's loving embrace, we find refuge. It's a love beyond our understanding, accepting us as we are and helping us become our best selves.

In our journey toward redemption, let's remember we're never alone. Even in our darkest times, God's love surrounds us, leading us toward the light. It sees our untapped potential waiting to be realized.

Choosing to embrace God's unconditional love isn't a one-time decision but a daily commitment. It means letting go of fears and insecurities and allowing his love to shine into our hearts. Though it may be challenging, the rewards are immense.

As we stand at life's crossroads, let's choose the path that draws us closer to God's unconditional love. Let his love heal our wounds, mend our brokenness, and transform our lives. In his love, we find redemption and the true beauty of our souls.

As you journey through your own darkness, hold onto the certainty of God's love. Let it guide, strengthen, and empower you as you discover your true self. May you find courage, hope, and strength in his unwavering embrace.

Love's Guiding Light: A Journey Of Encountering God

Embarking on the journey of experiencing God's love is truly remarkable. It's a journey that uncovers the depths of our souls, sparks hope in our hearts, and leads us toward healing and redemption. In this chapter, we'll explore practical steps and spiritual practices to help navigate this profound encounter.

The path to redemption may seem daunting, especially in life's darkest moments. Yet, it's precisely in these times that God's unconditional love shines brightest, offering solace, guidance, and purpose. This love goes beyond understanding, embracing us in our brokenness and gently guiding us toward restoration.

One practical step toward experiencing God's love is surrender. In society, surrender is often viewed as a weakness. However, in spirituality, surrender opens the door for God's grace to transform us. It's letting go, releasing burdens, and trusting in God's guidance toward redemption. Through surrendering to his will, we allow ourselves to be shaped and healed by his love.

Prayer and meditation are also vital practices on this journey. In moments of silence and connection with God, we hear his voice and feel his presence. These practices provide space for reflection, seeking guidance, and pouring out our hearts to God. Through prayer and meditation, we open ourselves to receive his love and find comfort in his embrace.

Additionally, cultivating gratitude profoundly impacts our journey. It shifts our focus from lack to abundance, reminding us of God's faithfulness even in darkness. Practicing gratitude helps us recognize and appreciate God's love in both big and small ways, fostering a deeper connection with him.

Seeking support and building community are essential on this journey. Encountering God's love isn't meant to be a solo venture. Often, God works through the people he brings into our lives, offering companionship, guidance, and motivation. By connecting with others who share our quest for God's love and redemption, we create a support system that strengthens us as we journey through life's challenges.

As you embrace the practical steps and spiritual practices shared in this book, remember that your path to encountering God's love is unique. Each step, each practice, and each moment of surrender brings you closer to the divine presence within your heart. May you find comfort, hope, and healing along this path, knowing that God's unconditional love accompanies you every step of the way.

As you continue this sacred journey, remember that despite the obstacles you face, you're never alone. The divine presence is ever-present, offering guidance, strength, and unwavering love.

A significant practice to adopt on this journey is self-compassion. Often, we're our own toughest critics, burdening ourselves with guilt, shame, and self-condemnation. However, God's love isn't condemning; it's unconditional and redemptive. It offers forgiveness and grace, allowing us to let go of past mistakes and embrace our humanity. By practicing self-compassion, we learn to forgive ourselves, treat ourselves with kindness, and trust in our worthiness of God's love and redemption.

Seeking wisdom and guidance from spiritual advisors, mentors, or trusted individuals who've walked similar paths is another crucial step. These wise souls, filled with God's love, can provide valuable insights, practical advice, and a listening ear. Their experiences and perspectives can illuminate your path, offering comfort and encouragement during moments of uncertainty.

Let's remember the power of Scripture on our transformative journey. God's Word offers comfort, truth, and life-giving wisdom. Dive into Scripture, and let the words sink into your heart, mind, and soul. Find solace and direction in stories of redemption, forgiveness, and love. Let these ancient words revive your spirit and fuel your quest to encounter God's love deeply.

Alongside these practices, it's crucial to care for your physical well-being. Body and soul are linked, so tending to your physical health greatly affects your spiritual journey. Rest, engage in joyful activities, nourish yourself with wholesome foods, and prioritize self-care. By honoring your body's needs, you create space within yourself to receive God's love and presence more fully.

May you find encouragement and strength knowing that the journey toward encountering God's love is transformative, illuminating, and profoundly beautiful. Through self-compassion, seeking guidance, Scripture immersion, and physical care, you lay the groundwork for a remarkable encounter with God's love, redemption, and healing.

Embrace these practices, knowing you're not alone. God's love surrounds you, and His grace carries you. Release expectations, open your heart, and embrace the possibility of encountering God's unconditional love in your darkest moments.

May the rest of this chapter and journey continue to lead you toward the embrace of God's redemptive love. You are worthy, loved, and on the path to healing and wholeness. Trust God fully, surrender to His plan, and let His love guide you every step of the way.

From Bitterness To Blessings: Unveiling The Transformative Power Of Forgiveness

In our darkest moments, when life feels like it's falling apart, finding a way forward can seem impossible. We might feel trapped, weighed down by regret, anger, and pain. But in these tough times, embracing God's unconditional love can be a beacon of hope. There's a powerful tool that can help us break free from the past and welcome divine love: forgiveness.

Forgiveness, whether we receive it or give it, has the power to heal our hurting hearts and open us up to God's immense love and grace. It's not always easy, and it might take some soul-searching, but the benefits are huge. When we forgive, we let go of the bitterness and resentment that have held us back for too long.

First, we need to accept forgiveness. As humans, we mess up; we stumble; we fall. Our imperfections might make us feel unworthy of love and forgiveness. But God's love doesn't have limits. He offers us forgiveness freely, embracing us in our brokenness and showing us we're worthy of redemption. Accepting this forgiveness helps us shed guilt, shame, and self-doubt, allowing us to move forward with purpose.

Then comes the harder part: forgiving others. When we've been hurt by someone else, it's natural to hold onto anger and crave revenge. But holding onto these negative feelings only keeps us trapped in a cycle of pain and darkness. Forgiving others is an act of freedom. It releases us from the toxic grip of resentment and gives us the power to break free from the past. Carrying resentment just weighs us down on our journey with God.

When we forgive others, we open ourselves to God's transformative love. It doesn't mean we excuse or forget the wrong that was done, but we choose to let go of its hold on us. Through forgiveness, we recognize our own humanity and embrace the chance to grow and heal. It takes courage and strength, but it sets the stage for a future filled with peace and joy.

When we embrace forgiveness, we let go of resentment and become channels of God's unconditional love. Our hearts are cleansed, and we start seeing ourselves and others with compassion. We no longer carry the weight of past mistakes or grudges. Instead, we embrace the freedom forgiveness brings, allowing us to fully feel the love God intended for us.

As we journey through darkness, facing pain and despair, let's remember the power of forgiveness. Let's accept God's forgiveness and share it with others, knowing it can transform lives. In this chapter, we'll explore practical ways to nurture forgiveness in our daily lives and embrace God's unconditional love.

For now, let's pause at the threshold of exploration, ready to discover the wonders of forgiveness. As we dive deeper into forgiveness, we'll uncover ways to nurture it in our lives and fully embrace God's love. These practices will help us experience the freedom and healing forgiveness brings.

Self-reflection is a crucial first step in cultivating forgiveness. Examining our actions and motives helps us understand how we've affected others and where we need forgiveness ourselves. It takes humility and facing our shortcomings to lead to a deeper grasp of God's grace.

Empathy is another key to forgiveness. Putting ourselves in the shoes of those who wronged us helps us see their humanity and the reasons behind their actions. It's not about excusing their behavior but understanding what drove them. By doing so, we can let go of anger and resentment and find compassion in our hearts.

Prayer is a mighty tool on the path to forgiveness. Through prayer, we can seek strength and guidance from God, asking Him to help us let go of the pain caused by others. Forgiveness might seem impossible on our own, but with God's grace, all things are achievable. In prayer, we find comfort and can lay down our burdens before the one who offers us unconditional love and forgiveness.

Besides prayer, seeking support from others is crucial in our journey toward forgiveness. Sometimes, the wounds we carry need the help and advice of trusted friends, family, or mentors. Sharing our stories with others who have gone through similar pains can bring validation and healing. It's through the support of others that we find the courage to forgive and move forward in our quest to embrace God's love.

Forgiveness is an ongoing process requiring daily commitment. It's not a one-time decision but a choice we must make every day. As we journey through life, new hurts and old wounds may resurface, testing our ability to forgive. But by consistently choosing forgiveness, we build strength and deepen our capacity for love and compassion.

Embracing forgiveness isn't easy, but it's transformative. Through self-reflection, empathy, prayer, seeking support, and daily commitment, we can nurture forgiveness in our lives and encounter God's unconditional love in the darkest moments. Through forgiveness, we find release from the burdens of the past and discover the joy and peace that come from embracing the transformative power of God's love.

Let's continue our exploration of forgiveness with open hearts and minds, ready to uncover the wonders that lie ahead in this journey of redemption and healing. As we embrace forgiveness, we not only change our own lives but also become sources of hope and love for those around us, reflecting the power of God's unconditional love. May the light of God's love shine through us as we extend forgiveness, and may we continue to witness the profound impact that forgiveness has on our souls and the world around us.

Perfectly Imperfect: Embracing Grace Amidst Flaws

In the midst of life's chaos and challenges, our imperfections often become sources of solace and redemption. In a world fixated on perfection, grace stands as a beacon of hope, urging us to accept our flaws and experience the unconditional love of God. This chapter dives deep into the essence of grace, encouraging us to let go of the pressure of performance-based love and revel in the unearned favor and acceptance bestowed upon us by God.

Too frequently, we find ourselves trapped in the pursuit of perfection. Society bombards us with unattainable standards, leaving us feeling inadequate and undeserving. We strive to meet these impossible expectations, desperately seeking approval and validation. Yet, in our relentless pursuit, we lose sight of a fundamental truth: God's love isn't contingent on our performance.

Grace, at its core, is a gift freely given by our loving creator. It's the divine declaration that we are worthy, not because of our actions or failures, but simply because we exist. This radical notion disrupts our ingrained thought patterns, challenging us to shift our focus from our deficiencies to the boundless love that surrounds us.

When we embrace grace, we release the grip of fear and shame on our hearts. We acknowledge that despite our flaws and missteps, there's redemption waiting for us. It's in our darkest moments, when we feel lowest that we encounter God's, unwavering love. It's a love that doesn't falter in the face of our imperfections but reaches out to embrace us, flaws and all.

Embracing grace demands surrendering our need for control and trusting in the mercy of a compassionate God. It's an act of vulnerability, laying bare our weaknesses and brokenness to the one who seeks to heal and restore us. Through this, we find the courage to forgive ourselves and extend grace to others, nurturing a cycle of love and acceptance that knows no bounds.

Within our imperfections lies the beauty of our humanity. It's through our fractures that the light of grace shines, illuminating the path to redemption. To fully embrace grace is to recognize that we aren't defined by our mistakes but by the infinite love that envelops us.

In our journey of embracing grace, we need to let go of the burdens we carry—the weight of guilt and self-condemnation. God's forgiveness and unconditional love call us to lay down our burdens at His feet. It's only by surrendering our imperfections that we can truly experience the transformative power of grace.

As we delve deeper into our journey of grace, we'll uncover the stories of individuals who, in their brokenness, found strength and hope through God's unconditional love. Their narratives reveal how grace can transcend our darkest moments, offering redemption and a way forward.

Here, we'll explore the stories of those who faced overwhelming obstacles yet discovered the extraordinary depth of God's grace. Their journeys will inspire and uplift us, reminding us that within our imperfections lies the potential for remarkable transformation.

We'll witness the incredible power of grace in action. In the depths of our imperfections, we often discover the profound depth of God's grace. It's in those moments when we feel completely broken and unworthy that we can truly encounter the transformative power of God's unconditional love. As we continue to explore grace, let's look at stories of those who faced unimaginable obstacles yet discovered the extraordinary depth of God's grace.

Here, we see the resilience of the human spirit and the undeniable presence of grace in adversity. We meet individuals who've battled addiction, abuse, and loss yet found the strength to rise above their circumstances. These journeys highlight the redemptive power of God's love, showing us that even in the darkest moments, grace can ignite a flame of hope.

One such story is that of Tom, a young man who struggled with addiction for years. His life had become a cycle of shame, guilt, and despair. He'd lost all hope and felt utterly undeserving of love. But in his brokenness, he encountered a community of believers who embraced him with open arms, showing him the unmerited favor of God. Through their love and acceptance, Tom began to understand that God's grace wasn't limited to the perfect and well-put-together but extended even to the most broken and wounded souls.

As Tom embraced this truth, he began a journey of healing and transformation. With the support of his newfound community, he faced the deep-rooted pain that led him to seek solace in addiction. Through prayer, counseling, and a renewed trust in God's unconditional love, Tom started to rebuild his life. It was a slow and often challenging process, but he saw firsthand how grace could bring restoration and renewal.

Then, there was Tammy, a woman who had experienced the devastation of domestic abuse. For years, fear had silenced her, and her sense of self-worth had been eroded by someone else's cruel actions. But as she found the courage to share her story, she realized that God's grace wasn't just a concept but a tangible reality. With the support and love of those around her, Tammy broke free from the chains of abuse and reclaimed her identity. In her journey to healing, she found comfort in the arms of a loving God who understood her pain intimately.

These stories, and many others like them, show the transformative power of God's grace in our lives. They remind us that no matter how deep our wounds or how far we've strayed, we still receive his unearned favor and unconditional love. By embracing grace, we let go of the weight of our imperfections and allow God's love to heal our brokenness, guiding us toward redemption.

In this journey of grace, let's hold onto the truth that perfection isn't required for God's love. Let's remember that his grace meets us in our brokenness, inviting us to accept our imperfections and find comfort in his unconditional acceptance. May the stories of those who've experienced God's grace be sources of hope, lighting the way to redemption and reminding us of the extraordinary depth of his love.

Pathways To Purpose: Navigating The Divine Blueprint

In life's vastness, everyone holds a unique purpose, a calling that speaks deeply to their soul. This purpose, often hidden beneath the surface, waits to be discovered, leading us to a life of deep fulfillment and boundless joy. It's through uncovering this divine purpose that we encounter the transformative power of God's unconditional love, even in our darkest moments.

Each of us carries special gifts, talents, and passions woven into the fabric of our lives. These remarkable qualities aren't random; they're intentional manifestations of the divine. As we journey toward self-discovery, we unearth these hidden treasures, revealing the dormant richness within us.

Yet, seeking our divine purpose can feel overwhelming. The world throws distractions our way, pulling us from our true path. Doubts, fears, and societal pressures blur our vision, hiding the road to our authentic selves. But in these dark moments, God's unconditional love shines bright, lighting our way forward.

Divine purpose isn't one-size-fits-all. Though it's easy to compare our journeys to others, we must remember that God has a unique purpose for each of us. Embracing God's unconditional love gives us the courage to embark on this deeply personal quest, unafraid to explore the depths of our souls.

God's love breaks the chains of self-doubt and fear, empowering us to embrace our true potential. It encourages us to take bold leaps of faith, replacing hesitations with the belief that we can fulfill our purpose. With every step toward our calling, we find new strength and resilience, knowing God's love sustains us.

As we dive into the depths of our being, we not only discover our purpose but also our interconnectedness with the world. God's unconditional love sparks compassion and empathy within us, urging us to make a positive impact on others' lives. We become agents of change, vehicles through which God's divine purpose shines in the world.

Every step we take on our journey toward uncovering divine purpose holds a sacred significance, a chance to align our lives with something greater than ourselves. In these moments, we realize we're not just spectators but active participants in life's grand symphony; each note played with love, purpose, and intention.

In the pursuit of divine purpose, there are no accidents or coincidences. Every experience, whether joyful or painful, serves as a stepping stone toward a deeper understanding of ourselves and our role in the world. Embracing God's unconditional love allows us to see the hidden lessons and blessings within life's darkest moments.

Remember, you're not alone on this journey. God's unconditional love surrounds you, guiding your steps and nurturing your soul. Trust the process, for it's through the unfolding of divine purpose that you'll find boundless joy, peace, and fulfillment. Stay faithful to the wonders that await.

In moments of uncertainty on our quest for divine purpose, we must lean on God's unwavering love and guidance. His presence comforts us, giving us solace and strength, reminding us that we're never alone.

As we grasp the realization of our unique calling, we understand it's not just for our own fulfillment but also for the betterment of the world. Embracing God's unconditional love enables us to recognize our interconnectedness with humanity and understand our purpose extends beyond ourselves. It's in the interplay of our individual purposes that we contribute to the collective beauty and unity of existence.

Amid life's noise, it's essential to create moments of stillness and reflection. These intentional acts of self-care provide fertile ground for divine inspiration to flourish. In the quiet of our hearts, we hear God's gentle guidance, leading us further on the path of self-discovery.

When we let go of our doubts and fears, allowing God's unconditional love to guide us, something amazing begins to happen within us and around us. We become channels through which his divine purpose flows into the world. It's in these moments, aligning with our calling, that we grasp the power we have to bring about positive change.

Every act of kindness, every extended hand, becomes an opportunity to share God's love with those we meet. Whether it's offering a listening ear, a comforting word, or a simple gesture of generosity, we can touch others' lives with love and compassion.

But let's not forget, this journey isn't always smooth sailing. There will be setbacks and times when we feel unsure or disheartened. It's important to remember these moments don't define us. Instead, they remind us of our shared humanity and the growth that comes from facing challenges.

In tough times, God's unconditional love remains unwavering. It's when things seem darkest that we lean on his strength, tapping into the resilience within us. We learn that the most profound lessons often emerge from our deepest struggles, and through them, we gain the wisdom and empathy to support others on their journeys.

As we continue on this path of discovering our divine purpose, take a moment to reflect on the truths revealed. Let it sink in: you have a unique calling woven into the fabric of who you are, waiting for you to fully embrace it.

Know that fulfilling your purpose won't always be easy, but with every step, God's love will light your way. Trust his guidance and embrace the limitless possibilities ahead.

Your journey doesn't end here. Embrace the wonder of discovering your divine purpose, knowing there's beauty and fulfillment waiting for you. Move forward with courage, knowing God's love will guide you, and your purpose will unfold in ways beyond imagination. Keep going, keep seeking, and never forget the transformative power of God's unconditional love.

Healing Hearts: The Journey Of Redemption In Relationships

When we look at the role relationships play in our journey toward redemption, we see how they can be both a source of struggle and a path to healing.

In our darkest moments, it's often our connections with others that bring us the most pain. We crave love, understanding, and acceptance but sometimes find ourselves caught in a web of hurt and brokenness. Yet, even in these difficult times, there's a chance for redemption within our relationships.

Relationships can deeply impact our lives, bringing joy, security, and support, but they can also cause turmoil and heartache. Whether it's strained family ties, shattered friendships, or fractured romantic relationships, the wounds we endure can leave lasting marks. But it's within these broken connections that we can encounter the love of God.

When we're open to redemption, we let God work through us and in us. Through God's love, we start to see the depth of our brokenness and the potential for healing in our relationships. But this journey isn't without its challenges.

One of the biggest hurdles we face is forgiveness. When we've been hurt by someone else's actions or words, letting go of our anger and resentment can be incredibly hard. We might hold onto the pain, unwilling to release the hurt. But forgiveness is where God's love steps in to mend the broken pieces of our relationships.

Forgiveness isn't simple, but it's crucial for our own growth and well-being. When we choose to forgive, we let go of bitterness and acknowledge that we're all imperfect. Just as we seek mercy and grace, we must extend them to others. By forgiving, we create room for healing and restoring our relationships.

Another challenge on the road to redemption is dealing with conflicts. Disagreements, differing opinions, and misunderstandings are inevitable in relationships. However, through these conflicts, we have a chance to learn and strengthen our connections. By facing the discomfort and seeking resolution, we create a space where God's love can bring transformation.

In times of conflict, it's important to approach with humility and grace. Instead of trying to win or prove ourselves right, we can prioritize understanding and reconciliation. Listening to the other person's perspective and being open to their feelings helps us see beyond our biases and allows room for healing. It's in these moments of vulnerability and humility that God's love can work in our relationships, bringing redemption.

On this journey toward redemption in our relationships, we must remember that it's not something we do alone. We need the support and guidance of God and our community. By seeking redemption, we let go of our pride and invite others to join us in the pursuit of healing.

This book and its chapters lay out the groundwork for understanding the challenges we face and the importance of embracing redemption in our relationships. We'll delve deeper into the healing and transformation that can happen when we let God's love mend and restore our connections with others. And we'll explore real-life stories and practical steps toward redeeming our relationships.

For now, let's consider that even in the darkness of broken relationships, there's hope for redemption. As we open ourselves to the possibility of change, hope emerges, promising healing and restoration. Let's embrace that hope and trust in God's unconditional love. In the depths of brokenness, when relationships seem beyond repair, we must cling to the hope that redemption is possible. As we journey toward transformation, we'll encounter real-life stories showing how God's love can mend and restore our connections with others.

Take Carol, for instance. She spent years estranged from her father due to unresolved conflicts and deep-seated resentment. Their relationship was fractured and distant, with wounds that seemed impossible to heal. Yet, Carol chose to embrace redemption in her relationship with her father.

With the help of a therapist, Carol began the painful but necessary process of forgiveness. She learned that forgiveness isn't about forgetting or excusing hurtful actions; it's about letting go of anger and resentment. Through prayer and reflection, Carol found the strength to extend mercy and grace to her father, recognizing their shared imperfections and the need for healing.

As Carol set aside her pride and ego, she opened herself up to vulnerability and authenticity. She had honest conversations with her father, expressing her hurt and desire for connection. In turn, her father acknowledged his mistakes and asked for forgiveness. They both understood that rebuilding trust would take time, but with humility and grace, they embarked on a journey of redemption.

Their relationship didn't magically transform overnight, but over time, they experienced moments of healing. They laughed together, shared memories, and slowly rebuilt a foundation of love and understanding. Their story shows the power of God's unconditional love, working through their willingness to be vulnerable and open to change.

Just like Carol found redemption in her relationship with her father, we can also discover hope in our own broken connections. By choosing to believe in redemption, we breathe new life into old wounds and scars. It's a courageous decision to let go of bitterness and resentment that only isolates us. Instead, we can opt for love and forgiveness, knowing that by doing so, we allow God's love to reshape and renew our relationships.

The journey to redemption requires deliberate steps. We must be ready to look inward, to acknowledge our own faults and imperfections. It's in recognizing our own brokenness that we can show compassion and understanding to those who have hurt us.

Moreover, seeking guidance and support from a trusted community can be crucial on this journey. Together, we can share our stories, offer comfort, and walk side by side toward healing. Opening ourselves to the vulnerability of community allows God's love to work through the hearts and hands of others.

The road to redemption in relationships isn't easy or straightforward. It demands great courage, humility, and vulnerability. Yet, within the darkness of broken connections lies the potential for transformative healing. As we embrace the redemptive power of God's unconditional love, we discover hope, restoration, and a deeper appreciation for the beauty that can emerge from our most wounded relationships. I pray you find encouragement to take the first steps toward redemption, knowing that God's love is ready to mend and transform your connections with others.

The Promise Of Tomorrow: Holding Onto Hope In Suffering

In the depths of despair, when darkness overwhelms our hearts and pain looms large, it's easy to feel abandoned by hope. But in those darkest hours, hope emerges as a guiding light, leading us back to the comfort of God's unconditional love.

Suffering touches everyone, regardless of age, background, or circumstance. It arrives uninvited, disrupting our lives and leaving us feeling shattered and adrift. Yet, it's precisely in these moments that hope becomes a powerful force, offering solace amidst the chaos.

When despair threatens to drown us, it's vital to remember that we're not alone. God's unwavering love stands beside us, even in our darkest hours. His love isn't based on our circumstances or mistakes. It transcends notions of worthiness, offering hope that redemption is always within reach.

Hope encourages us to trust in God's promises, even when our world feels shattered. It gives us strength to endure, grounding us in the belief that our suffering serves a purpose—for growth and spiritual transformation.

In the midst of suffering, hope helps us find meaning in our pain. It reminds us that our struggles aren't in vain but opportunities for God to reveal his love and power. Through trials, our faith is refined, our character strengthened, and our compassion deepened.

As we navigate suffering, hope shines a light into our darkest corners. It whispers reminders of God's unwavering presence and love, urging us to persevere. Hope assures us that, though we may stumble, we can rise again with God by our side.

Let's embrace hope with open hearts, knowing it's more than wishful thinking—it's a belief in God's goodness. In our darkest moments, when despair threatens, let's cling to hope as the bridge back to the warmth of God's unconditional love.

As you journey through the challenging wilderness of suffering, let hope be your guide. Trust that there's purpose in your pain and that redemption awaits. We'll explore practical ways to cultivate and sustain hope amidst hardship, uncovering the resilience within us as we embrace God's redemption in suffering.

For now, consider this an invitation to embrace hope tightly amid life's trials. Find solace in knowing that, even in your darkest moments, God's unconditional love shines bright, offering comfort, strength, and the promise of redemption. In the depths of suffering, when pain overwhelms, and it feels like there's no way out, hope can seem elusive. But it's in these moments that we can deepen our understanding of hope and let its power carry us through.

When despair grips us, it's easy to feel hopeless and weighed down by our circumstances. Yet, these are the moments when we must hold onto hope, for it's the lifeline guiding us back to God's love.

To nurture hope amid hardship, start by acknowledging and processing your pain. Allow yourself to grieve, to feel, and to seek support. In your vulnerability, you'll find resilience you didn't know you had. Through tears and prayers, open yourself to hope's transformative power.

Finding solace in God's love during dark times requires intentional trust in his plan. We may not understand our suffering, but we can trust that God has a purpose for it. In this trust, we gather the strength to move forward, even when the path seems impossible.

As we journey through the challenges of suffering, it's vital to have a supportive community around us. Connecting with others who've faced similar hardships and hearing their stories of resilience can offer comfort and inspiration. Together, we remind each other that we're never alone and that God's love is always there, even in our darkest moments.

To nurture hope, self-care is essential. Taking care of our physical, mental, and spiritual well-being helps replenish our strength to endure trials. Engaging in joyful activities, setting healthy boundaries, and finding moments of solitude and reflection all help keep our flame of hope burning.

Even when hope wavers, we must remember that God's redemption is within reach. His love for us is constant and profound. Our suffering isn't without purpose; it's a chance for growth, transformation, and a deeper understanding of God's love and plans.

I hope you've found comfort and encouragement in the power of hope amidst suffering. May you continue to hold onto the lifeline leading you back to God's unconditional love. May you find strength, peace, and, ultimately, redemption on your spiritual journey.

Remember, you're not alone. Many have walked the path of suffering before you, and as we come together, our collective strength grows. Let's face the darkest moments with hope, knowing that God's redemption is real, his love unwavering, and his promises true.

So, my friend, keep the flame of hope burning bright within you. Let it guide your journey, lighting the way and reminding you that even in the darkest nights, God's love and redemption are ever-present.

Restored Faith: Nurturing Resilience And Restoration

In our darkest moments, when it feels like everything is crashing down, there's resilience in embracing God's love. It's in these tough times that we find chances for restoration, where new beginnings can sprout amidst the challenges we face.

Throughout history, there are many stories of people transformed by God's love. They're like guiding lights, showing us the way to redemption and reminding us that even in the toughest times, there's hope for renewal.

Take Ava, for example. Her life was filled with pain and despair, stuck in a cycle of bad habits and toxic relationships. But in her lowest moments, she encountered a love so pure and unconditional that it changed everything. It sparked a journey of healing and restoration.

Ava's story shows the strength we find when we open up to God's love. In her darkest times, she found the courage to face her past, letting God's love reach deep into her soul. Through this encounter, she experienced the power of redemption firsthand.

As Ava walked the path of restoration, she learned that embracing God's love means letting go of pain and embracing forgiveness. True resilience isn't just about surviving tough times; it's also about forgiving ourselves and others and showing compassion along the way.

Ava's story isn't unique. Around the world, many find comfort in God's unconditional love. It's a love that goes beyond circumstances, embracing us in our brokenness and guiding us forward, even when things seem hopeless.

Let's reflect on the story of Elijah, a man who faced great loss and hardship. His dreams shattered, hope fading, and Elijah found himself at rock bottom. But in his darkest hour, he felt the enduring love of God, giving him renewed strength.

With God's love, Elijah found the courage to rise above his struggles and embrace a path of healing. He realized that resilience isn't about avoiding suffering but believing in a brighter tomorrow.

These stories remind us that tough times don't define us. They're just parts of a bigger story of redemption and fresh starts. By embracing God's love, we find the strength to keep going, the bravery to face challenges, and the optimism for better days ahead.

As we delve deeper into resilience and restoration, we'll uncover more tales of triumph over adversity. These stories will uplift and inspire, showing that even when the odds seem overwhelming, hope still shines through, guiding us toward a brighter future.

But for now, let's remember that embracing God's love can ignite resilience and restoration. As we journey through the stories ahead, may we find comfort in the knowledge that new beginnings are possible, even in our darkest moments. Ava's journey of healing continued, touching the hearts of all who heard it. Embracing the transformative power of God's love, she found herself surrounded by a community also seeking redemption.

Within the warm embrace of her community, Ava learned the value of being open and forming genuine connections. It was in sharing stories and heartfelt talks that she realized she wasn't facing her struggles alone. In her darkest moments, she found comfort in knowing others had also known pain and come out stronger.

Together, they created a space of compassion and empathy where brokenness wasn't judged but embraced. Through their combined strength, they became sources of hope and encouragement for each other, lighting the way toward healing. Ava's journey showcased the power of community, reminding us that together, we're stronger than we could ever be alone.

As Ava's healing journey progressed, she realized that restoration wasn't just about changing herself but also about showing love and compassion to others. She saw the impact she could make by listening, encouraging, and sharing her own story openly.

Ava became a voice for those stuck in the same cycles of pain she once endured. Through her journey, she inspired others to face their pasts, embrace forgiveness, and find their own paths to redemption. Her story reminded them that even in the darkest times, there's always hope.

But Ava's story isn't the only one of resilience and restoration. In the vast tapestry of human experience, there are countless tales of individuals touched by God's unconditional love, overcoming immense challenges.

Take Tammy, for instance, who escaped domestic abuse and rebuilt her life. Or Tom, who battled addiction but found the strength to seek help and start anew, all thanks to God's love.

These stories, and many others like them, speak of a love beyond comprehension. A love that meets us in our brokenness lifts us up and breathes new life into our weary spirits. They remind us that no matter how dire our situations may seem, God's love always offers us a chance for renewal.

Let's take a moment to consider the resilience and restoration experienced by individuals like Tammy, Tom, David, Elijah, and many others. Their stories remind us that God's love can penetrate even the deepest darkness and redeem the most profound pain.

By embracing God's unconditional love, we find the courage to confront our deepest wounds and the hope of new beginnings. May their stories and others like them continue to inspire us, reminding us to never lose hope, always believe in love's power, and embrace our own journeys of resilience and restoration.

Our lives are filled with unwritten chapters waiting to unfold. The story of redemption and fresh starts goes on, and with each step forward, we come closer to grasping the depth of God's love for us all.

Let us pray and persevere, knowing that even in our darkest moments, God's love brings light and healing. As we journey together, let's hold onto the truth that embracing God's love is indeed the key to resilience and restoration.

Forgiven And Free: Embracing Redemption

In life's darkest moments, when hope seems out of reach and despair looms large, the idea of redemption can feel distant and unreachable. Yet, it's precisely in these times of deepest pain and brokenness that we're offered an extraordinary gift—an invitation to truly encounter God's unconditional love and feel the transforming power of his grace and mercy.

Throughout this book, we've explored the ups and downs of our human journey, facing pain, loss, and struggle head-on. We've recognized our flaws and the mistakes we've made. But through it all, one undeniable truth remains: God's love for us is limitless. It reaches us at our lowest points and encompasses every part of who we are.

Redemption might seem abstract, but it's a real-life game-changer. It starts with admitting we need it, understanding that our past doesn't define us, and believing God's love can mend us from the inside out.

Encountering God's love means embarking on a journey of redemption—a journey of trust, vulnerability, and surrender. It's not easy, but it leads to freedom, healing, and finding our purpose anew.

In our darkest times, when despair clouds our minds, we may doubt if redemption is possible. The weight of our mistakes can feel crushing. But we must remind ourselves that redemption isn't about being worthy or fixing ourselves. It's a gift for anyone who's willing to accept it.

When we embrace redemption, we let go of our past's grip. We bring our brokenness to Jesus' feet, knowing he bore our sins so we could start afresh. It's through surrendering that we open ourselves to God's boundless love and transformative power.

As adults, life throws us curveballs—regrets, old wounds, and doubts. But in these struggles, we can experience God's love in ways beyond our understanding.

No matter what mistakes you've made or the pain you've felt, redemption is within reach. God wants to mend what's broken, heal what's hurt, and turn ashes into beauty. His love for you never wavers, and his grace knows no limits.

Take a moment to breathe in God's love. Let grace guide you toward the redemption waiting for you. As you move forward, face challenges with hope, knowing God's love can transform any situation.

In our darkest moments, when hope fades and despair looms large, it's hard to see a way out of the pain. The weight of our mistakes and wounds can feel overwhelming, making us wonder if redemption is truly possible. But I'm here to assure you it is.

As we journey toward redemption, let's recognize the incredible power of God's love and grace. Through his unconditional love, we can find healing, renewal, and purpose. Redemption isn't just a far-off idea; it's real and can transform our lives if we're open to it.

Let's explore practical ways to embrace redemption and feel God's love's transformative power. It starts with a genuine desire for change, letting go of the past, and accepting our brokenness. We must face our mistakes, the pain we've caused, and the hurts we carry. Only then can we fully surrender to God's redemptive work.

As we journey through life, we often carry heavy burdens—regrets, shame, and unresolved pain. But in God's love, we find strength to release these burdens, surrendering them to him. It's in this surrender that we discover the beauty of redemption, where our brokenness becomes a canvas for healing.

Don't be afraid to seek support on this journey. Surround yourself with a caring community—friends, family, or a faith group—who can walk with you with compassion and understanding. Healing and growth often come through relationships, as others speak truth into our lives and help us face our challenges.

In the journey of embracing redemption, be patient with yourself. It's not a quick fix or an instant change. It takes time, persistence, and grace. Give yourself room to grow and be kind when setbacks happen. Remember, redemption isn't a straight path—it's a series of steps, some forward and some backward. Every step, no matter how small, brings us closer to healing and freedom.

Above all, hold onto hope. Embracing redemption means believing in God's goodness and his power to restore and transform. Even when the future seems uncertain, or the past still hurts, let hope stay with you. Trust in God's faithfulness, knowing redemption isn't a one-time event but a journey of growth and renewal.

As we journey through this book, embrace the life-changing love of God and the redemption that awaits you. No matter how broken you feel, remember that God's love is endless. You are valued, forgiven, and called to a purposeful life filled with hope.

May your heart be filled with the certainty of God's love, and may you find the courage to embrace redemption in every part of your life. Let's carry the truth of his love with us, guiding us through the challenges and joys ahead. Embrace redemption, where new beginnings blossom and God's love transforms us.

CHAPTER 6
"Letting go of Judgment"

Letting Go Of Judgment

In Romans 14:10-12, it's said, *"Why do you pass judgment on your brother? Or you, why do you despise your brother? For we will all stand before the judgment seat of God; for it is written, as I live, says the Lord, every knee shall bow to me, and every tongue shall confess to God. So, then each of us will give an account of himself to God."*

This passage emphasizes that God will ultimately judge us based on our actions and intentions. It urges believers not to judge others but to focus on being accountable to God themselves.

Similarly, in Matthew 7:1-2, Jesus says, *"Judge not, that you be judged. For with the judgment you pronounce, you will be judged, and with the measure you use, it will be measured to you."* This verse warns against hasty judgments, as we'll be judged by God in the same way.

The concept of divine judgment is central in Christian theology, highlighting the belief in a final evaluation of our actions and intentions by God. It stresses moral accountability and the importance of humility and self-reflection.

Outside Christianity, other religions also have similar teachings about divine judgment, each with its own scriptures. This concept serves as a guiding principle for ethical living, reminding individuals to uphold their beliefs while leaving ultimate judgment to a higher power.

Breaking The Chains Of Judgment: Finding Freedom Within

In a world that bombards us with images of perfection and success, it's easy to get caught up in chasing impossible standards. We compare ourselves to others, basing our worth on society's superficial expectations. But what if we could break free from this cycle? What if we could learn to accept our imperfections and live authentically?

Embracing our imperfections isn't about settling for less or being complacent. It's about recognizing that flaws are part of being human. We all have strengths and weaknesses, and it's through our imperfections that we find our true selves. Accepting and embracing these imperfections allows us to live in harmony with who we are.

One important reason to embrace our imperfections is to let go of self-judgment. Constantly critiquing ourselves against unrealistic standards creates a cycle of dissatisfaction. It hinders us from appreciating our true worth. By embracing imperfections, we break free from self-criticism and open up to self-love and acceptance.

Moreover, embracing imperfections empowers us to live authentically. When we hide or deny our flaws, we deny a part of ourselves. We put on a façade, pretending to be someone we're not and lose touch with our true selves. Embracing imperfections lets our authentic selves shine. We stop conforming to society's expectations and celebrate our uniqueness, quirks, and vulnerabilities, knowing they define who we are.

Embracing imperfections also helps us develop compassion and empathy for ourselves and others. When we acknowledge and accept our own flaws, we become more understanding and tolerant of imperfections in others. We realize that imperfections are part of being human, making judgment less common in our interactions. Instead of criticizing, we can support each other, fostering self-acceptance and personal growth.

As we start this journey of embracing imperfections, it's essential to understand it's not a straight path. We'll have days when doubt creeps in and old habits of self-criticism resurface. But each time we embrace imperfections, we get closer to living authentically and meaningfully.

Here, we'll explore practical ways to embrace imperfections. We'll dive into mindset shifts and acceptance practices guiding us toward a more fulfilling life. But for now, let's reflect on why embracing imperfections is crucial. Remember, self-acceptance isn't a one-time achievement; it's a lifelong journey uncovering the beauty of our imperfect selves.

We'll also delve into practical tools aiding us in embracing imperfections. These tools empower us to navigate challenges on our journey of self-acceptance and growth.

One effective tool is mindfulness. It helps us stay present, noticing our thoughts, emotions, and judgments without getting caught in negativity. With practice, we develop a kinder inner voice, challenging self-judgment and offering understanding.

Another useful technique is reframing. It involves changing our perspective on flaws or imperfections. Rather than seeing them as weaknesses, we view them as unique traits defining us. For instance, instead of seeing sensitivity as a flaw, we recognize it as a strength, allowing us to connect deeply with others.

Self-compassion is crucial in accepting our imperfections. It means treating ourselves with the same kindness we'd show a loved one. We can practice it by giving ourselves encouragement, reminding ourselves that we're doing our best, and knowing we deserve love and acceptance just as we are.

Regularly reflecting on our strengths and achievements is also helpful. It helps build self-confidence and reminds us of the progress we've made, no matter how small. Positive affirmations can boost our self-image and overall well-being.

Having a supportive community is essential on our journey to self-acceptance. Surround yourself with people who lift you up and appreciate your imperfections. Honest conversations about our vulnerabilities foster trust and belonging.

As we embrace our imperfections, let's be patient and kind to ourselves. It's not about being perfect but accepting our flaws as part of being human. Setbacks are part of the process, offering opportunities for growth and self-discovery.

Remember, accepting imperfections is a lifelong journey. It takes reflection and letting go of societal pressures. With each step, we reclaim our authenticity and discover our inner richness.

So, let's embark on this journey together—embracing imperfections, finding strength in our vulnerabilities, and celebrating our wonderfully flawed selves. Self-acceptance isn't just for a select few; it's for everyone. Let's walk with courage and compassion, knowing that by embracing imperfections, we can live a more joyful, fulfilling, and authentic life.

Looking Inward, Seeing Outward: Recognizing Judgment's Impact

In our daily lives, judgment is everywhere, shaping how we see ourselves and others. It's deeply rooted in us, often driven by societal standards. But what if we could let go of judgment? What if we embraced imperfections and stopped comparing and criticizing? This chapter explores judgment's impact as we aim for a more accepting world.

At its core, judgment comes from insecurity and fear. When we judge others, we're projecting our own doubts onto them. We pick out flaws to feel better about ourselves, but it only breeds negativity and unhappiness.

Judgment affects how we see ourselves, too. Constantly comparing to others leads to self-criticism and lowers self-esteem. This harsh self-talk holds us back from growing and embracing our potential.

The first step is recognizing judgment. We must notice when we judge others or ourselves. Our judgments are often based on limited info and distorted views. Everyone's journey is unique and shaped by struggles and circumstances. Understanding this complexity helps us show empathy and compassion instead of judging.

To cultivate a more accepting mindset, we need to question our judgments. Are they fair and objective? Are we embracing diversity? By challenging our biases, we open ourselves to understanding and growth. It's important to remember that perfection is a myth. Embracing imperfections helps us accept ourselves and others.

On this journey, surround yourself with positive influences. Connect with people who value growth and acceptance. Creating a supportive environment makes it easier to explore ourselves authentically.

Mindfulness of our words and actions is crucial. Words can lift or hurt. Choose to encourage and inspire instead of criticize. Small acts of kindness can have a big impact.

As we navigate judgment, remember change starts with us. By addressing our own judgments, we contribute to a kinder society. We'll explore practical ways to release judgment and accept ourselves fully.

In our quest to embrace imperfections and let go of judgment, let's explore practical strategies. By implementing them, we can develop a more compassionate outlook on ourselves and others.

One powerful strategy is practicing self-awareness. Take time to notice your thoughts and feelings, especially when judgment arises. Identify what triggers your judgment. Reflect on why these triggers affect you. This reflection helps you choose a kinder response.

Another helpful way to let go of judgment is by practicing empathy. Try to understand others' experiences and perspectives. Remember, everyone has their own journey with its challenges and victories. To stop judging others, acknowledge that flaws are part of being human, for them as well as for you. Embrace the diversity of life and let go of the idea that everyone should fit into a certain mold. Celebrate the richness that different perspectives bring.

Besides empathy, it's crucial to show yourself compassion. Be kind to yourself and know that you're a work in progress. Accept your imperfections; they don't determine your worth. Treat yourself with the same kindness you give to others. Take care of yourself, engage in activities that uplift you, and surround yourself with positivity. Positivity fosters self-acceptance and growth.

Gratitude is another powerful tool to release judgment. Each day, take a moment to appreciate what you're grateful for, whether it's simple joys or profound lessons life has taught you. Gratitude shifts your focus from scarcity to abundance. By recognizing the beauty and goodness in your life, judgment fades, replaced by awe and appreciation.

As you progress on this transformative journey, remember that it's not about attaining perfection but about embracing growth. Be patient with yourself and others, understanding that change doesn't happen overnight. Surround yourself with a supportive community of like-minded individuals who foster personal growth and authenticity. Share your experiences and challenges, and remain open to learning from others' journeys.

By applying these practical strategies, you embark on a path of self-discovery, acceptance, and personal development. Keep in mind that embracing imperfections is an ongoing commitment, not a final destination. Embrace your uniqueness and extend the same acceptance and compassion to others, contributing to a more inclusive and empathetic society.

Continue to accept your imperfections, let go of judgment, and embrace the freedom to be authentically yourself. You have the power to not only transform your own life but also to positively influence those around you. Embrace this power, embrace who you are, and continue to spread love and acceptance wherever you go.

Finding Peace Within: Navigating The Path Of Self-Judgment

Self-judgment has a way of sneaking into our lives, like an unwanted guest overstaying its welcome. It often originates from our deep-seated desire to be flawless, to meet society's standards, and to constantly measure ourselves against others. But why do we subject ourselves to this relentless self-critique? What are the underlying factors that fuel our self-judgment?

One of the main culprits is our fear of failure. We inhabit a world that prioritizes success and accomplishments, leading to immense pressure to continually prove ourselves. Consequently, any stumble or perceived shortcoming becomes fodder for self-condemnation. We emerge as our own toughest critics, relentlessly chastising ourselves for falling short of unattainable standards.

Another contributing factor to self-judgment is our tendency to seek external validation. We frequently depend on others' opinions and approval to gauge our self-worth. When faced with criticism or rejection from others, we internalize their judgments, using them as ammunition against ourselves. Thus, we become ensnared in a cycle of pursuing external validation, only to deepen our self-judgment when it proves elusive.

The pursuit of external validation is a common part of human nature, stemming from our innate need for acceptance and acknowledgment from others. From early on, we're taught to seek approval from parents, teachers, peers, and society as a whole. This validation often comes through praise, recognition, or admiration for our accomplishments, appearance, or behavior.

While seeking external validation can momentarily boost our self-esteem and confidence, relying too heavily on it can pose challenges.

Firstly, it can create a perpetual need for validation, forming a cycle of seeking approval to feel worthy or sufficient. This dependency can erode our self-esteem and inner assurance, as our sense of self becomes contingent on others' opinions.

Moreover, relying on external validation can make us vulnerable to the influence of others' viewpoints, leading to self-doubt and insecurity when faced with criticism or rejection. It may also encourage us to prioritize others' expectations over our own desires and values, fostering feelings of discontent or resentment.

Furthermore, depending solely on external validation may impede personal growth and self-discovery. When we define our value solely based on others' judgments, we may neglect our own instincts, passions, and aspirations. True fulfillment arises from aligning our actions and choices with our authentic selves rather than seeking validation externally.

To break free from the cycle of seeking external validation, it's crucial to cultivate self-awareness and self-compassion. Recognize your intrinsic worth and value regardless of others' opinions. Practice self-validation by acknowledging your strengths, achievements, and progress, even in the absence of external affirmation.

Surround yourself with supportive individuals who uplift your growth and authenticity. Seek helpful feedback, but trust your own judgment and intuition. Focus on pursuing goals and activities that truly bring you joy and fulfillment rather than just seeking approval from others.

The journey toward self-validation is an ongoing process of self-discovery and acceptance. Prioritize your intrinsic worth and authenticity to nurture inner confidence and fulfillment beyond external validation.

Societal standards and expectations heavily influence self-judgment. We're bombarded with images and messages promoting a narrow definition of beauty, success, and happiness. These unrealistic ideals fuel self-doubt and self-criticism as we compare ourselves to seemingly flawless figures.

The roots of self-judgment are often traced back to our upbringing and early experiences. Childhood environments that emphasize perfection or criticize mistakes can embed self-judgment within us. While unraveling these deeply ingrained beliefs and patterns is challenging, it's possible with compassion and self-awareness.

How do we overcome pervasive self-judgment? It starts with self-compassion. Instead of berating ourselves over perceived failures, we cultivate a kind and understanding relationship with ourselves. Recognizing our humanity, flaws, and inherent worth allows for love and acceptance, just as we are.

Practicing self-awareness is another key step in overcoming self-judgment. Identifying negative self-talk, self-limiting beliefs, and judgments empowers us to challenge and reframe them. By questioning the fairness and validity of our self-judgments, we reveal them as mere illusions born from our insecurities.

It's vital to surround ourselves with a supportive network of people who champion our growth and accept us unconditionally. Seeking out individuals who uplift and encourage us creates an environment where self-judgment is less likely to thrive. Finding belonging and connection allows us to share in our struggles and triumphs.

Moving forward, we'll explore specific strategies and practices to foster self-acceptance and break free from the chains of self-judgment. We'll delve into practical steps for cultivating self-compassion, challenging negative self-talk, and reframing our beliefs. Together, we'll embark on a transformative journey toward embracing our imperfections and discovering our true power.

For now, let's pause and reflect on the profound impact of self-judgment in our lives. May this serve as a reminder to treat ourselves with kindness and understanding. It's through this lens that we unlock our true potential. The journey toward self-acceptance begins with embracing our humanity and celebrating the imperfections that make us uniquely beautiful.

Here, we'll delve deeper into specific strategies and practices that foster self-acceptance and help us break free from the grip of self-judgment. By integrating these tools into our daily lives, we can gradually loosen our hold on our thoughts and emotions.

One essential aspect of overcoming self-judgment is cultivating self-compassion. We must learn to treat ourselves with the same kindness we offer to others. Acknowledge imperfection without harsh self-criticism. Be gentle when you make mistakes or fall short of expectations. Offer words of reassurance and encouragement, as you would to a friend. Remember, self-compassion isn't a weakness; it's a catalyst for growth and transformation.

Another effective strategy in combating self-judgment is practicing self-awareness. Take time to observe your thoughts and notice when self-critical beliefs arise. Are these judgments rooted in reality, or are they distorted perceptions fueled by fear and insecurity? By questioning the validity of our self-judgments, we can begin to break free from their hold. Replace negative self-talk with affirmations, reminding yourself of your strengths and achievements. With persistence, you'll rewire your mind to focus on self-empowerment rather than self-criticism.

Equally important is surrounding ourselves with a supportive network of people who champion our growth and accept us unconditionally. Seek out individuals genuinely invested in your well-being and who believe in your potential. Their encouragement and positivity serve as a potent shield against self-judgment. Remember, you're not alone in your struggles. Connecting with like-minded individuals offers solace in shared experiences and lends perspective to your journey of self-acceptance.

In addition to these strategies, reframing our beliefs holds immense power. Often, self-judgment stems from deep-seated beliefs of inadequacy or worth tied to external validation. Challenge these limiting beliefs and embrace more empowering ones. Recognize your inherent worth, independent of others' opinions. Embrace imperfections as facets of your unique beauty, essential for personal growth and evolution.

As we traverse this transformative path toward self-acceptance, acknowledge it isn't always easy. Progress may be gradual, but setbacks are inevitable. Be kind and patient with yourself throughout. Celebrate every victory, no matter how small, and grant yourself the space to grow at your own pace.

Reflect on the profound impact of self-judgment in our lives, approaching ourselves with kindness and understanding. Embrace imperfections as facets of your humanity. By releasing judgment, you unlock your true potential, fostering a life rich in self-compassion, self-awareness, and genuine connection.

May this journey toward self-acceptance serve as a reminder that perfection is a myth, but self-acceptance is real and potent. Embrace every aspect of your being, for it's through embracing our imperfections that we radiate and lead lives brimming with joy, authenticity, and fulfillment.

Embrace Your Uniqueness: Breaking The Cycle Of Comparison

Comparison—a habitual act we often engage in unconsciously. Daily, we measure ourselves against others, be it in appearance, achievements, status, or happiness. Assessing our worth through this lens perpetuates a cycle detrimental to our well-being.

When we compare, we set ourselves up for failure. There will always be someone seemingly better, happier, or more successful. This pursuit of unattainable standards not only diminishes our self-esteem but also deprives us of the joy found in embracing our unique qualities and imperfections.

Comparison steals our happiness. Fixating on others' possessions or appearances breeds discontent in our own lives. We falsely believe fulfillment lies in possessing what they have or resembling them. Yet true happiness isn't found in comparison—it resides within accepting and cherishing who we are, flaws included.

Moreover, comparison breeds jealousy and resentment. Constantly measuring ourselves against others fosters resentment toward those who possess what we desire. This negativity damages relationships and impedes personal growth.

Now, liberating ourselves from the destructive grip of comparison may seem daunting. It's deeply ingrained in our culture, perpetuated by social media, advertising, and societal norms. However, with conscious effort and the right mindset, breaking this cycle is achievable, offering freedom from the ceaseless comparison game.

A powerful strategy to overcome comparison is to shift our focus inward. Rather than gauging our worth against others, let's cultivate self-awareness. Explore your strengths, talents, and passions. Celebrate your achievements, regardless of their size. By redirecting attention to our own progress and growth, we learn to appreciate our unique journey and release the urge to compare.

Practicing gratitude is another effective approach. Reflect on the blessings in your life instead of fixating on what others possess. Focus on your accomplishments and the experiences shaping you. With an attitude of gratitude, shift your perspective and realize the abundance already present in your life.

Surround yourself with positive influences. Choose companions who uplift and inspire rather than fuel comparison and competition. Being amidst those who celebrate your successes and support your growth significantly impacts your mindset, aiding in breaking free from comparison's grasp.

Breaking the cycle of comparison isn't instantaneous. It demands dedication, self-reflection, and a commitment to embracing imperfections. Recognize we're all on unique paths, navigating individual journeys. Let's delve deeper into strategies for freeing ourselves from comparison chains.

One powerful strategy is cultivating self-compassion. Often, we judge ourselves harshly, basing our worth on others' achievements or appearances. Through self-compassion, we learn kindness and acceptance toward ourselves.

Self-compassion starts with acknowledging our imperfections and accepting them. Instead of harsh self-criticism, offer yourself the same understanding and kindness you would to a loved one. When mistakes happen, or expectations aren't met, treating yourself with compassion is crucial. Recognize your humanity and learn from experiences.

Letting go of the need for external validation is another aspect of self-compassion. Seeking approval from others often leaves us feeling unworthy or incomplete. True validation stems from self-acceptance. By embracing imperfections and recognizing inherent worth, we break free from comparison and find contentment within.

Mindfulness of self-talk is vital. Our internal dialogue profoundly affects self-esteem and well-being. Constant self-criticism perpetuates the cycle of comparison. Challenge these limiting beliefs with compassionate and empowering thoughts. Affirmations like "I deserve love and acceptance as I am" or "My worth isn't defined by others' accomplishments" reshape our mindset, nurturing self-compassion.

To release comparison's grip, embrace your unique journey and redefine success. External achievements or societal standards shouldn't solely measure success. Honor and celebrate personal progress and growth. Recognize strengths, talents, and milestones, no matter how small. By shifting focus to inner fulfillment and growth, joy, and contentment are found in your journey.

Lastly, prioritize self-care to break free from comparison's destructiveness. Nurturing physical, mental, and emotional well-being fosters self-worth and appreciation. Engage in mindfulness, hobbies, seek professional help, or set healthy boundaries. Prioritizing self-care redirects focus inward, fostering a resilient foundation of self-worth, unaffected by comparisons.

Breaking the cycle of comparison is a continual journey of self-discovery and self-acceptance. It demands patience, self-reflection, and a dedication to embracing our imperfections. Remember, your uniqueness and worthiness stem from simply being. So, take a moment, release the comparison's grip, and welcome the exquisite journey of self-discovery ahead. You deserve love, acceptance, and happiness, just as you are. Forge ahead on your own path, releasing the urge to compare. Embrace imperfections, for they compose the beautiful and authentic you.

The Compassionate Heart: Cultivating Self-Love And Understanding

In life, understanding the power of self-compassion and adopting practical techniques to foster a compassionate and nurturing attitude toward oneself is crucial.

Often, we find it easier to show compassion to others than to ourselves. We set unattainable standards, criticizing ourselves for perceived flaws and missteps. But what if we opted for a different approach, one that embraced imperfections and released judgment? Cultivating self-compassion can be life-changing, offering a haven of kindness and acceptance.

It starts with acknowledging our shared humanity—our flaws and vulnerabilities. Embracing imperfections means acknowledging that mistakes are a natural part of growth. Rather than viewing them as personal shortcomings, we can see them as opportunities for learning and development. Self-compassion enables us to treat ourselves with the same care and understanding we'd offer a struggling friend.

Practicing self-compassion isn't about excusing our actions or evading accountability. It's about acknowledging our humanity and responding with kindness and understanding. When we approach ourselves with self-compassion, we're better positioned to learn from our mistakes, make amends when needed, and move forward with renewed purpose.

One potent technique for fostering self-compassion is self-observation without judgment. This involves becoming mindful of our thoughts, feelings, and actions in a compassionate, non-judgmental manner. Instead of criticizing ourselves for how we feel or the choices we make, we simply observe and acknowledge our experiences without attaching negative judgments. This practice deepens our understanding and acceptance of ourselves, laying the groundwork for self-compassion.

Another helpful technique is reframing our self-talk. Often, we're our harshest critics, inundated with negative thoughts and self-critical beliefs. By challenging these patterns and replacing them with kind, supportive statements, we nurture a more compassionate inner dialogue. For instance, rather than berating ourselves for mistakes, we remind ourselves that everyone errs and that growth arises from learning.

Additionally, self-compassion thrives through self-care practices. Tending to our physical, emotional, and mental well-being is an act of self-compassion. Engaging in activities that bring joy, practicing mindfulness, seeking support from loved ones, and establishing healthy boundaries prioritize our self-compassion.

By cultivating self-compassion, we foster a more compassionate and fulfilling relationship with ourselves. We release the weight of self-judgment and embrace imperfections as beautiful facets of our unique journey. Self-compassion empowers us to navigate life's challenges with resilience and grace, enabling us to treat ourselves with kindness and understanding.

As you embark on the journey of self-compassion, remember your worthiness of love, understanding, and forgiveness. Embrace the power of embracing imperfections, witnessing the unfolding of self-compassion within. Your relationship with yourself spans a lifetime, and treating yourself with kindness and compassion is the key to unlocking a life of self-acceptance and inner peace.

In our quest to cultivate self-compassion, patience, and persistence are paramount. Like any skill, developing self-compassion requires practice and gentle perseverance. Yet, the rewards of nurturing a compassionate relationship with ourselves are immeasurable.

A technique that profoundly impacts self-compassion is self-forgiveness. Often, we cling to past mistakes, burdened by guilt and shame. Embracing self-compassion involves releasing these burdens and extending the forgiveness we readily offer others.

Forgiveness doesn't condone our actions or erase their impact. It's about acknowledging our humanity, understanding our capacity for mistakes, and choosing to learn from them. Through self-forgiveness, we release the grip of self-judgment, creating space for growth and healing.

Cultivating self-acceptance is another vital aspect of self-compassion. Embracing imperfections means embracing all aspects of ourselves—the light and the shadow, strengths and weaknesses. Instead of comparing ourselves to unrealistic ideals or pursuing perfection, we can choose to love and accept ourselves just as we are in this moment.

Self-acceptance isn't about complacency; it's a foundation for growth and self-improvement. When we accept ourselves with kindness and understanding, we can recognize areas for change and set goals from a place of compassion rather than self-criticism.

In addition to self-forgiveness and self-acceptance, practicing gratitude can also wield significant power in nurturing self-compassion. Taking moments each day to reflect on things we're thankful for shifts our focus from lack or imperfection to the abundance and beauty already within and around us.

Gratitude cultivates a positive mindset, fostering self-compassion by reminding us of blessings and opportunities in our lives. It helps us recognize ourselves as deserving of love, abundance, and happiness, reinforcing our worthiness of self-compassion and life's goodness.

As we journey through this book and its chapter on cultivating self-compassion, let's remember it's not a destination but a lifelong journey. It's a continuous practice of nurturing and caring for ourselves with the same kindness, understanding, and love we'd offer our closest friends or loved ones.

By embracing imperfections, practicing non-judgmental self-observation, reframing self-talk, prioritizing self-care, and nurturing forgiveness, acceptance, and gratitude, we nourish self-compassion's roots within us. With each step, we rewrite our narrative with self-acceptance, self-love, and self-empowerment.

So, as you tread your path of self-compassion, be patient and gentle with yourself. Embrace the journey, knowing every small act of self-compassion contributes to growth and well-being. Trust in your resilience and capacity to learn, heal, and evolve.

May self-compassion become second nature, guiding you through life's challenges and allowing you to embrace imperfections with grace and courage. You're deserving of all the love, understanding, and forgiveness you extend to others. Embrace your unique journey, witnessing how self-compassion's power transforms your life in beautiful, unexpected ways.

Heart Wide Open: Embracing Vulnerability

In a world that often esteems strength and invulnerability, it can feel daunting to contemplate embracing vulnerability. We're taught to wear a brave facade to navigate our trials without revealing any hint of weakness. But what if a vulnerability isn't a weakness at all? What if it's a path to growth and connection with others?

Embracing vulnerability means allowing ourselves to be truly seen as we are. It entails shedding the masks and defenses we employ to shield ourselves. When we embrace vulnerability, we open ourselves to the potential for a profound connection, inviting others to witness our authentic selves.

At first glance, vulnerability may seem counterintuitive. It demands that we expose our fears, insecurities, and uncertainties to others. We fear judgment, rejection, and the possibility of emotional pain. However, when we embrace vulnerability, we foster an atmosphere of trust and empathy, enabling others to perceive us as human beings rather than mere embodiments of strength.

Embracing vulnerability doesn't entail recklessness or divulging our deepest secrets to everyone we encounter. Rather, it's a deliberate, conscious choice to lower our defenses in specific relationships and situations. By acknowledging our imperfections and embracing vulnerability, we cultivate an environment conducive to genuine connection and understanding.

Vulnerability also plays a pivotal role in personal growth. When we acknowledge our vulnerabilities, we create space for introspection and self-awareness. We can examine our fears, insecurities, and limiting beliefs with a compassionate, non-judgmental lens. This introspection empowers us to identify areas for growth, learning, and evolution.

Through embracing vulnerability, we open ourselves to new experiences and perspectives. We become more compassionate and understanding toward others' struggles and challenges. Rather than viewing vulnerability as a sign of weakness, we recognize it as a wellspring of strength and courage. It takes immense bravery to confront our fears head-on.

Embracing vulnerability also calls us to practice self-compassion. Often, we set standards impossibly high, fostering self-criticism and a fear of failure. But when we embrace vulnerability, we acknowledge our imperfections, just like everyone else. We learn to extend kindness to ourselves, understanding that mistakes and setbacks are natural facets of the human journey.

By embracing vulnerability, we pave the path for genuine connections with others. We foster a safe environment where others feel free to be vulnerable, too. This mutual vulnerability strengthens our bonds, nurtures empathy, and fosters meaningful relationships.

As you journey through embracing vulnerability, remember it's a route of growth and connection. It demands courage, self-compassion, and a readiness to be seen authentically. It's an ongoing process, yet one that offers immense rewards.

Now, take a deep breath, acknowledge your vulnerabilities, and step into this transformative journey with an open heart. The beauty and resilience inherent in embracing vulnerability await you, guiding you toward personal growth and deeper connections with others.

And with that, we leave you hanging, on the brink of discovery. Turn the page and uncover what lies ahead as we delve further into the embrace of vulnerability. Let's deepen our understanding of its transformative power in our lives. By shedding societal expectations and allowing vulnerability, we create space for growth, authenticity, and deeper connections.

Embracing vulnerability demands that we confront our fears directly. It's in these moments of discomfort and uncertainty that we unveil our true strength. By embracing our vulnerabilities, we embrace our humanity, fostering compassion and understanding for ourselves and others.

Within our vulnerabilities lies the opportunity for growth and self-discovery. When we embrace the possibility of failure or disappointment, we also embrace new experiences and perspectives. Through vulnerability, we challenge ourselves, broaden our horizons, and foster personal and professional development.

Furthermore, vulnerability invites us to step into authenticity. When we shed the masks we wear for protection, we grant others permission to do the same. In this space of vulnerability and authenticity, relationships are built on trust, understanding, and acceptance. We find comfort in knowing we're not alone in our struggles, and our vulnerabilities become bridges connecting us with others who share similar experiences.

It's important to remember that embracing vulnerability isn't a one-time event but an ongoing process requiring practice and self-compassion. We may stumble, face setbacks, or doubt ourselves along the way. Yet, through these challenges, we grow and learn. By showing kindness and understanding during vulnerable moments, we foster resilience and empowerment.

As we navigate this journey of embracing vulnerability, surrounding ourselves with supportive individuals becomes crucial. Seek out those who appreciate the beauty and strength found in vulnerability; they provide the foundation of trust and acceptance needed for growth.

In summary, embracing vulnerability isn't a sign of weakness; it's an act of courage and strength. It's a testament to our willingness to show up, be seen, and embrace authenticity. By acknowledging our vulnerabilities, we open doors to profound personal growth and connections with others.

Take a moment to reflect on the power of vulnerability in your own life. Recognize where you may be holding back and where you could allow yourself to be seen more fully and authentically. Embrace discomfort, knowing it's a step toward self-discovery and genuine connections. Embracing vulnerability is a lifelong journey, and as you continue, remember you're not alone. Let's celebrate imperfection, for within vulnerability lies our most authentic selves.

Letting Go and Living: Liberating Yourself from Perfectionism

As we journey through life, the allure of perfection often beckons us. We aspire to flawlessness, to maintaining control, and meeting sky-high standards. We convince ourselves that only in perfection can we find success, happiness, and acceptance. But what if I told you that this relentless pursuit of perfection does more harm than good? What if I shared how it impacts our mental well-being and relationships? And most importantly, what if I offered powerful tools to break free from this unrealistic standard?

Perfectionism, though seemingly desirable, can be detrimental to our overall well-being. At its core, it's fueled by fear and the craving for approval. We fret over making mistakes, fearing judgment from ourselves and others. This pressure to be faultless can lead to anxiety, depression, and a steep decline in our mental health.

Perfectionism doesn't just affect our mental well-being; it deeply impacts our relationships too. By setting unattainable expectations for ourselves, we inadvertently impose these standards on others. We become critical of those around us, always seeking flawlessness in their actions and behavior. This critical outlook creates a toxic atmosphere, straining our relationships and hindering genuine connections.

So, how do we break free from the clutches of perfectionism? How do we shed this distorted mindset and embrace our imperfections with acceptance? It starts with acknowledging the harmful effects of perfectionism in our lives. By realizing that our pursuit of flawlessness does more harm than good, we can begin to challenge this deeply ingrained belief.

A potent tool to combat perfectionism is self-compassion. Instead of chastising ourselves for our mistakes or shortcomings, we need to extend kindness and understanding. We must learn to treat ourselves with the same empathy and forgiveness that we offer to others. By embracing self-compassion, we can shift our perspective and foster a healthier relationship with ourselves.

Furthermore, reframing our perception of success is crucial. Perfectionism often makes us see success as an all-or-nothing endeavor. We believe that unless we achieve everything flawlessly, our efforts are futile. However, success can be found in progress, growth, and resilience. Embracing the notion that perfection does not define success allows us to value our journey and acknowledge even the smallest triumphs along the way.

Another valuable tool for shedding perfectionism is practicing gratitude. Dwelling on what we lack or where we need improvement perpetuates the perfectionism cycle. Instead, shifting our focus to what we're grateful for cultivates a mindset of abundance and contentment. Gratitude reminds us of the beauty in imperfection and encourages us to find joy in the present moment.

As we delve deeper into our exploration of letting go of perfectionism, let's remember that it's a journey, not a destination. It requires time, patience, and plenty of self-compassion to break free from perfection's grasp. However, the rewards are priceless.

In the following section of this chapter, we'll dive into practical strategies and actionable steps to further liberate ourselves from perfectionism. We'll explore techniques to silence our inner critic, nurture self-acceptance, and foster genuine connections with those around us. So, let's embark on this journey together, embracing our imperfections to lead lives filled with genuine happiness and fulfillment.

With an understanding of the detrimental effects of perfectionism and the initial tools to combat it, we can now delve deeper into practical strategies and actionable steps on our journey to let go of this unrealistic standard.

A pivotal strategy in conquering perfectionism is challenging our inner critic. Often, this voice within can be the toughest judge, incessantly pointing out our flaws and shortcomings. Yet, it's crucial to realize that this inner voice doesn't always reflect reality accurately. Take a moment to quiet that critical voice and replace it with self-compassion and understanding. Remind yourself that making mistakes is a natural part of our humanity, and growth often springs from these experiences. Practice shifting negative self-talk to positive affirmations, acknowledging your efforts and progress.

Nurturing self-acceptance is another crucial step in releasing the grip of perfectionism. Embrace the idea that inherent worthiness and deserving love exist within you, regardless of your achievements. Recognize that your value as an individual transcends external accomplishments. Begin by acknowledging and embracing your strengths and weaknesses. Instead of chasing perfection, focus on personal growth and improvement. Foster a mindset that values progress over flawlessness. Embracing self-acceptance as an ongoing practice, remind yourself daily that your worth isn't measured by external standards.

In the pursuit of freeing ourselves from perfectionism, fostering genuine connections with others holds significance. Peer beyond surface judgments, understanding that everyone carries their unique imperfections. Practice empathy and compassion towards others, granting them the freedom to be imperfect. Cultivate authentic connections by embracing vulnerability and sharing your own struggles and insecurities. Surround yourself with a supportive community that cherishes authenticity and empathy.

As we tread along this path, it's vital to celebrate the small victories along the way. Every step forward, no matter how small, deserves acknowledgment and applause. Adopt a growth mindset that focuses on learning and progress rather than fixating solely on achieving predefined outcomes. Remember that success takes various forms, and each stride towards your goals is worthy of recognition.

Last but certainly not least, in our pursuit of shedding perfectionism, practicing self-care takes precedence. Allocate time for activities that bring joy and replenish your energy. Prioritize rest, nourishing food, regular exercise, and practices that promote relaxation and stress relief. Establish boundaries that safeguard your mental and emotional well-being, making self-compassion a daily ritual.

In conclusion, embracing our imperfections and relinquishing perfectionism is a journey well worth undertaking. It demands self-reflection, self-compassion, and a dedication to personal growth.

Remember that progress is not linear, and setbacks are a natural part of the process. Be patient and kind to yourself as you navigate this transformative path.

You have the power to break free from the chains of perfectionism and lead a life filled with genuine happiness and fulfillment. Embrace your imperfections, for they are what make you beautifully human. Let go of judgment, both of yourself and others and open your heart to the beauty that lies within our flaws. Together, let us cultivate a world that celebrates authenticity, compassion, and acceptance.

Unbreakable: Cultivating Resilience For Life's Trials

Life unfolds as a beautiful journey, yet it's peppered with unexpected twists and turns. We all encounter setbacks and trials that can leave us feeling overwhelmed and disheartened. However, it's precisely during these challenging moments that we have the chance to cultivate resilience and unveil our inner strength.

Resilience embodies the ability to rebound from adversity, to adapt amid trials, and to emerge stronger from the experience. It's not an inherent quality bestowed upon a select few; rather, it's a skill that can be honed and nurtured.

To foster resilience, we must first recognize and embrace our imperfections. Many of us have been conditioned to pursue perfection as the ultimate goal, viewing any deviation as a failure. Yet, this mindset merely constrains our potential and fuels self-doubt and criticism. By embracing our imperfections, we liberate ourselves from the shackles of judgment. We begin to perceive setbacks and challenges as opportunities for growth and enlightenment rather than indicators of failure. It's through these imperfections that our distinctive strengths and capabilities come to light.

The subsequent step in fortifying resilience is cultivating a positive mindset. Our thoughts and beliefs wield significant influence over how we navigate turbulent times. When confronted with setbacks, it's easy to succumb to a spiral of negative thinking, questioning our abilities, and fearing the unknown.

Yet, with a deliberate focus on cultivating a positive mindset, we can reframe our thoughts and surmount these obstacles. It's crucial to highlight our strengths, acknowledge our progress, and have faith in our capacity to overcome challenges. Embracing an optimistic outlook empowers us to confront setbacks with unwavering determination and resilience.

Furthermore, establishing a robust support network proves indispensable in times of adversity. None of us are meant to navigate challenges in isolation. Surrounding ourselves with individuals who genuinely care about our well-being can offer the encouragement, guidance, and perspective needed during trying times.

Seek out those who inspire you, who have triumphed over their own adversities, and who grasp the significance of resilience. Together, you can exchange experiences, extend support, and serve as reminders of the inherent strength within each of you.

Moreover, prioritizing self-care and self-compassion is paramount in cultivating resilience. It's natural to feel overwhelmed and depleted when confronting setbacks and challenges. Setting aside time to recharge, nurture ourselves, and practice self-compassion allows us to replenish our energy and confront adversity with renewed vigor.

Whether through indulging in activities that bring joy, embracing mindfulness, or seeking professional assistance when necessary, self-care should remain a cornerstone throughout our resilience-building journey.

Building resilience unfolds as a transformative process, empowering us to navigate setbacks and challenges with grace and fortitude. By embracing our imperfections, fostering a positive mindset, fostering a robust support network, and prioritizing self-care, we enhance our capacity to bounce back and flourish amidst adversity.

Remember, esteemed reader, the setbacks you encounter don't define your worth or capabilities. They serve as opportunities for growth, resilience, and self-discovery. As you embark on your journey to build resilience, embrace the inherent power within you, recognizing that with each challenge, you emerge stronger, more empowered, and better equipped to embrace life's imperfections. With each setback encountered, we unveil our inner resilience, demonstrating our strength and capability. In the following sections, we'll delve into additional strategies and tools to further bolster our resilience and continue thriving in the face of adversity.

A fundamental aspect of fostering resilience lies in practicing emotional intelligence. Emotional intelligence enables us to comprehend and manage our emotions adeptly, a skill particularly crucial when confronted with setbacks. By acknowledging and validating our emotions, we prevent them from overpowering us and clouding our judgment. Rather than suppressing or disregarding our feelings, we can learn to process them in a constructive manner, channeling them into motivation for growth.

Moreover, engaging in self-reflection and nurturing self-awareness plays a pivotal role in resilience-building. Devoting time to scrutinize our thoughts, beliefs, and responses to challenging circumstances yields valuable insights into our resilience journey. Through self-reflection, we uncover patterns, unearth any limiting beliefs, and enact necessary adjustments to our mindset and behavior. Self-awareness empowers us to cultivate a deeper understanding of our inner strengths and values, serving as a steadfast anchor during adversity.

Another potent tool in resilience-building is cultivating gratitude and uncovering meaning amidst adversity. While setbacks may evoke pain and dismay, they also harbor the potential to impart invaluable lessons and mold us into improved versions of ourselves. By directing our focus toward the lessons gleaned and the personal growth forged through trials, we can shift our perspective and discover significance even in the most daunting of challenges. Expressing gratitude for the opportunities that setbacks bestow fosters resilience and optimism.

Furthermore, mastering the art of adaptation and embracing flexibility proves indispensable in resilience-building. Life unfolds unpredictably, and setbacks often necessitate adjustments to our plans and expectations. Embracing flexibility and embracing change enable us to confront challenges with an open mind and a willingness to explore fresh possibilities. Adaptability enables us to perceive setbacks as diversions rather than insurmountable obstacles, unveiling new avenues that we may not have previously considered.

In essence, it's vital to remember that resilience isn't a fixed destination but an ongoing journey. It demands patience, perseverance, and self-compassion. Throughout our resilience-building endeavors, we'll inevitably encounter highs and lows, underscoring the importance of treating ourselves with kindness during tough times. Practicing self-compassion entails extending to ourselves the same understanding, patience, and love that we readily offer to a cherished family member or close friend. It's about acknowledging that setbacks are a natural facet of life and recognizing that we're doing the best we can.

To recapitulate this chapter on resilience-building, remember that you possess the capability to navigate through any challenge that crosses your path. Embrace your imperfections, nurture a positive mindset, cultivate a robust support network, prioritize self-care, and foster gratitude and flexibility. By integrating these strategies into your life, you'll continually fortify your resilience, emerging stronger and more empowered with each setback encountered.

Looking ahead, we'll delve into the significance of self-acceptance and its profound impact on our overall well-being and happiness. However, for now, take a moment to reflect on your personal resilience-building journey, celebrate the strides you've made, and trust in your capacity to confront whatever lies ahead. Embrace the inherent strength within you, and rest assured that you possess the resilience to navigate life's imperfections with grace and fortitude.

Living In The Moment: Practicing Mindfulness For Inner Peace

In our quest to embrace our imperfections and relinquish judgment, one of the most potent tools at our disposal is mindfulness. Mindfulness embodies the art of residing fully in the present moment, devoid of judgment or attachment. It empowers us to observe our thoughts, emotions, and sensations with gentle curiosity, fostering a profound sense of self-acceptance.

At its essence, mindfulness beckons us to direct our attention to the here and now. Often, we find ourselves ensnared in the grasp of our past or anxiously projecting into the future. Our minds meander, replaying old narratives or fretting about what lies ahead. Yet, through mindfulness, we can tether ourselves to the present, embracing the richness and depth of each fleeting moment.

The practice of mindfulness commences with self-acceptance. We inhabit a world inundated with messages dictating who we should be, how we ought to appear, and what milestones we should attain. These external pressures fuel our inner critic, prompting harsh self-judgment. However, mindfulness offers an avenue to break free from this cycle.

Through mindfulness, we learn to observe our thoughts and emotions without entangling ourselves within them. We come to realize that thoughts are mere mental phenomena emerging and dissipating. Instead of chastising ourselves for harboring negative thoughts or feeling inadequate, we greet these experiences with compassion and empathy.

Mindfulness imparts the understanding that imperfections and judgments are inherent aspects of our human journey.

Furthermore, mindfulness nurtures a presence in the present moment. How often do we find ourselves physically situated in one place yet mentally absent? Our minds drift towards distant worries and distractions, depriving us of the richness of our immediate experiences. Yet, by redirecting our attention to the present moment, we can wholeheartedly engage with the world around us.

Through mindfulness, we learn to relish the simple pleasures that often elude our notice. We savor the flavor of a steaming cup of tea, the tender embrace of a loved one, or the splendor of a sunset. We become attuned to life's subtleties, discovering joy in the minutiae that comprise our everyday reality. As we cultivate present-moment awareness, we uncover the profound beauty nestled within life's imperfections.

Moreover, mindfulness serves to diminish judgmental tendencies. Our minds hasten to label and categorize, erecting rigid divides that segregate the world into binaries of good or bad, right or wrong. This inclination to judge extends to ourselves as well, as we scrutinize our actions, decisions, and appearance through a critical lens.

When we embrace mindfulness, we adopt a non-judgmental stance towards our experiences. We endeavor to observe without attaching labels or assigning values. Rather than categorizing an experience as "good" or "bad," we simply acknowledge it as it unfolds. This shift in perspective liberates us from the confines of judgment, fostering a deeper understanding and acceptance of ourselves and others.

As we immerse ourselves in the practice of mindfulness, we gradually recognize that self-acceptance, present-moment awareness, and a reduction in judgment are intertwined. With each breath we draw, we create space for self-compassion and growth. Mindfulness serves as our anchor, guiding us through life's turbulent waters with grace and composure.

As we journey through this chapter, we'll delve deeper into the practical facets of mindfulness. We'll explore specific techniques and exercises that can augment our ability to integrate mindfulness into our daily lives. Stay alongside esteemed readers as we traverse this transformative path together. The gift of mindfulness awaits, poised to unlock the door to self-acceptance and liberation from judgment.

To fully embrace mindfulness, it's imperative to weave it into our daily routines. One potent exercise is the practice of mindful breathing. Simply set aside a few moments each day to focus on your breath. If comfortable, close your eyes, place your hand on your belly, and observe the natural rise and fall with each inhale and exhale. Pay heed to the sensations, rhythm, and depth of each breath. With each breath cycle, gently guide your attention back to the present moment. This exercise not only quiets the mind but also grounds us in our bodies and the present reality.

Mindful eating stands as another valuable practice that enables us to fully engage our senses and foster gratitude for nourishment. Prior to eating, take a moment to observe the colors, textures, and aromas of your food. Savor each morsel, attentively noting flavors and their evolution as you chew. Observe how your body responds to different tastes and textures. This act of mindful eating not only heightens our enjoyment of food but also instills a sense of gratitude for the sustenance it offers.

One of the most effective methods for integrating mindfulness into our lives is through a formal meditation practice. Locate a quiet spot in your home, free from distractions, and allocate a few minutes each day to sit in tranquility. Close your eyes and direct your focus to your breath, a specific anchor point, or a sensation in your body. Permit thoughts to arise and fade without judgment, gently redirecting your attention to your chosen focal point whenever you realize your mind has wandered.

As we persist in our mindfulness practice, it's imperative to acknowledge that setbacks and challenges are inherent aspects of the journey. There may be instances where our minds wander more frequently than they remain present, or judgmental thoughts may surface unexpectedly. During these moments, it's crucial to approach ourselves with kindness and compassion.

Keep in mind, esteemed readers, that mindfulness isn't a fixed destination but rather a lifelong endeavor. Cultivating a profound sense of self-acceptance and releasing the grip of judgment necessitates time and patience. Be gentle with yourself and commemorate every small advancement. Embracing our imperfections demands a tender and nurturing disposition towards ourselves.

In essence, mindfulness stands as a potent instrument on our voyage towards self-acceptance and liberation from judgment. By integrating mindfulness into our daily lives through practices like mindful breathing, mindful eating, and meditation, we foster present-moment awareness and commence our liberation from the shackles of judgment. As we navigate this transformative odyssey, let us persist in embracing the bounty of mindfulness, cognizant that it holds the key to unearthing our inherent worth and unleashing our true potential.

I pray you start this journey with an open heart and a readiness to plumb the depths of your own essence. The practice of mindfulness awaits, poised to steer you toward a life brimming with self-acceptance, compassion, and the splendor inherent in each fleeting moment.

True To You: Embracing Authenticity In A World Of Expectations

Discover the liberation and joy found in embracing our authentic selves, releasing the grip of societal expectations, and living a life aligned with our true essence.

In a world inundated with images dictating who we should aspire to be, it's effortless to lose sight of our genuine selves. We often find ourselves contorting to fit predefined molds and conforming to societal norms, often sacrificing our authenticity in the process. But what if we dared to defy these expectations? What if we opted to embrace our imperfections rather than conceal them?

Embracing authenticity entails embarking on a voyage of self-discovery, a journey necessitating both bravery and vulnerability. It beckons us to peel away the layers of societal conditioning and instead embrace the essence of who we truly are. It entails relinquishing the shackles of perfectionism and shedding the fear of judgment. By embracing our authenticity, we unlock a realm of endless possibilities, discovering a newfound liberation that infuses joy and fulfillment into our existence.

One of the foremost hurdles encountered in this odyssey is the relentless pressure to conform to societal norms. We're inundated with messages dictating how we should appear, what accolades we should attain, and even whom we should love. These expectations can prove suffocating, leaving us feeling ensnared and estranged from our authentic selves. Yet, the truth remains—we're not meant to be carbon copies of one another.

Each of us is imbued with unique qualities, quirks, flaws, and talents. Embracing authenticity entails honoring these disparities and recognizing that they constitute the intricate tapestry of human existence. It entails realizing that our worth isn't measured by how seamlessly we fit into societal constructs but by our unwavering commitment to staying true to ourselves.

When we embrace our authentic selves, we inspire others to do the same. Our courage becomes contagious, encouraging those around us to discard their masks and embrace their own imperfections. Authenticity wields a profound influence, capable of fostering deep connections and nurturing a sense of belonging. By embracing our true selves, we grant others the freedom to do likewise.

Living authentically also entails embracing vulnerability as an integral aspect of the journey. It necessitates honesty with ourselves and others, even amidst discomfort or adversity. Yet, it is through vulnerability that we forge genuine connections and cultivate intimacy. By relinquishing the facade of invulnerability, we create space for authentic relationships to flourish.

Embracing authenticity is a continual process—not a sudden transformation or a final destination. It demands a lifelong commitment to honoring our essence and perpetually delving into the depths of our authenticity. It compels us to regularly introspect, confront difficult inquiries, and remain receptive to growth and evolution.

As we embark on this collective journey, let us recognize that embracing authenticity is far from selfish. Indeed, by authentically living our truth, we become guiding lights for others, illuminating their paths of self-discovery. Let us summon the courage to embrace our imperfections, release judgment, and forge a life that resonates authentically with our being.

We will delve further into uncharted realms on this expedition, exploring the potency of vulnerability and the transformative essence of self-acceptance. Here, we will unveil practical strategies to cultivate authenticity in our daily lives and navigate the hurdles that arise along the way. Brace yourself for an unparalleled journey of self-discovery as we continue to unravel the marvels of embracing authenticity. Within the depths of vulnerability lies a latent power, one capable of metamorphosing our lives and igniting a profound sense of self-acceptance. As we persist in our pursuit of authenticity, let us venture into the sacred realm of vulnerability and uncover the pragmatic steps to integrate it into our everyday existence.

Vulnerability is often misconstrued as weakness, yet it serves as the gateway to authenticity. It entails the courage to unveil our true selves, complete with flaws, to the world around us. It demands the audacity to relinquish the masks we don, the barriers we erect, and the fear of judgment that constrains us. When we embrace vulnerability, we foster an environment where genuine connection and personal growth can thrive.

A tangible step towards embracing vulnerability is cultivating self-compassion. As adults, we often subject ourselves to harsh scrutiny, incessantly reproaching ourselves for our missteps or perceived inadequacies. But what if we opted for self-kindness instead? What if we embraced the mantra, "I am enough," and bestowed upon ourselves the same tenderness and compassion we readily offer others? This act of self-compassion empowers us to relinquish the pursuit of perfection and embrace our imperfect yet beautiful humanity.

Another stride in nurturing vulnerability involves fostering a supportive network of relationships. Surrounding ourselves with individuals who embrace and celebrate our authentic selves creates a haven where vulnerability feels embraced. These connections furnish us with a supportive shoulder, a receptive ear, and unwavering love. They serve as a reminder that we are not solitary travelers on this journey and that seeking assistance or sharing our vulnerabilities with others is not only acceptable but encouraged.

Courting vulnerability also entails taking risks, venturing beyond our comfort zones, and allowing ourselves to be seen, even amid discomfort or uncertainty. It may entail pursuing a passion that elicits skepticism or articulating our beliefs, notwithstanding the potential for criticism or rejection. By embracing such risks, we affirm to the world and ourselves our commitment to standing firm in our authentic truth, irrespective of the repercussions.

Likewise, practicing vulnerability necessitates establishing healthy boundaries, recognizing our limits, and articulating them effectively. By delineating boundaries, we safeguard our emotional well-being while still permitting ourselves to exhibit vulnerability in suitable moments and with appropriate individuals. Boundaries empower us to prioritize our needs, ensuring that we remain steadfast in our authenticity even as we embrace vulnerability.

As we near the end of this chapter, it's important to remember that our journey toward embracing authenticity and vulnerability is ongoing. It's not a destination or a goal to achieve but a continuous exploration of who we are and what brings us joy and fulfillment. We need to stay open to growth and change as we peel back the layers of societal expectations and uncover our true selves.

With each step we take toward embracing vulnerability and authenticity, we become sources of encouragement for others. Our willingness to show up as our true selves inspires those around us to do the same, creating a ripple effect of authenticity and connection. By accepting our imperfections and letting go of judgment, we create space for others to embrace their uniqueness and find beauty in their authenticity.

As we continue on this journey, let's remember the power of vulnerability. Embracing our imperfections leads to liberation and joy. Let's move forward with courage and compassion, living lives that reflect who we truly are. May our commitment to authenticity not only transform our lives but also inspire others to embark on their own journey of self-discovery and self-acceptance. Let's live authentically, knowing that we are enough just as we are.

CHAPTER 7
"Embracing the Heart of God: Finding love in every moment"

Embracing The Heart Of God: Finding Love In Every Moment

In this chapter, we dive into the importance of embracing God's love as the bedrock for discovering peace and fulfillment in our lives.

Life can often feel like a rollercoaster ride, with its highs and lows, joys and sorrows, victories and defeats. We search for meaning, purpose, and happiness, often feeling lost in the chaos of the world. But amidst all the challenges, there's one constant: God's love.

Embracing God's love isn't just about recognizing it; it's about fully surrendering to it. It's about understanding that we're loved unconditionally, flaws and all. God's love is a safe harbor where we find comfort and strength in tough times. It's a guiding light that leads us to peace and fulfillment.

When we open our hearts to God's love, we welcome a connection that surpasses human comprehension. It's a boundless love, greater than any worldly experience. By embracing God's love, we invite His presence into every facet of our lives, allowing Him to mend our wounds and revive our spirits.

One of the most beautiful aspects of embracing God's love is its ability to empower us to love ourselves. It serves as a gentle reminder that we are intricately crafted with purpose. In God's eyes, we are never insignificant or overlooked; rather, we are treasured beyond measure.

Through the embrace of God's love, we unearth the truth that true peace and fulfillment reside within. In a world that clamors for external validation and achievements, God's love redirects our focus inward. It prompts a journey of self-discovery, where we recognize our inherent worth and find joy in life's simplest moments.

In this chapter, we embark on a journey to explore the myriad ways we can embrace God's love in our everyday lives. We'll delve into the potency of prayer, the value of gratitude, and the fulfillment found in serving others. Each of these components plays a pivotal role in nurturing our relationship with God and deepening our comprehension of His boundless love.

Through personal anecdotes, uplifting narratives, and practical insights, we'll glean wisdom on how to cultivate an unwavering faith and embrace God's love wholeheartedly. We'll uncover the transformative power that comes from relinquishing our worries and fears, allowing God's love to permeate every corner of our existence.

Before we press forward, take a moment for introspection. Have you truly embraced God's love in your life? Are there areas where surrender still feels challenging? Remember, embracing God's love is an ongoing journey—a daily commitment to align our hearts with His divine will. Let's embark on this expedition together, allowing God's love to lead us toward lives filled with peace, fulfillment, and divine purpose.

With these reflections, we pause our discussion here, teetering on the brink of understanding the profound impact of embracing God's love. We'll further explore practical strategies for fully embracing this love and basking in its abundance. Expectations will be shattered as we uncover remarkable insights and revel in its transformative presence. Until then, open your heart to God's love and let its radiant essence kindle your soul's flame.

In the depths of our being, we yearn for enduring peace and fulfillment—a love that transcends the transient pleasures of this world, steadfast and eternal. In our pursuit of this profound connection, we're drawn to the boundless love of God.

As we delve deeper into the embrace of God's love, we unearth a wealth of practices to nourish our souls and uplift our spirits daily. Among these, prayer stands as a powerful tool. Through prayer, we engage in a sacred dialogue with our Creator, opening ourselves to divine communion. It's within these moments that we truly encounter God's love and discover the peace and guidance we seek.

Prayer is more than a laundry list of requests or a plea for divine intervention; it's a chance to sync our hearts and minds with God's boundless wisdom and love. In the quiet moments of prayer, we release our worries, fears, and doubts, inviting God to work wonders in our lives. We find solace in His presence, reassured that His love is ever-present and accessible to us.

Gratitude stands as another crucial pillar in embracing God's love. By nurturing a thankful heart, we shift our focus from scarcity to abundance. Gratitude opens our eyes to the myriad blessings that grace our lives each day, both grand and small. It allows us to revel in life's simple pleasures and recognize the beauty woven into every facet of our existence.

As we embrace God's love and embody gratitude, we uncover the profound significance of serving others. Through acts of kindness and compassion, we become conduits through which God's love flows. In service, we manifest the essence of God's love, becoming vessels of His peace and fulfillment in the lives of those around us. Serving others not only brings us boundless joy but also allows us to tangibly experience the depth and transformative power of God's love.

Through personal anecdotes, uplifting narratives, and practical guidance, we navigate the journey of embracing God's love with wisdom and insight. We learn that surrendering our worries and fears isn't a sign of weakness but rather an expression of trust and faith in God's divine plan. As we relinquish control and entrust our burdens to Him, He fills us with His love, peace, and resilience.

Yet, embracing God's love isn't devoid of challenges. It demands a daily commitment to relinquish our own desires and align our hearts with His will. It necessitates confronting our doubts and fears, allowing God's love to permeate every corner of our lives. But the rewards are immeasurable—a life brimming with peace, fulfillment, and divine purpose.

Take a moment to ponder your own path. Have you genuinely embraced God's love in your life? Are there areas where surrender still feels daunting? Remember, embracing God's love is an ongoing journey—a daily commitment to align our hearts with His will. It's never too late to embark on this exploration of love and allow God's transformative presence to kindle your soul.

As we press forward, keep in mind that embracing God's love surpasses mere acknowledgment; it's about allowing His love to saturate every fiber of our being. It's about wholeheartedly surrendering to His divine embrace. The journey of embracing God's love is a profound personal metamorphosis, one that opens our hearts to receive the abundance of love, peace, and fulfillment He desires for each of us.

May you continue to embrace God's love in your life, discovering eternal peace and fulfillment as you journey hand in hand with Him. And in this sacred odyssey, may you unearth the profound truth that you are cherished, valued, and loved beyond measure.

Unveiling Your Intrinsic Value: Understanding Our Worth

Let's journey into the concept of our worth in God's eyes and how acknowledging it can bring us peace and fulfillment. Understanding our values is pivotal to discovering genuine inner peace and leading a fulfilled life. So, let's uncover this beautiful truth together.

In a world where worth often seems measured by external accomplishments and comparisons, it's all too easy to lose sight of our intrinsic value as individuals. We often find ourselves chasing validation from others, striving to meet societal standards, only to feel hollow and adrift. But here's the comforting truth: our true worth isn't defined by what we achieve or how others perceive us; rather, it's rooted in God's steadfast, unwavering love for each of us.

As our Creator, God has instilled His love and purpose deep within our souls. We are fearfully and wonderfully crafted in His image, each endowed with unique gifts, talents, and a divine purpose. Embracing this truth is the gateway to finding lasting peace and fulfillment.

Acknowledging our worth can sometimes feel like navigating through a maze of obstacles. Many of us carry the heavy burdens of past mistakes, failures, and feelings of inadequacy. We might have endured rejection, betrayal, or abandonment, leaving indelible marks on our hearts and minds. However, it's precisely in these fractured places that God's love shines brightest. He meets us in our brokenness, whispers words of affirmation, and gently reminds us of our immeasurable worth.

As we turn our gaze inward and ponder God's love for us, we begin to see ourselves through His eyes. We realize that our worth isn't tethered to our past, our achievements, or the opinions of others. Rather, it's rooted in our identity as beloved children, recipients of His unfailing love and grace.

Recognizing our worth in God's eyes brings profound peace to our souls. It liberates us from the relentless pursuit of validation and the wearisome cycle of performance-driven living. We no longer need to chase after approval, for we are already fully embraced and cherished by our heavenly Father. This revelation lifts the weight of striving to prove ourselves and grants us the freedom to find rest in God's loving embrace.

Moreover, as we grasp our worth, we begin to walk in our divine purpose. Instead of seeking fulfillment in external accolades, we feel compelled to align our lives with God's plans for us. We discover that genuine satisfaction arises when we utilize our unique gifts and talents to honor Him and serve others. Embracing our worth propels us into the fullness of our God-given identities, ushering in a profound sense of joy and contentment that surpasses worldly possessions and achievements.

In the chapters ahead, we'll delve into practical strategies for embracing and deepening our understanding of our worth in God's eyes. We'll explore the transformative power of self-compassion, the importance of saturating our minds with God's truth, and the role of a supportive community in affirming our values. There's a wealth of wisdom waiting to be unearthed and applied to our lives, so let's eagerly anticipate the journey ahead as we venture onward together.

Remember, you are worthy. You are seen, cherished, and loved beyond measure by your heavenly Father. May this truth resonate deep within your soul, bringing you peace and fulfillment in the light of God's infinite love. Together, let's explore practical ways to embrace and deepen our understanding of our worth in God's eyes. These methods will enable us to fully embody the peace and fulfillment that comes with recognizing our true value. Let's embark on this journey of transformation together.

First and foremost, cultivating self-compassion is crucial in our quest to understand our worth. Often, we find ourselves as our harshest critics, fixating on past mistakes, faults, and shortcomings. Yet, God's love surpasses our imperfections. Just as He extends boundless compassion and forgiveness to us, we must learn to grant ourselves the same grace. Embracing self-compassion liberates us from self-judgment, allowing us to fully grasp our worth as beloved children of God.

Moreover, renewing our minds with God's truth is pivotal in comprehending our worth. In a world teeming with negative messages and unrealistic expectations, it's essential to immerse ourselves intentionally in the truth of God's Word. By consistently meditating on His promises and delving into His character, we can silence the lies that seek to diminish our worth. God's truth reaffirms that we are fearfully and wonderfully made, empowering us to live boldly in our divinely appointed purpose.

Furthermore, community plays a vital role in affirming our worth. Surrounding ourselves with loving, supportive individuals who reflect God's love can strengthen our understanding of our inherent value. Sharing our struggles, hopes, and dreams with others allows us to receive encouragement, accountability, and affirmation. Together, let's cultivate a community that uplifts one another, reminding us of our worth and equipping us to confront life's challenges with confidence and joy.

As we embrace these practices, we begin to unlock the fullness of God's love and the depth of our worth. We realize that our value isn't defined by external achievements, possessions, or other's opinions. Instead, it's rooted in our identity as cherished children of the Most High, forever embraced by our Heavenly Father.

With this newfound understanding, we can boldly step into our divine purpose. True fulfillment isn't found in worldly success but in using our unique gifts to serve God and others. Aligning our lives with His desires brings deep joy and satisfaction, surpassing material gains or societal praise. Our work becomes a reflection of God's love, a heartfelt gratitude for the immeasurable worth He has bestowed upon us.

May these words resonate deeply within your soul. Your worth isn't determined by your actions or others' judgments but by your status as God's beloved child. Embrace this truth, nurture self-compassion, delve into God's wisdom, and surround yourself with a supportive community. As you do, may you discover enduring peace and fulfillment in the boundless love of your Heavenly Father.

Embracing Boldness: Letting Go Of Fear And Doubt

In our quest to find peace and fulfillment in God's love, we often face a daunting challenge: overcoming fear and doubt. These emotions can immobilize us, hindering our ability to fully embrace the abundant love and joy that God offers. Yet, it's crucial to recognize that we're not alone in this struggle. God, in His boundless wisdom, equips us with the tools and guidance needed to conquer these obstacles and discover His peace.

The first step in overcoming fear and doubt is acknowledging their presence in our lives. We often attempt to suppress or ignore these emotions, hoping they'll vanish on their own. But by doing so, we unwittingly empower them. Instead, we must confront them head-on, acknowledging their sway over our thoughts, beliefs, and actions.

Once we confront fear and doubt, we can delve into their origins. These emotions frequently stem from past experiences, negative beliefs, or insecurities. However, as God's children, we possess the power to challenge and transform these limiting beliefs. Through prayer, reflection, and seeking God's guidance, we can pinpoint the sources of our fear and doubt, replacing them with thoughts grounded in God's love and truth.

Furthermore, it's important to have a supportive community of faith around us. Sharing our struggles and fears with trusted individuals can give us encouragement and wisdom. Knowing we're not alone in our journey brings comfort. Our fellow believers can guide us, share their own stories of overcoming fear and doubt, and remind us of God's faithfulness throughout history.

Another effective way to let go of fear and doubt is by deepening our connection with God through prayer and meditation. These practices help us enter God's presence, letting go of our fears and doubts. When we open our hearts to God, we invite His love and strength into our lives, giving us the courage to face any challenge. Through prayer, we find reassurance in God's promises, knowing He's with us, even in our darkest moments.

Additionally, it's crucial to realize that fear and doubt can hinder us from fully experiencing God's blessings. Instead of relying solely on our understanding, we must trust in God's plans for our lives. Surrendering control to Him allows us to let go of fear and doubt, allowing His guidance to lead us toward peace and fulfillment.

As we set out on the journey to conquer fear and doubt, it's crucial to recognize it as a gradual process. There might be setbacks, but each step forward brings us closer to the freedom and peace God promises. Let's not lose heart or become discouraged but rather persist in seeking God's love and the abundant life He assures us.

For those grappling with these struggles, anticipation fills the air as they embrace new strategies to overcome fear and doubt, eager to taste the peace and fulfillment awaiting them. Little do they realize that their journey is poised for an unexpected turn, revealing a deeper comprehension of God's love and transformative power. However, that revelation must wait as we continue our journey through this chapter and book. Stay open to the divine surprises awaiting you on your path.

For many, the journey to conquer fear and doubt and discover peace and fulfillment in God's love led them to unexpected challenges that tested their resolve. It seemed as though every obstacle conspired to push them to their limits, compelling them to confront their deepest fears and doubts. Yet, they soon realized that these challenges were essential for their growth and a deeper understanding of God's love.

Amidst these trials, they clung to their faith and the wisdom they had acquired. Each setback became an opportunity to demonstrate their trust in God's plan and rely on His strength. They came to understand that true peace and fulfillment didn't stem from the absence of challenges but from an unwavering belief in God's goodness and His constant presence in their lives.

In the face of adversity, they turned to prayer and meditation with increased fervor, seeking solace in the quiet moments of connection with God. Pouring out their hearts, they released their fears and doubts into His loving hands. Surrendering to His will, they discovered a renewed sense of peace and a deeper understanding of His transformative power.

Their supportive community became an even more valuable source of encouragement and wisdom during this trying time. The individuals they confided in not only shared their own testimonies but also reminded them of countless stories throughout history where God had shown His faithfulness. Surrounded by love and support, they found the strength to endure and the reassurance that they were never alone on this journey.

While navigating these challenges, they learned to cling to God's promises with unwavering faith. Holding onto His words, they understood that in His perfect wisdom, He was orchestrating all things for their good. They discovered that when they relinquished control and surrendered their fears and doubts, they created space for the miraculous to unfold.

Amidst their struggles, they began to notice the small blessings and signs of God's presence that had previously escaped their notice. Simple joys took on new significance, reminding them that God's love and fulfillment could be found in the most ordinary moments. They learned to embrace the present fully, trusting that God was guiding their lives, even amid uncertainty.

Their journey through fear and doubt had changed them profoundly. They emerged stronger, more resilient, and closer to God. They understood that finding peace and fulfillment in His love was not a destination but an ongoing process of surrender, growth, and trust.

This chapter ends with a profound sense of hope and a newfound appreciation for the transformative power of God's love. They emerged from the depths of fear and doubt with firm faith and resilience, ready to welcome the divine surprises that awaited them on their quest for true peace and fulfillment.

As we bid farewell to our protagonists for now, we, too, are encouraged to embrace our own journey of releasing fear and doubt and discovering the abundance of God's love. Let's embark on this path with open hearts, eager to uncover the peace and fulfillment that await us. Remember, no matter the challenges we encounter, we are never alone, for the light of God's love guides us. Keep moving forward, knowing that divine surprises await just around the corner.

Daily Delights: Finding Joy In Every Moment

Life comprises moments, big and small, shaping our journey and defining our essence. Often, we seek happiness and fulfillment in grand achievements or extraordinary occurrences. But what if true joy and peace lie in the simplicity of our everyday lives? Let's embark on a journey to explore the significance of finding joy in ordinary moments and recognizing God's love in the beauty that surrounds us each day.

Each day presents numerous opportunities for experiencing moments of pure joy. Amidst life's chaos and busyness, it's easy to overlook these moments. We become engrossed in routines and responsibilities, neglecting to appreciate the blessings unfolding before us. Yet, by shifting our perspective, we can uncover the extraordinary within the ordinary.

One simple way to find joy in everyday moments is by cultivating gratitude. Pause to reflect on the blessings bestowed upon you—the shelter over your head, the warmth of the sun on your face, the sound of laughter. Gratitude enables us to recognize the beauty and goodness in life's simplest aspects, reminding us of God's abundant love and provision.

Amidst the hustle and bustle of our lives, it's easy to overlook the magnificent tapestry of creation that surrounds us. Take a stroll outside and marvel at nature's wonders—the vibrant colors of flowers, the melody of birdsong, and the gentle dance of trees in the breeze. These small yet awe-inspiring moments remind us of the intricate design and breathtaking beauty of the world crafted by God. Such inspiring moments abound. Step outside and witness the daily gifts of beauty bestowed upon us, embracing the love that envelops us.

Finding joy in everyday moments also entails cherishing the relationships that enrich our lives. Pause and truly connect with those around you—family, friends, even strangers. Engage in meaningful conversations, share laughter, and moments of vulnerability. These simple acts of connection draw us closer to one another and fill our lives with joy and love.

Amid life's ebb and flow, nurturing a spirit of mindfulness becomes crucial. Be fully present in each moment, relishing the sights, sounds, and emotions that unfold. By doing so, we open ourselves to joy even in the simplest of activities. Whether sipping a cup of tea, taking a leisurely stroll, or listening to soothing music, immerse yourself fully in these moments, allowing tranquility to wash over you.

In the pursuit of joy, it's vital to realize that it doesn't always reside in the extraordinary or grandiose. True joy often lies within the quiet moments, the seemingly insignificant instances that fill our days. It's in these moments that God's love shines brightest, guiding us towards inner peace and fulfillment.

Learning to appreciate the beauty in the ordinary teaches us that joy isn't a destination but a state of being. It's a daily choice—to actively seek and embrace moments that bring us happiness, contentment, and purpose. Let's journey together, treasuring the joys found in everyday moments and uncovering the depth of God's love hidden within them.

In our quest to find joy in everyday moments, we must also learn to release expectations and embrace mindfulness. Often, our minds dwell on future worries or past regrets, causing us to overlook the beauty unfolding before us. The past is done, and the future remains a mystery. Embrace the moment you're in and the beauty around you.

Mindfulness entails being fully present in the current moment without judgment or attachment. It's about immersing ourselves in the here and now, awakening our senses to the richness of each experience. By practicing mindfulness, joy naturally finds its way into our lives.

Begin by taking a deep breath and grounding yourself in the present. Close your eyes and feel your breath entering and leaving your body. Notice the rhythm of your heartbeat and the sensation of air filling your lungs. As you focus on your breath, let go of any thoughts or worries, simply allowing yourself to be.

With a calm mind, open your eyes and engage with your surroundings. Observe the colors, textures, and shapes around you. Notice sunlight filtering through leaves, casting a warm glow. Take a moment to appreciate the intricate details of everyday objects, finding beauty in the ordinary.

As mindfulness deepens, we start to discover joy in unexpected places. It might be the warmth of water in the shower, the taste of a favorite meal, or the laughter of a child. These small, seemingly insignificant moments hold immense power to bring joy and fulfillment.

Alongside practicing mindfulness, discovering joy in everyday moments involves nurturing a sense of wonder and curiosity. Approach each day with the enthusiasm of a child, eager to uncover something new and inspiring. Let yourself be captivated by the smallest wonders—a butterfly hovering over a flower, a breeze through the leaves, or the first snowflake of the season.

Finding joy in everyday moments doesn't belittle the importance of grand achievements or extraordinary events. Rather, it's a gentle reminder that true fulfillment lies not only in those big moments but also in life's simple pleasures. It's an invitation to appreciate and treasure the ordinary, where the extraordinary often resides.

In the midst of our busy lives, it's easy to forget the essence of joy and lose sight of God's love and presence. But by intentionally seeking joy in the every day, we welcome God's love into every part of our lives. We become more aware of His guiding hand, recognizing His grace in even the smallest details.

So, let's continue on this journey of discovering peace and fulfillment in God's love. Let's remember that joy isn't something to attain but a precious gift already within our grasp. Let's embrace the beauty of the ordinary, practicing gratitude, mindfulness, and wonder. And in doing so, may our hearts overflow with joy, and our souls find true peace in each day.

Forgiveness: The Pathway To Healing

In our quest for peace and fulfillment in God's love, forgiveness holds significant power. By forgiving ourselves and others, we open the door to healing. Though it may seem daunting, with God's enduring love guiding us, we can find the strength and courage to release our pain and embrace healing.

Forgiveness isn't merely about letting go or forgetting hurtful experiences. It's about acknowledging our emotions and recognizing their impact on our lives. By facing our pain, we allow God's love to transform us in the healing process. Ultimately, forgiveness is an act of freeing ourselves.

At times, forgiving ourselves for past mistakes or failures can be challenging. Guilt and shame weigh heavy on our hearts, hindering our progress. Yet, God's love is unconditional, offering forgiveness and redemption. We must extend the same compassion to ourselves. Acknowledging our flaws, we find the strength to grow and heal.

Similarly, forgiving others can be difficult. Their actions may have left lasting scars, making forgiveness seem almost impossible. But holding onto resentment prolongs our pain and stifles our growth. Choosing to forgive breaks the cycle of bitterness, allowing God's love to mend our hearts and restore inner peace.

It's important to note that forgiveness doesn't excuse hurtful actions. It's a conscious decision to release anger and resentment, freeing ourselves from emotional burdens. By forgiving, we reclaim our power and find peace in God's love.

The journey of forgiveness and healing takes time. It requires patience, self-reflection, and surrendering to God's guidance. As we embark on this journey, it's crucial to seek God's presence and trust His divine plan.

Here, we'll explore practical steps toward forgiveness and delve into the profound impact of God's love. We'll discover how forgiveness aligns with our fulfillment and enables us to cultivate a life of peace, love, and joy.

We'll continue exploring forgiveness and healing, unlocking the transformative power of God's love to find the peace and fulfillment we seek.

As we delve deeper into forgiveness and healing, we'll explore how God's love impacts our journey. In this chapter, we'll uncover practical steps toward forgiveness, understanding how it aligns with our fulfillment and helps us cultivate a life of peace, love, and joy.

A crucial step in forgiveness is developing empathy and understanding for those who've caused us pain. It means stepping back from our hurt and trying to grasp their motives, experiences, and struggles. It's not about excusing their actions but recognizing their humanity and understanding they, too, carry burdens.

Seeking understanding reveals that hurtful actions often stem from brokenness, fear, or ignorance. Remembering that the one who hurt us also needs love and healing opens us to forgiveness. Extending forgiveness breaks the chains binding us to pain, offering liberation.

Forgiveness also requires self-reflection. It prompts us to examine our role in the situation and own our emotions. Sometimes, our resentment may stem from insecurities or unresolved issues. Addressing these emotions fosters compassion not only for ourselves but also for those who hurt us.

Forgiveness isn't a one-time event; it's an ongoing process. Old wounds may resurface, triggering emotions we thought we'd dealt with. During these times, it's essential to be gentle with ourselves, understanding that healing isn't linear. We may need to revisit forgiveness, reminding ourselves to release pain and embrace God's love.

In our journey of forgiveness and healing, it's crucial to seek God's presence and guidance. He is our ultimate source of strength, love, and wisdom. Through prayer, meditation, and surrendering to His plan, we open our hearts to His transformative power. He walks beside us, offering comfort in our darkest moments and showing us the path to forgiveness and wholeness.

As we conclude this chapter on forgiveness and healing, let's remember that finding peace and fulfillment in God's love is an ongoing journey. It requires continual growth, self-reflection, and a sincere desire to align with His will. Through forgiveness, we experience the transforming power of His love, finding liberation, inner peace, and profound fulfillment.

I pray you find the strength and courage to forgive others in your life, allowing God's love to heal your wounded heart. May His love guide you toward a life of peace, love, and joy. Remember, you're never alone on this journey; God's love is always with you, ready to embrace and uplift you.

The Heart Of Togetherness: Nurturing Relationships

We all crave deep connections and meaningful relationships in our lives. Yet, in our quest for peace and fulfillment, we often overlook the importance of nurturing relationships with both God and others. These connections are vital for our self-discovery, understanding, and, ultimately, finding true peace and fulfillment.

At the heart of nurturing relationships is the understanding that we're not meant to journey through life alone. As social beings, we're designed to give and receive love, to offer and receive support. Nurturing relationships requires intentional effort—a genuine willingness to invest time, energy, and emotions. It's an ongoing process that demands care and attention.

Above all, nurturing our relationship with God is essential for lasting peace and fulfillment. His love is boundless and unconditional, and by nurturing our connection with Him, we uncover the depths of His love for us. Spending time in prayer and meditation, diving into His teachings, and seeking His guidance empower us to navigate life's challenges with strength and resilience.

Building a relationship with God isn't a one-way street. As we offer our devotion and trust, we receive an abundance of grace, love, and peace from Him. This divine connection brings solace and a sense of belonging, filling our hearts with joy and contentment. Nurturing our bond with God allows us to let go of fears, worries, and burdens, finding inner peace and fulfillment in His presence.

Beyond our connection with God, relationships with others are equally important for our well-being. Nurturing bonds with family, friends, and acquaintances contributes to our overall fulfillment. These connections provide support, a sense of belonging, and opportunities for growth and learning.

Investing time and effort in nurturing relationships plants seeds of love, compassion, and understanding. We lend an ear, extend a hand, and offer a shoulder to lean on during tough times. We celebrate victories and share in life's joys and sorrows. In nurturing relationships, we create spaces where trust and vulnerability can thrive, allowing us to be our authentic selves without fear.

Yet, nurturing relationships also means being mindful of our needs and boundaries. Balancing giving and receiving ensures we have emotional energy for others while caring for ourselves. Self-care and reflection enable us to engage fully in relationships, nurturing them with authenticity and genuine care.

In our journey of nurturing relationships, we realize our impact on others reaches beyond what we see. Our words, actions, and presence influence those around us. By nurturing relationships with love, compassion, and understanding, we create a ripple effect that extends beyond our circles, shaping a world of kindness, harmony, and acceptance.

Here, we'll explore practical steps for nurturing relationships with God and others, offering insights on deepening these connections. But for now, let's pause and reflect on the importance of nurturing relationships to find peace and fulfillment. Let's embrace the power of connection and its transformative impact on our lives.

We'll delve deeper into practical steps for nurturing relationships with God and others. These insights will help strengthen your connections, leading to more peace and fulfillment in your life.

To nurture your relationship with God, continue investing time in prayer and meditation. These practices quiet your mind, open your heart, and connect you with the divine. Set aside daily time to commune with God, reflecting on His words and seeking His guidance. In these moments, find solace, strength, and reassurance, knowing you can surrender fears and worries and find inner peace in His embrace.

Exploring scripture is another powerful way to nurture your relationship with God. Delve into His words, finding inspiration, guidance, and comfort. Whether reading, studying, or discussing scripture, you'll discover wisdom and insights illuminating your spiritual journey.

In nurturing relationships with others, cultivate empathy, compassion, and understanding. Consider their experiences and perspectives, being present in both joy and struggle. Listen actively, without judgment, providing a supportive space for expression. Small acts of kindness and service show others they're valued and loved.

Building trust is crucial in nurturing relationships. Be reliable and keep your commitments, respecting confidentiality. Trust grows over time through consistent actions and integrity, strengthening connections and fostering vulnerability.

Prioritize self-care and reflection as you nurture relationships. Engage in activities that rejuvenate you and reflect on your needs and boundaries. Understanding yourself prevents burnout and allows you to fully engage with others.

Recognize your impact on others—it extends beyond what you see. Show gratitude and kindness, celebrating not only your victories but those of others. Your encouragement inspires others to pursue their dreams.

By nurturing relationships with love and understanding, you create a ripple effect of kindness and acceptance. Understand that your actions contribute to a more peaceful world.

Reflect on the significance of nurturing relationships. Embrace the power of connection and its transformative impact on your life and others. Strengthen bonds of love, compassion, and understanding for deeper peace and fulfillment.

Passionate Living: Embracing Purpose With Zeal

In a world often filled with chaos and uncertainty, discovering our purpose and passion can bring clarity and fulfillment to our lives. It's through self-discovery and aligning our passions with God's love that we experience profound peace and contentment.

Each of us possesses unique gifts, talents, and interests waiting to be uncovered. This discovery sometimes requires stepping back from life's distractions and listening to our inner voice. In moments of reflection, we unearth the desires and dreams within us.

God has instilled in us a divine purpose tailored to our individuality. Yet, societal expectations can obscure our true selves. By seeking God's guidance and aligning with His plan, we open ourselves to endless possibilities.

Discovering purpose and passion begins with self-reflection. Assessing our interests, values, and joys guides us in the right direction. But this journey isn't solitary—we invite God, seeking His wisdom and guidance.

Through scripture and prayer, we tune into God's voice, discerning His will. Surrendering our desires allows Him to reveal His purpose. In this surrender, we find true freedom and peace, trusting in His plan.

Discovering purpose and passion involves risk-taking and stepping beyond comfort zones. It may mean exploring new interests or acquiring new skills. With God's presence, we find courage and strength for these challenges, knowing He equips us.

As we connect our passions with God's love, something remarkable occurs. What once seemed disjointed and unrelated now weaves together, forming a purposeful tapestry. Our passions, when infused with God's love, become a force for impacting not just our lives but also those around us.

With each step in this journey, we learn more about ourselves and draw closer to God. His presence becomes evident as we pursue our passions, realizing they're not separate from His will but an integral part of it. In His love, we find the drive, inspiration, and strength to chase our dreams and make a difference.

As we dive deeper into exploring purpose and passion, we grasp its significance. It's not just about personal fulfillment but also aligning with God's greater purpose for humanity. Pursuing our passions rooted in His love becomes a force for good, bringing hope, joy, and transformation.

So, as we embark together, let's open our hearts to boundless possibilities. Let's embrace uncovering our purpose and passion, knowing it aligns us with God's plan. Follow along as we delve deeper into this exploration, discovering the transformative power within.

In our pursuit of purpose and passion, we realize it's not just about personal fulfillment but also aligning with God's greater purpose for humanity. It requires dedication, perseverance, and unwavering faith. Yet, God's love remains the source of our motivation and the bedrock of our endeavors.

On this journey, obstacles and doubts may arise. The road may seem uncertain, prompting questions about our path. But in these moments, we turn to God's wisdom and guidance. Through prayer and meditation, we seek His direction and find comfort in His presence.

In our quest to align with God's purpose, we often face the challenge of letting go of our own plans. It means trusting in His timing and surrendering our will. By releasing the need for control, we find freedom and witness the wonders He unfolds in our lives.

Discovering our purpose and passion isn't a one-time thing but a continuous journey of growth. It requires constant self-reflection and adapting with God's guidance. Our interests may change over time, and so may the direction of our purpose. But with God beside us, we navigate through these changes, becoming who He intended us to be.

Aligning our passions with God's love reveals their transformative power. They become instruments of hope, joy, and change for others. Our pursuit of purpose isn't meant to be self-centered but to bring light to the world.

Each step on this journey brings us closer to God. We realize our desires are part of His will. He's planted these passions in us, providing the strength, inspiration, and motivation to make a difference in others' lives.

So, let's keep our hearts open to endless possibilities. With faith as our guide and passion as our fuel, and with God's love as our strength, we align our purpose with His plan. In doing so, we find a sense of peace and fulfillment beyond measure.

Let's embrace this journey of purpose and passion, knowing it's not just personal but also a way to bring positive change to the world. Hand in hand with God, let's make a difference, one step at a time.

Gratitude Attitude: Rewiring Your Brain For Happiness

In today's demanding world, it's easy to overlook the blessings around us, making it hard to find peace and fulfillment. We get caught up in chasing success, stuff, and meeting expectations, forgetting about the power of gratitude and contentment. But when we pause to embrace these qualities, we tap into a transformative force that helps us see God's love in everything.

Gratitude is like medicine for our discontent. It shifts our focus from what's missing to what we already have. When we practice gratitude, we start seeing the world differently, appreciating even the smallest joys, and feeling thankful for the beauty around us.

By practicing gratitude, we recognize and appreciate the blessings in our lives, big and small. Each day becomes a chance to be grateful for the little things, like the air we breathe, the people we love, and the moments that shape us. Gratitude opens our hearts, helping us feel content and connected to God's love.

Contentment comes from finding inner peace, not from chasing material things. It's about being happy with what we have, finding joy in the present, and trusting God's plan for us. Contentment isn't about being lazy but about understanding that true happiness isn't about what we own or achieve but about following God's path.

When gratitude and contentment come together, they become a powerful force for anchoring our lives in God's love. By appreciating our blessings and living in the present with gratitude, we find a peace that's beyond words. In tough times, gratitude reminds us of how many times God has helped us through life's storms.

Gratitude and contentment change how we see things, helping us notice God's love in everyday moments: a hug from a loved one, the beauty of nature, or unexpected blessings. They help us unravel the tapestry of God's love, always there, always faithful.

As we journey into nurturing gratitude and contentment, let's embrace their transformative power and seek God's presence in each moment. Here, we'll explore practical ways to cultivate these virtues. But for now, let's hold onto gratitude's seed, eager for what's to come.

Life's like a tapestry woven with many threads, and gratitude and contentment help us unlock its vibrant colors. Let's keep exploring their transformative power, embracing blessings, and discovering God's boundless love in every part of our lives.

May your hearts be full of gratitude as we continue our journey, seeking peace and fulfillment in God's love. In this chapter, we'll delve into practical ways to nurture gratitude and contentment, turning these ideas into real practices that bring more peace and fulfillment into our lives.

To nurture gratitude, take a moment each night to reflect on the good things that happened during the day. Think about moments of joy, acts of kindness, or unexpected surprises, and feel grateful for them. This practice helps us see God's love in everything around us and strengthens our connection with Him.

Another way to cultivate gratitude is by journaling. Write down three things you're thankful for each day, big or small. This creates a record of God's love and faithfulness in your life. When you're feeling down, you can look back on these entries and remember how blessed you are.

Contentment comes from focusing on the present moment instead of worrying about the past or future. Practice mindfulness by paying attention to what's happening right now. Enjoy simple things like a cup of coffee, a chat with a friend, or the beauty of nature. Mindfulness helps us find contentment in the little things.

Simplify your life to find contentment. Let go of things that don't matter and declutter your physical and mental space. When we have fewer distractions, we can focus on what truly brings us joy and fulfillment.

As we wrap up our discussion on gratitude and contentment, let's carry these qualities forward on our journey toward peace and fulfillment in God's love. By practicing reflection, journaling, mindfulness, and simplicity, we can turn these ideals into practical tools for changing our lives.

Let's keep nurturing gratitude and contentment every day, reminding ourselves of the many blessings we have. This opens us up to God's love and brings a deep sense of peace and fulfillment.

May gratitude fill your heart, and may contentment guide you toward a stronger connection with God. As we continue seeking peace and fulfillment in God's love, let's be thankful for the present and hopeful for what lies ahead. Embrace the blessings around you—they show us the endless love of our Creator.

I pray you find comfort in God's love and stay committed to your journey toward peace and fulfillment. Let gratitude and contentment transform your life, leading you to a deeper connection with God.

Rising Above: Overcoming Life's Challenges

Life is a journey full of ups and downs, with plenty of challenges along the way. These hurdles can be tough to handle and may leave us feeling lost. But in these tough times, it's crucial to remember that we're not alone. We have God's love to lean on, a constant source of strength and guidance.

When we're in the midst of tough times, it's easy to get caught up in negativity. Yet, by embracing God's love, we can find comfort and the bravery to face any obstacle head-on.

One way to tackle challenges is by changing how we see them. Instead of viewing them as roadblocks, we can see them as chances to learn and grow. Each challenge is an opportunity to become better, stronger versions of ourselves.

Furthermore, it's important to cultivate a mindset of gratitude and trust in God's plan. By focusing on the blessings and lessons in each situation, we can start to see the positive side even in chaos. Trusting that there's a purpose behind every challenge brings us peace, knowing our struggles serve a greater good.

Another effective way to overcome challenges is by relying on our faith and turning to prayer for guidance. When we open up to God, we invite His wisdom and support into our lives. Through prayer, we gain clarity, strength, and divine assistance, guiding us toward solutions.

Additionally, finding solace in scripture and drawing inspiration from saints and spiritual leaders can offer valuable guidance and encouragement. Their teachings remind us of the resilience that comes from trusting in God's love.

It's important to recognize that overcoming challenges isn't always straightforward. There will be moments of doubt, but it's during these times that we need to hold onto our faith even tighter. It's in our darkest moments that we can experience profound transformation and strength.

On our journey toward peace, surrounding ourselves with a supportive community is crucial. Connecting with those who share our beliefs can offer encouragement, accountability, and companionship. Together, we can uplift and inspire each other, reminding ourselves of the power of God's love.

Life throws challenges our way, but we have the capacity to conquer them. By finding comfort in God's love, changing our perspective, practicing gratitude, and seeking guidance through prayer, we can navigate through even the toughest times. Remember, we're not alone, and with God's love, we can find the strength, peace, and fulfillment we seek.

Life's journey is full of ups and downs, presenting us with challenges we must confront along the way. We've discussed strategies for overcoming these challenges by relying on God's love. Now, let's explore how to find peace and fulfillment, even in the toughest times.

One effective way to tackle challenges is by cultivating resilience. Resilience helps us bounce back from setbacks, seeing them as opportunities for growth. Instead of feeling defeated, we can view each challenge as a chance to learn and become stronger. This mindset shift allows us to focus on the lessons rather than the problems, empowering us to overcome obstacles with determination.

Additionally, maintaining an attitude of gratitude is key to finding peace in God's love. Gratitude helps us see the blessings and lessons in every situation, even amidst chaos. When we appreciate what we have, our perspective shifts, and we can find silver linings in the storm. Gratitude also fosters contentment and trust in God's plan, reminding us of His love and guidance.

Prayer remains a powerful tool for facing challenges. Through prayer, we establish a deep connection with God, finding solace, strength, and guidance. Our prayers offer clarity in confusion, peace in turmoil, and direction toward solutions. Moreover, prayer cultivates humility, acknowledging our reliance on God's wisdom and grace.

Drawing inspiration from the lives of saints and spiritual leaders can also guide us through challenges. Their faith journeys offer timeless wisdom, showing us how to overcome struggles with unwavering faith. By studying their examples, we gain insight and encouragement to persist, even when the path seems uncertain. Their stories remind us that we're not alone in our struggles, inspiring us to keep moving forward.

As we navigate the journey of overcoming challenges, we must acknowledge that it won't always be smooth sailing. Doubts may arise, uncertainty may cloud our thoughts, and we may stumble along the way. Yet, it's in these tough moments that our faith becomes even more crucial. It's when we're at our lowest that we often experience the most growth. So, we cling to our faith, trusting in God's love to guide us through.

In our quest for peace and fulfillment, having a supportive community is vital. Surrounding ourselves with people who share our beliefs gives us the strength and encouragement to face challenges. Together, we lift each other up, reminding ourselves of the power of God's love.

Remember, the journey toward finding peace in God's love isn't without its obstacles. But by staying resilient, staying grateful, praying for guidance, finding inspiration in others, and having a supportive community, we can overcome anything. You're not alone in your struggles, and with God's love, you have all the strength, peace, and fulfillment you need. Keep moving forward with faith as your guide.

The Path To Purpose: Embracing A Meaningful Life

In life's journey, we're always searching for meaning and direction. We long for clarity and fulfillment to guide us. Luckily, we have a guiding light: God's love.

Understanding and embracing God's love lays the groundwork for a purposeful life. It's through His love that we discover our true calling and reach our potential. His love empowers us, drives us, and helps us overcome obstacles.

Living with purpose begins with deepening our connection with God. Through prayer and scripture, we open our hearts to His voice and understand His plan for us. Spending time with Him makes us more receptive to His guidance, leading us toward a life that aligns with our purpose.

When we let God's love fill us completely, we undergo a transformation. His love gives us a fresh outlook on life, allowing us to see beyond the ordinary. We realize that our purpose isn't just about personal success but about making a positive impact on the world.

Living with purpose means living deliberately. It means aligning our actions, thoughts, and desires with God's plan. As we surrender our own agendas to Him, we find a deep sense of peace and fulfillment we never knew before. It's in this surrender that our true purpose unfolds.

God equips us with everything we need to fulfill our purpose. He blesses us with talents and passions that shape who we are and drive us to make a difference. When we use these gifts to help others, we fulfill our purpose and touch lives.

Discovering our purpose also means embracing the journey. There will be challenges and uncertainty, but it's in those moments that God's love shines the brightest. Through trials, we grow and become better equipped to fulfill our purpose.

Living with purpose isn't a one-time thing; it's a lifelong pursuit. It means staying open to God's guidance and trusting His timing. Sometimes, our purpose may change, and that's okay. It evolves as we grow closer to God.

As we journey on this path guided by God's love, we not only find peace and fulfillment but also deep joy. Our lives become a testament to His transforming love, inspiring those around us to seek their own purpose.

So, let's embrace the call to live purposefully, guided by God's love. Let's trust His plan, knowing that true peace and fulfillment await us. With open hearts, let's continue this adventure, one step at a time, as we explore practical ways to live with purpose.

Aligning ourselves with God's love and surrendering to His will allows for transformation. Through this process, we can fully embrace our purpose and step into the person God intended us to be.

Living purposefully means living intentionally in every aspect of our lives. It's about aligning our thoughts, words, and actions with God's plan and becoming more aware of how we impact others and the world.

As we navigate life's seasons, our purpose may evolve. What once drove us may change as we grow. This shouldn't discourage us but instead should prompt us to seek God's guidance in every season.

Living purposefully also means being open to opportunities and challenges. Sometimes, unexpected turns lead to profound discoveries about ourselves and our purpose. These moments of uncertainty can fuel growth and resilience.

Living a purposeful life offers us the chance to impact others positively. As we recognize and use our God-given gifts, we become agents of change. Whether it's in our families, workplaces, or communities, our actions can inspire and uplift those around us.

Living purposefully comes with its challenges. There may be setbacks and doubts that threaten our journey. But in those moments, we lean on God's love and wisdom. With His strength, we rise above adversity and keep pursuing our purpose with determination.

To live purposefully, we need a supportive community. Surrounding ourselves with like-minded people who encourage and challenge us keeps us on track.

As we wrap up this chapter and reflect on what we've learned, let's remember that living with purpose is a lifelong commitment. It's a continual process of refining, surrendering to God, and trusting His plan.

So, as you embark on this journey, be encouraged. Hold onto the truth that God's love guides you, bringing peace and fulfillment. Embrace this adventure, knowing you're never alone. God's love is with you every step of the way as you seek to live a purposeful life.

CHAPTER 8
"Embracing Hope: Finding Light in the Darkness"

Embracing Hope: Finding Strength And Purpose In Every Moment

Hope is a powerful force that can change our lives in profound ways. It guides us through tough times, reminding us of the possibilities ahead. In spirituality, hope is even more significant as it brings peace through God's salvation.

At its core, hope is a strong belief in something beyond ourselves. It's the belief that there's goodness and purpose in the world, even when things seem bleak. For many, hope is a light in dark times, urging us to keep going and find comfort in God's embrace.

In the face of challenges, hope gives us the strength to carry on. It helps us confront our fears, knowing there's a higher power guiding us toward a brighter future. The power of hope lies in how it changes our perspective and response to tough situations rather than changing the circumstances themselves.

In spirituality, hope shines brightest through God's salvation. His love and grace assure us of eternal life and redemption. This promise brings comfort and hope amid life's challenges, reminding us we're not alone.

To find peace in God's salvation, we must delve deep into our faith. It means letting go of doubts and insecurities, allowing hope to transform us. It's a journey of trust, knowing that despite challenges, we're held in our Creator's loving embrace.

Hope in God's salvation prompts us to let go of our burdens and find solace in His grace. It encourages us to release past mistakes, embracing forgiveness and redemption. By shedding guilt and shame, hope fills us with the assurance of God's love and mercy.

As we explore the transformative power of hope and its role in finding peace through God's salvation, let's approach it with wonder and anticipation. Let's open our hearts to the possibilities ahead, knowing hope isn't just wishful thinking but a path leading closer to the divine.

In the pages ahead, we'll dive deeper into hope's intricate connection with God's salvation. We'll see how it brightens our darkest moments, renews our spirits, and guides us to purpose and joy.

For now, let's pause, reflecting on hope's profound impact. Let's cherish the peace it brings, knowing God's salvation ensures we're never alone. As we journey through this chapter, let's explore hope's depths together, allowing its flame to illuminate our path.

In the depths of our souls, hope burns bright, guiding us through life's complexities. Through our unwavering belief in God's salvation, we find solace and peace amidst turmoil. Hope anchors us and propels us forward, reminding us of eternal love and redemption.

As we embrace hope, let's remember it requires action. We must trust God, surrender doubts and fears, and cultivate deep faith. Knowing there's a divine plan guiding us, let's step forward with purpose, trusting in the journey ahead.

In the face of adversity, hope becomes our guiding light, urging us to rise above challenges and discover strength within our vulnerabilities. It reveals God's enduring presence, reminding us of his boundless love and everlasting mercy.

Hope reminds us of our intrinsic value and boundless potential, empowering us to pursue our aspirations with unwavering determination. It inspires acts of kindness and compassion, reflecting the love bestowed upon us by God.

Within the depths of hope lies the courage to confront our past, embracing the promise of forgiveness and redemption. Through God's unyielding love, we shed the burdens of guilt and shame, finding healing and renewal.

Amid life's complexities, hope assures us of God's unwavering companionship. With hope as our guide, we navigate life's storms with purpose and resolve, anchored in God's faithful promises.

Each day, hope molds us into vessels of love and light, drawing us closer to God and enriching our faith. As we embark on this journey of embracing hope, let us nurture it with steadfast faith in God's salvation.

In the chapters ahead, we will explore hope's transformative power through stories of resilience and divine intervention. But for now, let us revel in the embrace of hope, knowing that God's love is our eternal companion.

God's Saving Grace: Exploring The Depths Of Redemption

Exploring the profound impact of God's salvation on our lives.

In a world rife with uncertainty, hope stands as a beacon of solace and comfort, guiding us through life's complexities. Amid our search for meaning, we are drawn to something greater, a purpose beyond the mundane—a longing rooted in the divine essence within us.

God's salvation offers fulfillment to this yearning, extending grace and love to humanity. Rooted in the Christian faith, it finds its essence in Jesus Christ, embodying God's sacrificial love and bridging the gap between the divine and the human.

At its heart, God's salvation is an act of grace, offering not only deliverance from sin's consequences but also restoration to a profound relationship with God. It invites us to experience the transformative power of grace, forgiveness, and redemption, altering the course of our lives forever.

In embracing God's salvation, we find hope—hope that transcends circumstances and empowers us to weather life's storms with courage and resolve. It assures us of peace, joy, and purpose, grounded in the unwavering character of God.

Through God's salvation, we are called to participate in his divine plan, spreading healing and love in a broken world. As vessels of hope, we extend the same salvation we've received, embodying Christ's love in our words and deeds.

Exploring God's salvation brings us face-to-face with the tension between divine sovereignty and human free will. While salvation is a gift from God, our acceptance or rejection of it is a reflection of our own choices. This dynamic invites us to ponder deeply our relationship with God and the responsibility we carry as recipients of his grace.

As we delve into the first part of our journey into God's salvation, I encourage you to consider its profound implications for our lives. It's not just a theological concept; it's a reality that can transform our identities and infuse our lives with meaning. I'll explore how embracing God's salvation impacts our daily lives, revealing the beauty of living in his grace.

Embracing God's salvation changes us forever. It shapes our identities and gives meaning to our lives. As we dive deeper into its practical implications, we uncover the richness of living in God's loving grace.

One significant aspect of God's salvation is its power to restore broken relationships. In our brokenness, we often find ourselves separated from others by resentment and unforgiveness. But through God's salvation, we're called to extend the same grace and forgiveness we've received.

By embracing God's salvation, we become agents of reconciliation, healing brokenness, and restoring harmony in our relationships. This requires humility and a willingness to let go of pride. As we embrace God's grace, we find the strength to forgive others, just as we've been forgiven.

Moreover, embracing God's salvation equips us to navigate life's complexities with wisdom and discernment. In a world filled with fleeting pleasures and instant gratification, God's salvation serves as a steadfast moral compass.

Through a close relationship with God, we gain clarity to make decisions aligned with his will. We're guided to choose what's right, even in difficult times, prioritizing eternal values over momentary temptations. Embracing God's salvation empowers us to live with integrity and pursue righteousness, even amid challenges.

Furthermore, God's salvation offers an unwavering hope that transcends life's uncertainties. In times of hardship, it's easy to lose sight of our purpose. Yet, anchored in God's salvation, we find meaning and significance in his plan.

This hope gives us strength to weather life's storms, finding peace amidst chaos. It assures us of security in God's love and sovereignty. Embracing God's salvation fills us with enduring hope that shines bright, even in darkness.

As we conclude our exploration of God's salvation, let's be grateful for this immeasurable gift. May we continually embrace God's saving grace, letting it shape every aspect of our lives.

God's salvation isn't just a theological concept; it's a transformative reality that deepens our relationship with Him. Through it, we're restored, empowered, and filled with hope. Embracing this salvation brings peace and meaning amid life's chaos. Let our lives reflect its transformative power as we extend love and grace to others, embodying Christ in all we do.

Fearless: Conquering Doubt And Fear

Addressing doubts and fears that hinder our embrace of God's salvation and offering guidance to overcome them.

Doubt and fear can be formidable barriers to our spiritual growth, inhibiting our full acceptance of God's salvation. They often loom large, prompting us to question our beliefs and wrestle with uncertainty. Yet, by confronting and addressing these doubts and fears, we open ourselves to a deeper sense of peace and hope in God's saving grace.

A common doubt many face is whether they are truly deserving of God's love and salvation. Past mistakes and shortcomings may weigh heavily, leaving us feeling unworthy of forgiveness. Yet, it's vital to recognize that God's love is unconditional and freely given to all. Embracing this truth allows us to shed self-doubt and receive God's love with open hearts.

Fear, too, can hinder our embrace of God's salvation. Fear of the unknown, loss of control, or stepping out of our comfort zones may hold us back. Confronting and overcoming these fears requires placing our trust in God. Remember, faith and fear cannot coexist. By choosing faith, we can release our fears and find comfort in God's unwavering guidance.

External influences, like skepticism and intellectual debates, can also fuel doubt in our faith. In a world rife with skepticism, doubts may arise from scientific discoveries or personal hardships. However, faith is not stagnant but a journey of growth and understanding.

Embracing doubt as part of our journey allows us to seek answers, deepen understanding, and strengthen faith. Rather than fearing doubt, we can see it as a chance for growth and a catalyst for a stronger relationship with God.

Finding guidance to overcome doubts and fears is crucial in our spiritual journey. Engaging with scripture, prayer, and seeking support from fellow believers greatly aids us in this process. God's word offers comfort, wisdom, and reassurance, helping us overcome doubts. Through consistent prayer, we open ourselves to God's guidance, understanding his intentions for us. Connecting with a community of believers provides valuable insights and support during moments of doubt.

Continuing this journey of overcoming doubt and fear, it's vital to remember that God's salvation encompasses both our earthly life and eternity. Embracing hope in his salvation requires courageous faith that transcends challenges. By acknowledging doubts, trusting in God's love, and seeking guidance through prayer and scripture, we experience peace beyond understanding.

With each step to overcome doubt and fear, we draw closer to embracing God's salvation fully. In this chapter, we'll explore additional strategies and perspectives to aid us on this transformative journey.

In moments of doubt, reflecting on others' testimonies can be helpful. Hearing how God has worked in their lives reinforces faith and offers reassurance. Reach out to fellow believers, sharing stories of God's love and salvation. Remember, you're not alone in doubts or fears; believers support and encourage one another.

Moreover, nurturing a relationship with God through prayer and meditation can offer the clarity and guidance we seek. Set aside daily dedicated time to commune with the divine. Pour out your doubts and fears before Him, knowing He's always ready to listen and respond with love and understanding. Through prayer, we open ourselves to receiving His peace and wisdom, which can help us find the strength to overcome doubts and fears.

As we continue our journey, it's crucial to remind ourselves that doubt isn't a sign of weak faith but an opportunity for growth. Embrace the questions within you and seek deeper understanding. Explore resources like theological texts, podcasts, or sermons to delve into challenging aspects of faith. Engage in dialogue with others, understanding that diverse perspectives can enrich our spiritual journey.

Remember, embracing God's salvation is an ongoing process of surrender and trust. We may face setbacks or doubts, but these moments can reveal God's faithfulness in unexpected ways. Allow doubts and fears to deepen your relationship with Him.

Lastly, be gentle and patient with yourself as you navigate doubt and fear. It's natural to feel overwhelmed, but God's love and grace are boundless. He meets us where we are and walks with us in our struggles. When doubt arises, remind yourself of His love and forgiveness. Lean into the hope of salvation, knowing God is always working for your good.

As we progress through this chapter on overcoming doubt and fear, let's hold onto the truth that God's salvation surpasses any doubt or fear. By addressing and seeking guidance through doubts and fears, we open ourselves to a profound sense of peace and hope in His salvation. Embrace the journey, trusting God every step of the way. May your faith strengthen, and may you find enduring peace in His amazing love.

In His Word We Trust: Finding Strength In Biblical Promises

As we journey through life, facing countless challenges and uncertainties, it's normal to feel overwhelmed and exhausted at times. The weight of the world often bears down on us, leaving us seeking comfort, strength, and hope. In these moments, turning to the promises found in God's word can bring a unique sense of peace and encouragement.

In the Bible, we discover a wealth of promises that speak directly to our hearts and experiences. These promises aren't just empty words; they're solid assurances from a loving and faithful God. They're meant to anchor our souls and lift our spirits, reminding us that we're never alone in our struggles.

In God's word, we find reassurance in His constant presence with us. Isaiah 41:10 says, "So do not fear, for I am with you; do not be dismayed, for I am your God. I will strengthen you and help you; I will uphold you with my righteous right hand." These words offer comfort, affirming that no matter how challenging life gets, God remains by our side, ready to support us.

Moreover, God promises to equip us with the strength we need for each day. Philippians 4:13 declares, "I can do all this through him who gives me strength." This verse reminds us that we don't have to rely solely on our own capabilities. Instead, we can draw on God's power within us, enabling us to tackle obstacles and find serenity amidst turmoil.

In God's promises, we discover the assurance of His provision for our needs. Matthew 6:26 shares Jesus' words, "Look at the birds of the air; they do not sow or reap or store away in barns, and yet your heavenly Father feeds them. Are you not much more valuable than they?" This reminder underscores that if God cares for the smallest creatures, He will surely provide for us according to His perfect will.

Additionally, God assures us of His gift of peace amidst life's storms. In John 14:27, Jesus says, "Peace I leave with you; my peace I give you. I do not give to you as the world gives. Do not let your hearts be troubled, and do not be afraid." This promise gently reminds us that worldly peace is fleeting, but true and enduring peace is found in a relationship with God.

In moments of doubt and uncertainty, we find solace in God's promises, which serve as an anchor for our souls, grounding us in truth and hope. As we journey towards embracing hope and seeking peace, let's cling tightly to the promises within God's word. Let's meditate on them, speak them aloud, and allow them to fortify us for whatever lies ahead.

Remember, these promises aren't just words on a page; they're living truths from a God who loves you more deeply than you can fathom. He understands the depth of your struggles, the weight of your burdens, and the weariness of your soul. Rest in His promises and find the strength and comfort you need on this journey toward peace and hope.

Let's continue exploring the specific promises that offer strength and hope in times of need. These assurances are like a soothing balm for our weary souls, reminding us of the unwavering and faithful nature of our God.

One promise that brings profound comfort is found in Romans 8:28, which states, "And we know that in all things God works for the good of those who love him, who have been called according to his purpose." This verse assures us that even amidst trials and challenges, God is actively working for our ultimate good. He can transform our brokenness into beauty. Trusting in this promise enables us to release fear and rest in the knowledge that God is orchestrating all things for our benefit.

In Jeremiah 29:11, God declares, "For I know the plans I have for you, plans to prosper you and not to harm you, plans to give you hope and a future." This verse assures us that God has a purposeful plan for our lives, brimming with hope and goodness. Even when the path ahead seems unclear, we can trust that God is leading us toward a future filled with His blessings.

During moments of doubt and discouragement, we find comfort in the promise of God's faithfulness. Lamentations 3:22-23 beautifully states, "The steadfast love of the Lord never ceases, his mercies never come to an end; they are new every morning; great is your faithfulness." These verses illustrate the enduring nature of God's love and faithfulness towards us. Despite changing circumstances, we find solace in the unwavering love and mercy He extends to us.

Moreover, 2 Corinthians 12:9 offers a reassuring promise: "My grace is sufficient for you, for my power is made perfect in weakness." This reminds us that we need not rely solely on our own strength. Instead, we can humbly lean on God's grace, knowing His power is magnified in our moments of weakness. In surrender, His strength empowers us to confront any obstacle.

As we reflect on these promises, let's cling to them tightly, allowing them to permeate every aspect of our lives. Let God's word anchor your soul in truth, hope, and peace. In moments of weariness and doubt, remember that God's promises are not hollow words but living truths with the power to transform.

Continuing on this journey, may we find strength and comfort in God's promises, allowing them to renew our minds and uplift our spirits. And let's always remember that our Heavenly Father walks with us, guiding us every step of the way.

In conclusion, find rest in these promises, propelling you forward with hope and renewed strength. Trust in the unchanging character of our God, who never forsakes us. With these promises in our hearts, we face the future knowing we are loved, protected, and cherished.

Remember, within the pages of God's word lie countless promises awaiting your discovery. Let's journey together, seeking His promises and embracing the hope and peace that come from knowing Him.

Letting God Lead: Surrendering Control For Spiritual Growth

In our journey of faith, we inevitably confront the concept of control. We often strive to manipulate circumstances, people, and even divine intervention to fit our limited understanding of what's best for us. However, deep within, we recognize that true peace and hope reside in surrendering our desires and control to God.

Surrendering control isn't admitting defeat; it's a profound act of trust and faith. It acknowledges that God's ways surpass ours, and His plans for us exceed our own. When we release our grip on control, we open ourselves to the boundless possibilities God has in store.

Surrendering control of God is vital because it prompts us to embrace humility. It asks us to let go of our ego and acknowledge that we aren't the ultimate authority in our lives. Instead, we trust in a higher power, understanding that God's wisdom far surpasses our own. Through surrender, we often find genuine peace as we release the burden of trying to navigate life's complexities alone.

When we surrender control, we also invite God to reveal His grace and love in our lives. We understand that His plans for us are rooted in love and a desire for our ultimate good. By surrendering our desires, we allow God to work in ways beyond our imagination. This surrender deepens our intimacy with our Heavenly Father as we learn to rely solely on His guidance and provision. Finding solace in His constant presence, we are led towards a future brimming with hope.

Moreover, surrendering control empowers us to live free from anxiety and worry. Releasing our grip on control, we shed the weight of the world and embrace the peace of being held in the palm of God's hand. Though surrendering control requires vulnerability, it leads to liberation. Entrusting our burdens to God brings profound relief as we acknowledge His superior ability to carry them.

In our journey of surrender, it's important to remember it's not a one-time event but a daily practice. Surrendering control to God demands constant renewal of our commitment to trust Him completely. It means allowing Him to guide us in every moment, even amidst uncertainty or difficulty. Through surrender, we align our will with His, finding perfect peace amidst life's storms.

As we embark on this path of surrender, let's recall that our salvation is intricately tied to our willingness to let go of control. Surrendering our desires and yielding to His divine plan unlocks abundant blessings and the promise of salvation He offers. May we find the courage to surrender, for in doing so, we discover true peace, hope, and the fulfillment of our deepest longings.

Here, we delve deeper into the transformative power of surrendering control to God. Embracing this act of faith, we witness remarkable ways in which God molds us into the individuals He created us to be.

Every day, we encounter opportunities to surrender control, whether in our relationships, careers, or dreams. It entails submitting our plans and desires to God and trusting His will over our own. This surrender doesn't diminish our individuality or ambition; rather, it invites God to refine and align them according to His purpose.

Through surrender, we also learn patience—an invaluable lesson in a world of instant gratification. When we relinquish control, we let go of the need for immediate answers, allowing God to work in His perfect timing. Practicing patience and trusting Him, we see His plans unfold with precision, leading us to a future filled with blessings.

Moreover, surrendering control to God frees us from the burden of self-reliance. We no longer carry the weight of navigating life solely by our own strength and wisdom. Instead, we embrace the truth that we're not alone in this journey. With God by our side, offering guidance, support, and unwavering love, we face challenges with courage, knowing we're equipped with divine wisdom and strength.

In our surrender, we also find healing and restoration. Letting go of control opens us to God's transformative power. He takes our brokenness and shapes it into beauty. Yielding to His plans, He restores our souls, guiding us toward wholeness and revealing the path to lasting peace and joy.

Finally, surrendering control to God lets us experience His full salvation. Through our willingness to let go, we become vessels for His love and light. Our surrendered lives testify to His faithfulness and goodness. Embracing hope and finding peace in His salvation, we discover a life rich in blessings and purpose and grounded in His unwavering love.

As we conclude this chapter on surrendering control to God, let's remember it's an ongoing journey requiring continual commitment. Daily, let's release our desires and trust in His plans, knowing surrender isn't a one-time event but a beautiful process of surrendering, receiving, and becoming. Through it all, may we find solace, peace, and hope, secure in our Heavenly Father's embrace.

For truly, in surrendering control, we discover a life surpassing our wildest dreams, fully experiencing God's transformative love and salvation.

The Power Of Forgiveness: Healing From Within

Understanding the transformative power of forgiveness and seeking healing through God's salvation leads to inner peace.

Within each of us lies a remarkable power capable of transforming even the most wounded souls: forgiveness. It's through forgiveness that we find the path to healing and, ultimately, inner peace.

Life often brings encounters that cause pain, disappointment, and heartache. These experiences leave us feeling broken, lost, and burdened by bitterness. In these moments, forgiveness becomes the key to unlocking our own healing.

To truly embrace forgiveness, we must grasp its essence. It surpasses merely pardoning others for their wrongs. Forgiveness is a deliberate choice, a decision to release the resentment and anger that weigh us down. It's an act of self-liberation, recognizing our own humanity. By forgiving others, we empower ourselves to move forward, breaking free from the chains of the past.

As we journey toward forgiveness, we must also consider the role of God's salvation in this process. God's salvation forms the foundation upon which forgiveness and healing rest. Through His divine grace and unconditional love, we find the strength to forgive, even amidst deep pain and betrayal.

Surrendering to God's salvation helps us realize that forgiveness isn't solely about the person who wronged us; it's about our own growth and transformation. By extending forgiveness, we acknowledge that we, too, have been forgiven by a loving and merciful God. Through His salvation, we find comfort in knowing we're not alone in our suffering. His grace gives us the courage to release our burdens and embrace healing.

In the journey of forgiveness and healing, we discover inner peace—a peace that transcends understanding. It radiates from within, lighting our path. Embracing forgiveness and seeking healing through God's salvation invites the powerful presence of peace into our lives.

The transformative power of forgiveness and healing isn't exclusive; it's accessible to all who seek it. Whether we've endured deep wounds or carried the weight of regret, forgiveness offers a lifeline to freedom. No mistake is too great, no pain too immense, for the power of forgiveness is limitless. It's a divine gift, an opportunity to rejuvenate our spirits and reclaim joy.

In this chapter, we'll explore practical steps toward embracing forgiveness and seeking healing. We'll navigate the complexities of remorse and resentment, opening our hearts to God's love. But for now, let's reflect on the transformative power of forgiveness and the promise of inner peace on this sacred journey.

Within our souls resides a longing for healing and wholeness, a desire to be liberated from the burdens of our past. As we journey toward embracing forgiveness and seeking healing through God's salvation, we must now look inward and explore practical steps to aid in this transformative process.

The first step toward embracing forgiveness is acknowledging our own pain and the pain we've caused others. It's an act of humility to confront the wounds we've inflicted and take ownership of our actions. Reflecting on the consequences of our choices compels us to seek forgiveness, not only from God but also from those we've wronged.

In seeking healing, we must learn the art of self-forgiveness. Often, we carry the weight of guilt and regret, punishing ourselves for past mistakes. Yet, God's salvation invites us to release this self-imposed burden and embrace the forgiveness He freely offers. Through self-forgiveness, we begin to heal from within, allowing God's transformative love to mend our fractured souls.

Empathy and compassion are also crucial in the journey of forgiveness and healing. Extending understanding and compassion to those who've hurt us creates space for healing to flourish. By empathizing with others and acknowledging their struggles, we find the strength to forgive. Understanding their complexities helps us cultivate forgiveness and foster healing.

To fully embody the transformative power of forgiveness and healing, we must cultivate an attitude of gratitude. By focusing on the blessings in our lives and the lessons learned through our experiences of pain and forgiveness, we shift our perspective. Opening our hearts to the healing power of God's grace, gratitude helps us see beyond our past wounds and embrace the beauty of the present moment.

Lastly, in our pursuit of forgiveness and healing, we must never underestimate the power of prayer. Through heartfelt communication with God, we find solace, guidance, and the strength to forgive and seek healing. Prayer connects us to

God's divine wisdom, empowering us to tap into the endless reservoirs of love and forgiveness.

Uniting these practical steps with the foundation of God's salvation, we discover a path toward profound healing and inner peace. It's a journey that demands bravery and vulnerability as we confront our brokenness and extend forgiveness to others. Yet, in this sacred journey, the rewards far outweigh the challenges.

The transformative power of forgiveness and healing calls to us all, regardless of the depth of our pain or the weight of our mistakes. It's an invitation to shed the shackles of resentment and embrace the freedom of forgiveness. Guided by God's salvation, we move toward a life of wholeness, abundance, and profound peace.

As we close, let's carry with us the understanding that forgiveness is not a one-time act but a lifelong commitment. It requires constant effort and a willingness to let go of past hurts. Yet, with each step toward embracing forgiveness and seeking God's healing, we draw nearer to the peace and joy awaiting us on this sacred journey.

Walking With God: Nurturing Your Relationship

In our quest for lasting peace and hope, cultivating a strong, meaningful relationship with God is vital. This relationship serves as a guiding light, an unwavering support system, and a source of immense comfort. Fostering this bond allows us to experience the profound love and guidance He offers.

Taking the first step toward nurturing this relationship involves honestly evaluating our beliefs and understanding of God. Letting go of preconceived notions or misunderstandings, we approach God with an open heart and a willingness to learn and grow. This creates space for Him to reveal Himself to us in new and transformative ways.

One of the most powerful ways to nurture our relationship with God is through prayer. Prayer is the language of the soul, our direct line of communication with the Almighty. Through prayer, we can express our gratitude, share our deepest struggles, and seek His divine guidance. In the stillness of prayer, we hear God's whispers and feel His presence. Cultivate a regular prayer routine to connect with God intimately and authentically.

Another essential aspect of nurturing our relationship with God is studying His word. The Bible isn't just a book; it's a living testament to God's love, grace, and wisdom. Through the scriptures, we gain insights into His character and find comfort in His promises. Invest time in exploring the Bible, meditating on its teachings, and allowing its truths to penetrate your heart. Engage in Bible studies and prayer groups, or find a spiritual mentor to navigate its treasures.

To nurture a relationship with God, surrender yourself completely to His will. This surrender isn't weakness but trust in His divine plan. Let go of your desires and align with His purpose. Surrendering brings freedom and peace as we allow God to guide our steps, knowing His plans surpass ours.

Cultivating gratitude is integral to nurturing a relationship with God. Gratitude unlocks our hearts, helping us appreciate His daily blessings. Reflect on God's goodness, dwelling on the ways He shows love and faithfulness. Gratitude strengthens our bond with God and fills our lives with joy and contentment.

Nurturing our relationship with God is a lifelong process, requiring time, effort, and a genuine desire for connection. Be patient and persistent, knowing each step brings you closer to the peace and hope He abundantly offers.

As we venture into this chapter, we will delve deeper into specific practices and exercises to enrich your relationship with God. Stay tuned for a more intimate exploration of the tools and techniques that will empower you to find solace, strength, and unending hope in His salvation.

And so, our journey continues as we embrace hope and seek the transformative power of a profound relationship with God. May each step we take be guided by the love and grace of our Heavenly Father.

Here, we will explore specific practices and exercises aimed at enriching your relationship with God. These tools and techniques aim to empower you to find solace, strength, and unending hope in His salvation.

Daily meditation serves as a profound means to strengthen our bond with God. Dedicate a specific time each day to reflect quietly, allowing your mind to calm and your heart to open. In this sacred silence, welcome God's presence, inviting Him to reveal His truth and love to you. As you make this a regular practice, you'll find that meditation deeply impacts your thoughts, emotions, and overall well-being, fostering a deeper peace and a more intimate connection with God.

Another impactful practice is journaling. Take pen to paper and express your innermost thoughts and feelings to God. Write down your prayers, aspirations, challenges, and joys. Pour out your heart, sharing your deepest desires and anxieties. Through journaling, not only do you gain clarity on your emotions and thoughts, but you also have the chance to reflect on God's unwavering presence in your life. Upon revisiting your entries, you'll witness His comforting hand, His guiding light, and His responses to your prayers.

Engaging in acts of service plays a crucial role in nurturing our relationship with God. Whether it's volunteering or offering a helping hand, we demonstrate God's love in action by reaching out to those in need. Through serving others, we not only draw closer to God but also gain a deeper understanding of His compassion and grace. By touching the lives of those who are suffering, we embody the hope we've found in His salvation, making a tangible impact in the world.

Additionally, fostering a spirit of forgiveness is essential. Holding onto grudges and resentment can hinder our connection with God and steal away the peace and hope He offers. Choose to let go of any bitterness or anger, whether directed towards others or ourselves. Embrace the freedom that forgiveness brings, recognizing it as a gift from God that allows us to experience His mercy and restoration. Release the past, forgive wholeheartedly, and open your heart to the healing power of God's love.

Finally, fostering a sense of awe and wonder in our daily lives can deeply impact our connection with God. Take moments to marvel at the beauty of creation – whether it's the vibrant hues of a sunrise or the soothing melody of birds chirping. Embrace these instances of awe and gratitude, allowing them to draw you nearer to the Creator. By recognizing God's craftsmanship in the world around us, we open our hearts to His presence and rediscover the inspiration to walk each day with hope and purpose.

In closing, remember that nurturing a relationship with God is an ongoing journey. It requires dedication, persistence, and a sincere desire for connection. Embrace the practices and exercises discussed in this chapter, tailoring them to fit your personal path. Seek support and guidance from a spiritual mentor or a community of fellow believers who can accompany you along the way.

We'll continue to delve into the depths of this profound relationship, uncovering its transformative power. Hold onto the hope found in knowing a God who loves you unconditionally and desires to walk beside you at every turn. Let this chapter serve as a source of encouragement, reminding you that by nurturing your relationship with God, you can discover lasting peace and hope in His salvation.

The Faithful Path: Embracing Trust

During moments of uncertainty, when doubt and fear grip our hearts, we find ourselves at a pivotal juncture. We can allow worries to overwhelm us, stealing our joy, or we can opt for hope, grounding ourselves in God's salvation and journeying forward in faith and trust.

Stepping out in faith and trust, though seemingly daunting, is a courageous endeavor with boundless rewards. It beckons us to release our burdens, doubts, and fears in exchange for a peace that defies comprehension.

But how do we initiate this journey? How do we summon the strength to trust amidst life's tempests? The answer lies in relinquishing our grip on control and acknowledging that we're not traversing this path alone.

God's boundless love for us serves as an unyielding beacon. It navigates us through the darkest of nights and illuminates our path. Entrusting ourselves to Him signifies our recognition that He holds the answers, solutions, and peace we fervently seek.

However, walking in faith and trust doesn't guarantee a smooth journey devoid of challenges. Often, it's the uncertainties and trials that shape our character, deepen our faith, and expand our capacity for hope.

In these moments, we must cling to God's promises. He pledges to never abandon us, to carry us through valleys, and to fight for us when our strength wanes. We're called to embrace these assurances, anchoring our faith and trust upon them.

Aligning our hearts with God's unleashes courage, peace, and hope within us. Our circumstances don't define us; rather, it's our response to them that reveals the depth of our faith.

So, let's rise with confidence, recognizing that God's salvation isn't remote, reserved only for the devout or flawless, but a freely offered gift to all who accept it. Let's step out in faith, trusting that God orchestrates all things for our good.

As we journey along the path of faith and trust, we'll inevitably encounter fresh challenges and uncertainties. Yet, let's cling to the assurance that we're not alone, our hope remains steadfast, and God's divine purpose unfolds, even when unseen.

In our ongoing exploration of faith and trust, may you find encouragement today. Draw comfort from God's promises and gather strength as you step forward with unwavering trust. Though the road ahead may seem uncertain, our faith and trust in God will guide us, leading to a peace that surpasses understanding.

Take a moment to let this truth sink in. Embrace the uncertainty, hold onto hope, and trust in the unfolding story ahead. In the next chapter, we'll delve into practical ways to nurture faith and trust in our daily lives. So, remain steadfast in faith as we continue this transformative journey toward embracing hope and discovering peace in God's salvation.

In our journey of faith and trust, we confront obstacles that test our beliefs to the core. Doubts may arise, and fears may threaten to immobilize us. But in those moments, remember our strength doesn't stem solely from ourselves.

It's rooted in the boundless power of God's love that surrounds us, sustains us, and ignites hope within our hearts.

As we journey through this transformative chapter, let's explore practical ways to nurture faith and trust in our daily lives. Amidst uncertainty, we can ground ourselves in the truth of God's Word. Scripture serves as a wellspring of wisdom, comfort, and guidance, offering reassurance and direction for each step we take.

Within the pages of scripture, we encounter tales of ordinary individuals whose faith and trust transformed them into beacons of hope. Abraham, confronted with the daunting command to sacrifice his son, chose to trust God's plan and witnessed miraculous deliverance. David, amidst enemies and inner turmoil, found solace in God as his refuge and strength. The disciples, facing storms at sea, turned to Jesus, who stilled the raging waters and assured them of His presence.

Just as these faithful individuals clung to God's promises, we, too, can opt to trust in His faithfulness. When uncertainties arise, we can immerse ourselves in His Word, allowing its truths to wash over us and penetrate our hearts. As we absorb the accounts of God's faithfulness, our trust in Him strengthens, and our fears and doubts fade in the radiance of His boundless love.

Furthermore, in the realm of prayer, we encounter a potent means to foster faith and trust. Prayer transcends mere ritual; it's a sacred dialogue with our Heavenly Father. It provides a platform to pour out our hearts, voice our doubts and fears, and seek God's guidance and fortitude. Through prayer, we invite God to intervene in our lives, aligning our desires with His will and surrendering our vulnerabilities to His sovereign care.

Acknowledging the gift of community is another crucial facet of nurturing faith and trust. Surrounding ourselves with fellow believers who uplift and support us is vital for spiritual growth. We're meant to journey together, bearing each other's burdens and encouraging one another toward love and good deeds. In the fellowship of believers, we find accountability, solidarity, and a reminder that we're not alone in our quest to embrace hope and discover peace in God's salvation.

As we persist in our journey of faith and trust, may your heart find strength and your spirit be lifted. Take courage in knowing that God's promises stand firm and reliable despite the circumstances that may seem daunting. Remember, you're never alone on this path.

Let's embrace this truth as we venture boldly into the unknown, guided by faith and trust in our loving Heavenly Father. He's the architect of our faith, the orchestrator of miracles in our lives, and the source of unwavering peace. Walk assured that you're cherished, esteemed, and upheld by the Creator of the cosmos.

May your journey press onward, leading you toward boundless hope and profound peace. May the words within these pages serve as a beacon of encouragement, reminding you that even amid uncertainty, you can journey in faith and trust, assured of God's nearness. Embrace this truth, allowing it to spark a profound transformation within you.

Unshakable Hope: Triumphing Over Life's Trials

Life is a tapestry of highs and lows, joys and sorrows, triumphs and challenges. We all encounter trials and difficulties at some juncture, and often, the burden of adversity feels too immense to bear. These trials can overwhelm us, leaving us feeling helpless and adrift. Yet, as believers and followers of Christ Jesus, we discover solace and strength in the embrace of God's salvation.

When life hurls its curveballs our way, we may be tempted to question our purpose or doubt our capacity to overcome it. We might find ourselves engulfed in sorrow, pain, or even despair. However, it's precisely in these moments that the potency of God's salvation shines brightest.

God's salvation not only liberates us from sin and bestows upon us eternal life but also equips us to confront the challenges of our daily existence. It empowers us to transcend our circumstances and discover hope and peace amid the tempest. By embracing God's salvation, we unearth the fortitude to endure and the resolve to persevere.

One of the most profound gifts bestowed by God's salvation is the assurance of His perpetual presence. In moments of trial, when we feel isolated and forsaken, the truth endures: God is ever by our side. He walks alongside us, guiding us through the darkest valleys and speaking peace into our troubled souls.

Embracing God's salvation unveils a deeper truth: trials are not meant to shatter us but to refine us. They serve as the crucible where our faith is tested and fortified. Just as gold is purified by fire, we too are refined through the trials we encounter, emerging more resilient and unwavering in our trust in God.

Furthermore, God's salvation bestows upon us a perspective that transcends earthly circumstances. It reminds us that this life is but a fleeting moment compared to eternity. We're called to fix our gaze on the unseen rather than the seen. By doing so, we anchor our hope not in fleeting conditions but in the enduring love and faithfulness of our Heavenly Father.

The story of Joseph in the Old Testament serves as a poignant illustration of overcoming trials and discovering hope in God's salvation. Despite enduring the hardships of slavery, false accusations, and imprisonment, Joseph never surrendered hope. He clung steadfastly to the promise of God's faithfulness, ultimately emerging as a prominent leader in Egypt and saving countless lives during a severe famine.

In the same vein as Joseph, we, too, can unearth hope amid our trials. We can rely on the assurance that God's salvation is at work, even when the broader picture eludes us. Amid adversity, we're afforded the opportunity to develop character, deepen our faith, and embody a living testament to God's grace.

As we traverse life's journey, trials will inevitably intersect our paths. We'll encounter tribulations of diverse forms, each presenting unique challenges. Yet, by embracing God's salvation, we can discover hope, peace, and the strength to prevail.

As we progress through this book, we'll delve deeper into specific strategies and principles to navigate our trials and discover hope amid adversity. For now, let this truth anchor your heart: God's salvation isn't merely a distant promise for the future but a present reality we can embrace for strength in every step of our journey. Stay tuned as we further explore the transformative power of God's salvation in overcoming trials and finding lasting hope.

As we delve deeper into the transformative power of God's salvation in overcoming trials and discovering lasting hope, we uncover invaluable strategies and principles applicable to our individual journeys, irrespective of the specific trials we face. These principles offer solace, strength, and hope within the embrace of God's salvation.

Foremost, when navigating trials, it's crucial to anchor ourselves in the truth of God's Word. Scripture serves as a guiding light in times of darkness, offering wisdom and reassurance when needed most. By immersing ourselves in the promises and teachings of the Bible, we gain perspective and understanding beyond our earthly circumstances. The Psalmist beautifully captures this sentiment, declaring, "Your word is a lamp to my feet and a light to my path" (Psalm 119:105). Even amidst shadows, God's Word illuminates our way, reminding us of His faithfulness and leading us to hope beyond our trials.

Prayers wield immense power, serving as an essential tool in our journey through trials. Through prayer, we pour out our hearts to God, expressing our fears, doubts, and pain. In return, we discover solace as we entrust our burdens to His divine wisdom and guidance. The apostle Paul urges us, stating, "Do not be anxious about anything, but in everything by prayer and supplication with thanksgiving let your requests be made known to God. And the peace of God, which surpasses all understanding, will guard your hearts and your minds in Christ Jesus" (Philippians 4:6-7). Through prayer, we find solace and encounter the incomprehensible peace of God, granting us renewed strength and hope to confront our trials.

Another principle to embrace is the power of community. When confronted with trials, we must acknowledge that we're not alone. God has designed us for fellowship with one another, and through the support and encouragement of fellow believers, we discover strength and renewal. The writer of Hebrews reminds us, "And let us consider how to stir up one another to love and good works, not neglecting to meet together, as is the habit of some, but encouraging one another, and all the more as you see the Day drawing near" (Hebrews 10:24-25). In the company of fellow believers, we encounter the encouragement and support necessary to continue our journey with hope and revitalized determination.

As many of us navigate through trials, cultivating a heart of gratitude becomes paramount. Amidst our difficulties, gratitude shifts our perspective, allowing us to discern the blessings and goodness of God in every season. It enables us to look beyond our immediate circumstances and witness His faithfulness in action. The Apostle Paul urges us with these words, "Rejoice always, pray without ceasing, give thanks in all circumstances; for this is the will of God in Christ Jesus for you" (1 Thessalonians 5:16-18). Gratitude redirects our focus from our trials to the faithfulness of our Heavenly Father, filling our hearts with renewed hope and peace.

Remember, embracing God's salvation equips us with invaluable strategies and principles to navigate trials, find strength, and endure hope amidst adversity. By anchoring ourselves in the truth of His Word, surrendering our burdens through prayer, seeking support in the community, and cultivating a heart of gratitude, we discover that God's salvation is not merely a future promise but a present reality that sustains us in every step of our journey. As you face life's trials, remember that you possess the tools to overcome, drawing on the transformative power of God's salvation.

Whisper Of Hope: Encounters With God's Salvation

As believers and followers of Christ Jesus, we are called to live lives infused with hope, embracing God's salvation and sharing the transformative power of His love with those around us. Our journey of faith isn't solitary, but one meant to be shared, weaving together the threads of hope and salvation into the tapestry of our lives, casting light into a world shadowed by darkness.

Living with hope amidst life's trials isn't always simple, especially when surrounded by news of unrest, injustice, and suffering. Yet, in these moments, we must cling tightly to the unwavering promises of God. Hope isn't just an emotion; it's a firm trust in God's faithfulness. His salvation serves as our steadfast anchor, grounding us in the certainty of His love.

Embracing God's salvation requires humility and recognizing our inability to save ourselves. It's a profound acknowledgment of our dependence on a Savior. In His boundless love, God extends His hand to rescue us from darkness, offering salvation through His Son, Jesus Christ. This salvation isn't a one-time event but an ongoing journey of renewal and transformation.

As we delve deeper into God's boundless love and grace, we witness the profound impact of His salvation unfolding in our lives. No longer ensnared by the shackles of sin and despair, we're liberated to bask in the richness of His love. Through this divine transformation, our very existence becomes a testament to His enduring kindness and compassion, illuminating the path of hope for all to see.

Living with hope and embracing God's salvation propels us to share this remarkable gift with those around us. Our journey isn't solitary but communal, woven into the fabric of relationships where we can extend the warmth of God's love and redemption. Just as we've been touched by His grace, our hearts ache for others to encounter the same life-altering power.

Sharing God's salvation isn't about imposing our beliefs but extending a heartfelt invitation. It's about living authentically, radiating the hope, peace, and love we've discovered in Christ. Through our transparency and openness, we become living testaments to the transformative work of God in our lives.

The acts of love and kindness that spring from a heart touched by God's salvation hold a profound power, often reaching depths we may never fully grasp. Whether through a comforting word, a compassionate deed, or simply lending an ear, these gestures can ignite a spark of hope in others. By sharing God's salvation, we become vessels of His love, catalysts for transformation in a world yearning for healing.

The journey of living with hope and sharing God's salvation is both a tapestry of beauty and a path strewn with challenges. There will be valleys of doubt and moments of uncertainty along the way. Yet, let us cling steadfastly to the assurance that we are never alone. As we embrace hope, accept God's salvation, and extend His love to others, we find ourselves drawn closer to Him, discovering deeper intimacy and fulfillment.

May our lives be beacons of hope, illuminating the truth that God's salvation is available to all who are open to receive it. Let us walk alongside others, extending grace and compassion, ultimately guiding them toward the wellspring of eternal hope found in Him.

As we journey through life with hope and embrace God's salvation, we encounter challenges that test our resolve. Moments of doubt, struggles, and disappointment may arise, serving as opportunities for our faith to deepen and our reliance on God to strengthen.

Living with hope entails entrusting ourselves to God's plan, even when it diverges from our own desires. It requires surrendering our will and yielding to His perfect guidance. In this surrender, we invite His transformative love to shape our lives, leading us to unexpected places and fortifying us to confront whatever trials may come.

Moreover, it's crucial to recognize that hope isn't solely for our own benefit; it's meant to be shared with others. When we encounter individuals grappling with loss, brokenness, or despair, we have the chance to embody hope in their lives. Through our actions, words, and attitudes, we become living testimonies to God's redeeming power, drawing others closer to Him.

In our endeavor to share God's salvation with others, humility and love should guide our approach. Our task isn't to judge or condemn but to extend an invitation to experience the hope and peace found in Christ. This involves fostering intentional relationships, demonstrating kindness, lending a sympathetic ear, and sharing our own struggles and victories authentically. Sometimes, it's through our vulnerability that others find the courage to seek hope and salvation themselves.

Living with hope and sharing God's salvation makes us vessels of His love and grace. Our lives become a testament to His goodness and mercy, directing others to the wellspring of eternal hope. Every act of kindness and every word spoken in love holds the potential to profoundly impact someone's life in ways beyond our comprehension.

The journey of living with hope and sharing God's salvation demands perseverance and resilience. It's not always easy, but with God's strength and guidance, we can press on. As we continue, we'll witness the beauty of transformation not only within ourselves but also in the lives of those around us.

So, let's forge ahead with steadfast hope, knowing that God's salvation isn't exclusive but open to all who seek it. May we persistently extend the love and hope we've discovered in Christ, understanding that our actions hold the power to touch lives, transform hearts, and, ultimately, reshape the world.

As I draw this chapter to a close, I offer a prayer that you carry with you the enduring reminder that hope transcends mere concepts or fleeting feelings; it's the very cornerstone of our existence. By embracing and sharing God's salvation, we become agents of everlasting change. Therefore, continue to embrace hope, journeying alongside God and lighting the way for others until we arrive at the eternal joy awaiting us in His presence.

CHAPTER 9
"The Prayer Warriors Guide"

The Prayer Warrior's Call: Igniting The Flame Of Spiritual Battle

In this chapter, we will explore how to access your inner strength and awaken the warrior within to confront life's challenges head-on.

Life often presents formidable hurdles that can leave us feeling overwhelmed, fearful, and directionless. Yet, deep within each of us resides a formidable force—a wellspring of strength awaiting release: our inner warrior.

What does it entail to awaken this inner warrior? It involves recognizing and harnessing the potent energy inherent within you. It entails acknowledging your inherent resilience, courage, and resolve and directing them towards triumphing over the adversities that cross your path.

It all starts with a shift in mindset. Instead of viewing obstacles as barriers, see them as chances for personal growth and transformation. Embrace them as challenges that can mold you into a stronger, wiser individual. By tapping into your inner warrior, you'll find the courage to confront these obstacles head-on, unafraid to embrace the lessons they offer.

So, how do you awaken your inner warrior? Begin by nurturing self-belief. Have faith in your abilities and trust in your potential to overcome any obstacle. Remember, you're capable of more than you realize. Push aside self-doubt and replace it with unwavering confidence. Once you truly believe in yourself, there will be no limit to what you can achieve.

Next, draw upon your inner resilience. Life's challenges may knock you down, but it's your ability to bounce back that truly defines you. Resilience isn't about avoiding hardships; it's about growing stronger through them. Embrace setbacks and failures as opportunities for growth, letting them fuel your determination. Remember, a warrior doesn't surrender in the face of adversity; they emerge stronger.

To awaken your inner warrior, it's crucial to embrace fear. Fear is a natural aspect of life; it can either paralyze you or propel you forward. Opt for the latter. Embrace fear as a catalyst for growth and transformation. Let it nudge you out of your comfort zone and into a world of endless possibilities. Take risks, confront your fears, and uncover the remarkable strength that lies within.

Furthermore, never underestimate the power of perseverance. The path to awakening your inner warrior won't be smooth. There will be setbacks, moments of uncertainty, and instances when quitting seems tempting. Yet, it's in those moments that your true resilience shines. Persist, cling to your vision, and keep pushing ahead. Warrior never gives up; they persist until the very end.

As you embark on this journey of awakening your inner warrior, remember that you're not alone. Seek guidance and encouragement from those who believe in you. Surround yourself with individuals who uplift and motivate you to unleash your full potential.

Now, take a moment to pause and reflect. Close your eyes and sense the power stirring within you. Envision the warrior residing deep within, poised to tackle any challenges that lie ahead. Though the journey has just commenced, with each forward stride, you awaken a strength that has long slumbered within.

So, embrace your inner warrior. Stir awake that fierce, untamed spirit nestled in your heart. Allow it to lead you through life's twists and turns. Draw upon your inner reservoir of strength, and witness as you conquer obstacles that once loomed insurmountable. The adventure beckons; are you prepared to unleash your inner warrior?

Now that you've embarked on the journey of awakening your inner warrior, it's time to delve deeper into the process. In this segment of the chapter, we'll explore additional strategies and practices to help you fully unleash your inner strength and overcome obstacles.

One vital aspect of awakening your inner warrior is nurturing a positive mindset. Your thoughts and beliefs shape your reality, making it crucial to foster a mindset that empowers and uplifts you. Replace negative self-talk with affirmations and encouragement. Remind yourself of your strengths, talents, and past accomplishments. Practicing gratitude and focusing on the positives in your life can also shift your mindset toward optimism.

Another potent tool in awakening your inner warrior is fostering resilience through self-care. Taking care of your physical, mental, and emotional well-being is essential for building the strength and endurance needed to tackle life's challenges. Prioritize adequate sleep, proper nutrition, regular exercise, and breaks to recharge. Cultivate your spirit through activities that bring joy, like spending time in nature, practicing mindfulness, or pursuing hobbies you're passionate about. Remember, self-care isn't selfish—it's an investment in your overall health.

As you progress on your journey, practicing self-compassion is crucial. Be kind and understanding toward yourself, especially during tough times. Recognize setbacks and failures as opportunities for growth. Treat yourself with the same compassion and forgiveness you'd offer a dear friend. Embracing self-compassion enhances your resilience, enabling you to rebound from challenges and keep moving forward.

In addition to self-compassion, conquering self-doubt is crucial for awakening your inner warrior. Confront and challenge any negative beliefs or doubts that hinder your progress. Reflect on the strides you've already taken and the obstacles you've conquered. Cultivate a mindset that believes in your abilities and trusts your potential. You possess the capability to surpass your perceived limits and transform your aspirations into reality.

Keep in mind that awakening your inner warrior is an ongoing journey. It's not a destination but a continual process that demands dedication and perseverance. Celebrate each step forward, no matter how small, and let them propel you onward.

The journey to unlocking your inner warrior is indeed challenging, but the rewards are immense. By accessing your inner strength, you'll discover the courage, resilience, and determination necessary to conquer any obstacle. Embrace the lessons gleaned from each experience, allowing them to shape you into a stronger, wiser individual.

Know that you're not traversing this path alone. Lean on your support system for guidance, encouragement, and inspiration. Share your dreams and aspirations with those who wholeheartedly believe in you. Surround yourself with individuals who uplift and empower you as you continue to unleash your full potential.

As you reflect on these words, remember that within you resides a potent force waiting to be set free. Embrace your inner warrior, allowing its fierce spirit to lead you, and witness as you triumph over obstacles that once seemed insurmountable. The adventure beckons, and you stand poised to embrace your true strength.

The journey to unlocking your inner warrior is indeed challenging, but the rewards are immense. By accessing your inner strength, you'll discover the courage, resilience, and determination necessary to conquer any obstacle. Embrace the lessons gleaned from each experience, allowing them to shape you into a stronger, wiser individual.

As you reflect on these words, remember that within you resides a potent force waiting to be set free. Embrace your inner warrior, allowing its fierce spirit to lead you, and witness as you triumph over obstacles that once seemed insurmountable. The adventure beckons, and you stand poised to embrace your true strength.

Never underestimate the power within you or the immense strength you hold. Access your inner warrior, embrace the journey, and witness the transformation of not just your own life but also the lives of those around you. You are capable, you are resilient, and you are prepared. Unleash your inner warrior and conquer the world with your steadfast determination.

Prayer: A Pathway To Inner Peace

Unlock the profound power of prayer to transform your life and provide guidance and support in times of need. Prayer is an incredible tool that connects us to something greater, enabling us to access our inner strength and overcome any obstacles that come our way.

Here, we'll explore the deep impact that prayer can have on our lives and delve into strategies for cultivating a strong prayer practice.

Prayer has been practiced for centuries across diverse cultures and religions. It serves as a universal language, transcending boundaries and uniting individuals in their quest for connection with the divine. Regardless of our spiritual beliefs, prayer offers solace, hope, and encouragement. It's a profound act of surrendering our worries, fears, and desires to a higher power, allowing us to find peace amidst life's turmoil.

The power of prayer extends beyond mere comfort; it holds a transformative essence. Through prayer, we open ourselves to receive guidance and strength from the universe, engaging in a sacred dialogue between our soul and the divine. This communion aligns our intentions with a higher purpose, enabling us to access the profound wisdom and energy within.

A remarkable aspect of prayer is its capacity to cultivate deep faith and resilience within us. Active participation in prayer serves as a reminder of our inherent connection to something greater, fueling our inner strength to confront life's challenges with courage and determination. Prayer empowers us to navigate difficult times, anchoring our belief in a guiding light that leads us forward.

Building a robust prayer practice demands consistency and intention. Dedicate a sacred space or time exclusively for prayer. Whether it's a serene corner of your home, a tranquil outdoor setting, or a personal altar adorned with meaningful items like candles or scripture, let it be a tangible reminder of the divine presence you seek.

When you engage in prayer, begin by grounding yourself and entering a state of mindfulness. Take a few deep breaths, allowing your body and mind to relax. Feel the weight of the world lifting off your shoulders as you surrender your worries and fears. Open your heart and mind to the vast possibilities that prayer can bring forth.

As you start to pray, express gratitude for the blessings in your life. Gratitude is a powerful force that can shift your perspective and ignite a sense of joy and abundance. Acknowledge the lessons learned from past experiences and embrace the opportunities for growth that lie ahead. Let your prayers encompass gratitude, requests for guidance and words of affirmation. Trust that the universe hears your prayers and will respond in its perfect timing.

Remember, prayer isn't solely about asking for help; it's also about actively listening. Be open to receiving messages, signs, and insights from the divine. Pay attention to synchronicities and the subtle whispers of intuition. God hears your prayers, knows your heart, and communicates with us in various ways. Through prayer, we create the space to hear His gentle voice guiding us.

As we embark on this journey of exploring the power of prayer, let's set aside our doubts and skepticism and embrace the boundless possibilities that lie ahead. Prayer holds the remarkable ability to transform our lives, providing us with strength, guidance, and a profound sense of connection. It serves as a gateway to our innermost selves and the divine. Open your heart, tap into the power within, and allow prayer to become a cornerstone of your life's journey.

Continuing our exploration of prayer, it's important to recognize its transformative impact on our mindset and emotions. Prayer isn't just a one-sided conversation; it's a dynamic exchange of energy that allows us to release negative emotions and cultivate inner peace and joy.

Here, we'll delve into practical tips and techniques to enhance your prayer practice and fully unleash your inner power. Let's begin by discussing the importance of mindfulness and visualization in prayer.

When engaging in prayer, take a moment to ground yourself in the present moment. Focus solely on your connection with the divine, letting go of distractions and worries. This mindfulness opens the door for a deeper, more meaningful prayer experience. Visualize yourself surrounded by a radiant light, symbolizing the divine energy within and around you. Envision this light, enveloping you with love, strength, and guidance.

Another way to boost your prayer practice is by using affirmations. Affirmations are positive statements that help reprogram your mind to align with your intentions. You can integrate affirmations into your prayers by saying them out loud or silently to yourself. For example, instead of just asking for healing, you can affirm, "I am now experiencing vibrant health in every part of my body." This helps you align your energy with what you want to happen.

Gratitude is also really important in prayer. Expressing gratitude not only strengthens your connection with God but also helps you appreciate the good things in your life. Take a moment to thank God for the support, guidance, and opportunities you've received. Gratitude brings more positive energy and opens the door for even more blessings.

Now, let's talk about faith and surrender in prayer. Having strong faith in prayer is key. Trust that the universe is always working in your favor, even when things seem uncertain. Surrender your worries and desires, knowing that things will work out for the best. Let go of trying to control everything, and let the universe guide you towards your goals and dreams.

Lastly, prayer is strengthened by the support of a like-minded community. Connect with others who share your beliefs and values, and join groups where you can pray together. Collective prayer boosts its effectiveness and fosters a supportive environment for spiritual growth.

As we wrap up our discussion on prayer, I urge you to make these practices a part of your daily life. See prayer as a positive conversation with God, surrendering to its potential for transformation and trusting the process. Remember, prayer is a lifelong journey that deepens your connection with God and equips you to overcome challenges.

You've now discovered the key to unlocking your inner strength and facing life's challenges with grace and resilience. Embrace prayer as a constant source of hope and guidance on your journey.

Unshaken: Standing Firm Through Life's Storms Of Fear And Doubt

Fear and doubt are powerful emotions that can hold us back from reaching our dreams and living our best lives. They sneak into our minds, building barriers and limiting beliefs that hinder our progress. But what if we could find practical ways to overcome these challenges? What if we could tap into our inner strength and push past these obstacles, stepping into our full potential and achieving greatness? This chapter explores these aspects of our lives in detail.

In today's fast-paced world, fear and doubt can show up in many forms. We might fear failure, rejection, or uncertainty about what lies ahead. Doubt whispers in our ears, questioning our abilities and sowing seeds of uncertainty. Yet, it's crucial to recognize that fear and doubt are natural emotions. They don't signal weakness but rather opportunities for growth and self-discovery.

The first step in overcoming fear and doubt is acknowledging their presence. It's tempting to bury these feelings, hoping they'll fade away. But they don't. Instead, they grow louder, threatening to overshadow our potential. By acknowledging them, we take back control of our emotions and pave the way for transformation.

Once we acknowledge fear and doubt, we can start questioning their validity. Often, these feelings arise from past experiences or external influences. It's important to ask ourselves whether these anxieties are based on truth or just illusions. By examining their source closely, we can diminish their hold on us and take steps to overcome them.

Developing resilience is also key in facing fear and doubt. Resilience helps us bounce back from setbacks with renewed determination. It means seeing failure as a chance to learn and grow, fostering a positive outlook. When we view challenges as opportunities rather than obstacles, we can navigate toward our goals with greater resilience.

Self-reflection is crucial on the journey to conquering fear and doubt. Understanding our values, strengths, and weaknesses lays a solid foundation. When we truly know ourselves, we can tap into our inner strength to combat fear and doubt. Reflecting on past successes and moments of overcoming obstacles reminds us of the potential within us.

Finally, seeking support from others can be a crucial source of encouragement and motivation when facing fear and doubt. Surrounding ourselves with people who believe in us and our goals can give us the strength to keep moving forward. Sharing our fears and doubts with trusted friends or family members not only lightens the burden but also brings fresh perspectives and potential solutions.

As we continue exploring this topic, we'll delve into practical techniques and exercises aimed at helping you conquer fear and doubt. Together, we'll uncover the hidden potential within you and tap into a strength that can overcome any obstacle. Get ready for the journey ahead, as your true potential awaits, ready to be unleashed.

The path to overcoming fear and doubt isn't always straightforward. It's filled with highs and lows, challenges and breakthroughs. But as we navigate this transformative journey, it's important to remember to be kind to ourselves. Practicing self-compassion is a powerful tool in conquering fear and doubt.

When we encounter challenges, it's natural to feel disheartened and doubt our abilities. But in those moments, we should remind ourselves that we're only human and that it's okay to stumble. Practicing self-compassion means acknowledging our fears and doubts without judgment and treating ourselves with the same kindness we'd offer to a close friend.

Boost self-compassion by using positive self-talk. Replace negative thoughts with gentle and encouraging words. Reflect on your past achievements and recognize your strengths. Celebrate even the smallest victories along the way. By nurturing self-compassion, we lay a strong foundation of self-belief that helps us tackle fear and doubt.

Visualization is another effective technique for overcoming fear and doubt. Close your eyes and picture yourself standing tall, confident, and capable. Visualize yourself triumphantly overcoming obstacles that once seemed daunting. Envision achieving your goals and realizing your dreams. By consistently imagining these positive outcomes, we retrain our minds to focus on possibilities rather than limitations.

In addition to visualization, practicing positive affirmations can have a significant impact on shifting our mindset. Repeat uplifting statements to yourself, such as "I am strong," "I am capable," and "I am worthy of success." By reinforcing these affirmations, we cultivate a positive internal dialogue that counteracts the negative influence of fear and doubt.

As we continue on the journey of overcoming fear and doubt, it's important to remember that we don't have to walk this path alone. Look for a supportive community that shares your aspirations and values. Surrounding yourself with like-minded individuals who understand your challenges can offer valuable encouragement and motivation.

Beyond finding support in communities, consider seeking guidance from a mentor or coach. These individuals can provide valuable insights, strategies, and encouragement tailored to your unique journey. They can help you navigate obstacles and offer the accountability needed to stay focused on your goals.

Remember, overcoming fear and doubt isn't about completely eliminating these emotions but rather learning to handle and utilize their power. Embrace the discomfort that comes with confronting your fears, as it's in these moments that real growth happens.

Take a moment to look back on your journey. Reflect on the progress you've already made in conquering fear and doubt. Recognize the inner strength and resilience within you. Trust that you have the ability to achieve greatness despite any fears or doubts that may arise.

With the right strategies, mindset, and support, you have the ability to unlock your true potential. Embrace challenges, step into the unknown, and always remember that life's purpose isn't to avoid fear and doubt but to rise above them.

Keep moving forward, for the next phase of your transformation awaits, ready to be revealed.

Rising Strong: Embracing Resilience To Bounce Back Stronger

Arm yourself with the tools necessary to rebound from setbacks and cultivate resilience to confront challenges with unwavering determination.

Resilience is a vital trait that guides us through life's ebbs and flows, enabling us to surmount obstacles and emerge stronger in the face of adversity. It equips us with the capacity to persist, adapt, and ultimately thrive. In this chapter, we'll explore various strategies and techniques to nurture resilience, empowering you to embrace challenges and emerge stronger than before.

One of the initial steps in fostering resilience is fostering a positive mindset. It's important to recognize that setbacks and challenges are inherent to life. Instead of viewing them as insurmountable barriers, see them as opportunities for growth. Focus on the lessons gleaned from each experience and approach them with curiosity and a thirst for knowledge. By reframing your perspective, you can transform obstacles into catalysts for personal growth.

Another effective method for building resilience is through self-reflection and self-awareness. Take time to understand your strengths, weaknesses, and triggers. Recognize how you typically react to stress and setbacks and pinpoint any negative thought patterns that might hinder your progress. By being self-aware, you can gain a deeper understanding of yourself and develop strategies to navigate challenges more effectively.

Creating a solid support network is also essential for fostering resilience. Surround yourself with people who uplift and motivate you. Seek out mentors and role models who have overcome adversity and emerged stronger. Their experiences can offer valuable insights and guidance as you face your own challenges. Additionally, rely on your friends and family for emotional support during tough times. Knowing that you have a support system that believes in you can boost your courage and resilience.

In moments of setback, practicing self-compassion is crucial. Be gentle with yourself and understand that it's okay to stumble along the way. Treat yourself with the same kindness and empathy you would extend to a close friend. Remember, resilience isn't about being invincible but about having the strength and determination to pick yourself up each time you fall.

An essential part of developing resilience is being able to adapt to change. Life is always changing, and being able to adjust and embrace new situations is crucial. Understand that change can bring opportunities for growth and learning. Keep an open mind and be flexible in your thinking. Embracing change can help you overcome obstacles and thrive in an ever-changing world.

As you begin your journey to develop resilience, remember that it's a lifelong process. It takes consistent effort, but the benefits are huge. By having a positive mindset, reflecting on yourself, building a strong support system, and embracing change, you'll equip yourself with the tools to bounce back from setbacks. Challenges will come, but with resilience, you'll navigate through them and come out stronger.

So, as you start on this path of resilience, have faith that you already have the inner strength to overcome any obstacle. The journey may be tough, but the growth and transformation you'll experience will be worth it.

Stick with me as I delve into specific techniques to build resilience and conquer even the toughest challenges. Until then, hold onto your determination and embrace the journey ahead. Now, let's dive into those specific techniques that will help you build resilience and overcome any challenge. These strategies will empower you to tap into your inner strength and unleash your limitless potential.

A powerful way to build resilience is by reframing your mindset. Train yourself to see setbacks as opportunities for growth, as stepping stones toward personal development. Instead of focusing on the negatives, concentrate on the lessons learned and the potential for self-improvement. This change in perspective will help you approach obstacles with renewed determination and curiosity, pushing you forward on your journey.

Another effective strategy is to develop coping skills. Identify techniques that help you manage stress and maintain balance amidst life's chaos. This could involve physical activities like exercise or yoga, practicing mindfulness and meditation, or journaling to express your emotions and thoughts. By exploring different coping mechanisms, you'll discover what works best for you and be better prepared to face challenges head-on.

As you build resilience, cultivate optimism and hope. Believe in your ability to overcome obstacles and in brighter days ahead. Even in adversity, remind yourself that setbacks are temporary and that you have the strength to persevere. Surround yourself with positive affirmations and inspirational quotes that fuel your determination and remind you of your inner strength.

Furthermore, maintaining healthy boundaries is vital for building resilience. Be aware of your limits and learn when to say no. Prioritize self-care and heed the needs of your body and mind. Resilience starts with a solid foundation, and that foundation begins with taking care of yourself. Remember, you can't pour from an empty cup, so make self-care an essential part of your daily routine.

In the face of challenges, it's normal to feel overwhelmed or disheartened at times. During such moments, practicing self-compassion is crucial. Be kind and understanding with yourself, just as you would with a close friend. Remind yourself that it's okay to stumble and that setbacks don't define your worth. Treat yourself with the same love and kindness you would offer to someone you deeply care about.

Lastly, embrace the power of gratitude. While it's easy to dwell on what's going wrong, shifting your focus to what you're grateful for cultivates a mindset of abundance and resilience. Make expressing gratitude a daily habit, whether through journaling or simply taking a moment to appreciate the blessings in your life. Gratitude lays a sturdy foundation for navigating challenges, reminding you of the strength and blessings within your reach.

As you continue your journey, remember that building resilience is a lifelong process. It requires consistent effort, but the benefits are invaluable. Through a positive mindset, coping skills, optimism, healthy boundaries, self-compassion, and gratitude, you're arming yourself with the tools to bounce back from setbacks and overcome any obstacle with unwavering determination.

So, have confidence in yourself and the strength you possess within. Embrace the challenges ahead, knowing that you have the ability to conquer them. May this journey of resilience not only cultivate incredible inner strength but also foster growth, transformation, and a life brimming with endless possibilities.

Stay encouraged, and keep unleashing your inner warrior.

The Power Within: Cultivating A Resilient Positive Mindset

Discover the strength of a positive mindset and uncover how to reframe negative thoughts, empowering you to tackle obstacles with optimism and composure.

In life, we'll inevitably encounter hurdles and challenges that leave us feeling overwhelmed and deflated. These obstacles come in various shapes and sizes, from personal setbacks and professional letdowns to unforeseen circumstances that push us to our limits. While it's tempting to let negativity take hold, it's precisely during these moments that nurturing a positive mindset becomes essential.

A positive mindset isn't just about plastering on a smile and pretending everything is okay. It's a deliberate choice to shift our perspective and confront challenges with optimism and resilience. When adversity strikes, our initial reaction may be to dwell on the negatives, sinking into a sea of self-doubt and pessimism. However, fostering a positive mindset allows us to transform these negative thoughts into opportunities for growth and personal advancement.

One effective method for nurturing a positive mindset is through reframing. It involves consciously shifting our perspective to find the silver lining in even the toughest situations. By reframing our thoughts, we can uncover meaning and purpose in our experiences, enabling us to tackle obstacles with poise.

When faced with a setback, ask yourself: What lessons can I take from this? How can this experience contribute to my growth? Instead of dwelling on the negatives, focus on the opportunities for learning and development that exist within. By reframing our outlook, we can turn setbacks into stepping stones toward personal and professional advancement.

Another crucial aspect of fostering a positive mindset is the practice of self-affirmation. The way we speak to ourselves profoundly influences our thoughts, emotions, and behaviors. Affirmations, which are positive statements we repeat to ourselves, can help rewire our subconscious mind by challenging negative beliefs and reinforcing positive ones.

Remember, your mind holds more power than you may realize. It follows its most dominant thoughts. What does this mean? It reflects the principle that our predominant thoughts shape our experiences and perceptions. This concept is often linked with the law of attraction and the influence of positive thinking. By focusing on empowering thoughts, we can attract more positive outcomes and foster a more optimistic mindset. Conversely, dwelling on negative thoughts can spiral into negativity, hindering personal growth and happiness. Hence, being aware of our dominant thoughts and intentionally shifting them towards positivity can profoundly impact our well-being and success.

Incorporating positive affirmations into our daily routine helps counteract the negative self-talk that often clouds our minds. Repeat statements such as, "I am capable and resilient" or "I embrace challenges as opportunities for growth." These affirmations serve as gentle reminders of our inner strength and potential, empowering us to confront obstacles with confidence and optimism.

Furthermore, cultivating a positive mindset involves practicing gratitude. Gratitude redirects our focus from what's lacking to what we already have. It's a potent tool that nurtures contentment, resilience, and an appreciation for abundance in our lives.

Take a moment each day to reflect on what you're grateful for, no matter how small or seemingly insignificant. It could be as simple as a warm cup of coffee in the morning or a supportive friend. Through gratitude, we foster an appreciation for the present moment and develop the ability to find joy even amidst adversity.

As we delve deeper into the power of a positive mindset, we'll explore various techniques and practical exercises to help you navigate obstacles with optimism and grace. Through these practices, you'll begin to unlock your inner strength and tap into your boundless potential.

Remember, cultivating a positive mindset is a journey, not a destination. It demands patience, self-compassion, and a readiness to challenge our own limiting beliefs. By embracing positivity, we unlock a realm of possibilities where obstacles morph into opportunities, and setbacks pave the way for personal growth.

We've only just skimmed the surface of what it takes to nurture a positive mindset. The road ahead promises even more valuable insights and practical tools for facing challenges with grace and optimism. Prepare yourself for this journey as we delve deeper into the techniques and strategies that will guide you toward cultivating an unshakeable positive mindset. Brace yourself for the transformative potential that lies ahead. As we progress on this transformative journey, remember that fostering a positive mindset isn't about ignoring or denying our challenges but about facing them with optimism and grace.

A potent technique for nurturing a positive mindset is visualization. It involves crafting vivid mental images of yourself triumphantly overcoming obstacles and achieving your goals. By visualizing positive outcomes, we can rewire our brains to believe in our own potential and boost our motivation to take action.

Spend a moment each day closing your eyes and picturing yourself confidently facing challenges, finding innovative solutions, and relishing the joy and fulfillment that accompany overcoming obstacles. Envision the steps you need to take and the actions required to turn your goals into reality. Through consistent visualization, you'll align your thoughts and actions with your desired positive outcomes, ultimately bringing them to fruition.

Another valuable technique for fostering a positive mindset is reframing setbacks as opportunities for personal growth and learning. Rather than seeing challenges as barriers, start viewing them as stepping stones that propel you forward. Embrace the notion that setbacks aren't failures but valuable lessons that refine and shape your character.

When confronted with a setback, ponder: How can I turn this experience into a stepping stone for personal growth? What insights can I glean from this situation? By shifting your perspective and focusing on the lessons and opportunities for growth, you'll rebound from setbacks with resilience and determination.

Alongside reframing setbacks, practicing self-compassion is crucial for fostering a positive mindset. We all encounter obstacles and make mistakes, and it's vital to treat ourselves with kindness and understanding during such times. Instead of falling into self-criticism and blame, extend self-compassion by acknowledging and embracing your emotions, failures, and imperfections.

Treat yourself as you would a dear friend or cherished loved one facing a challenging moment. Offer yourself words of encouragement, forgiveness, and empathy. Remember that mistakes and setbacks are part of life's journey and don't define your worth or potential. Through practicing self-compassion, you'll nurture a positive mindset rooted in self-love and acceptance.

Finally, immerse yourself in positivity. Your surroundings wield a significant influence on your mindset, so consciously craft a positive and uplifting environment. Surround yourself with individuals who inspire and motivate you; their energy will propel you forward on your journey.

Explore resources like books, podcasts, or online communities that foster positivity and personal growth. Infuse your space with objects, quotes, or visuals that remind you of your goals, strengths, and the boundless opportunities ahead.

In wrapping up, remember that cultivating a positive mindset demands ongoing commitment and practice. Embrace the techniques and strategies discussed here, allowing them to guide you toward unleashing your inner strength and facing obstacles with optimism and grace.

The transformation sparked by a positive mindset extends far beyond this chapter. It's an ongoing journey that will continually enrich your life in profound ways. Embrace this journey, trust in your abilities, and recognize your capacity to overcome any challenge.

With an unyielding positive mindset, you'll navigate life's challenges with resilience, believing in your potential and forging a path toward personal growth and fulfillment. Stay dedicated, stay inspired, and embrace the endless possibilities that await on your journey toward becoming the best version of yourself.

The Power Of Faith: Strengthening Your Relationship With God

Explore avenues to fortify your faith and enhance your spiritual bond, laying a sturdy groundwork to navigate life's challenges. Life's journey is often unpredictable and fraught with trials, yet our faith stands as a beacon in times of uncertainty. Strengthening our faith grants us the inner resilience to confront obstacles and approach the world with optimism and bravery.

At its essence, faith embodies belief in something beyond ourselves—a steadfast trust in a higher power, whatever form it assumes for each individual. While faith remains deeply personal, there exist practical steps to cultivate and reinforce it in our lives.

The initial stride in fortifying your faith involves engaging in spiritual practices. Regular prayer, meditation, and contemplation foster a deeper communion with the divine. Allocate time daily for these rituals, fashioning a sacred sanctuary where you can commune with your higher power and heed the whispers of your heart, spirit, and soul.

Furthermore, delving into scripture and spiritual teachings serves as a potent means to bolster your faith. Every religion brims with profound wisdom and guidance, capable of inspiring and uplifting us. Select a sacred text that resonates with you and delves into its teachings. Let its words permeate your being, guiding you along your spiritual odyssey.

Community plays a vital role in nurturing faith. Surrounding yourself with like-minded individuals who share your beliefs offers support, encouragement, and inspiration. Whether through spiritual groups, religious services, or meaningful conversations, engaging with others deepens your understanding of faith. Together, you grow and learn, fostering a sense of belonging and connection.

In moments of doubt or adversity, gratitude becomes a guiding light. It's easy to lose sight of faith during challenging times. Cultivating gratitude shifts our focus from scarcity to abundance. Take a daily moment to reflect on life's blessings. Embracing gratitude strengthens faith as you recognize the myriad ways your higher power guides and supports you.

Faith isn't mere optimism; it's a proactive belief empowering us to confront life's challenges. Strengthening faith means stepping beyond comfort zones and embracing growth opportunities. Through such experiences, we uncover the depths of our inner strength and the resilience of our spirit.

In your faith journey, setbacks and doubts are natural. Even the strongest believers face moments of uncertainty. Embrace these moments as opportunities to deepen your trust in your higher power. Have faith that you are being guided, even when the path seems unclear. Trust that each challenge shapes you into the person you're meant to be.

In this chapter and throughout the book, we'll explore practical ways to deepen your spiritual connection and overcome obstacles to your faith. Together, we'll delve into rituals, self-reflection, and service, uncovering tools to unleash your inner strength. Join us on this transformative journey as we explore the power of rituals, self-reflection, and service in deepening our spiritual connection and overcoming obstacles. These practical strategies will nourish your soul and strengthen your faith.

Rituals have stood as pillars of faith for centuries, offering structure and significance to our existence. Whether it's a daily prayer, the lighting of candles, or participation in religious ceremonies, rituals create sacred moments that draw us closer to God. These practices not only fortify our faith but also usher in a sense of peace and calmness. Discover rituals that resonate with you and weave them into your daily life. Through these consistent acts of devotion, we invite the divine into our midst.

In tandem with rituals, self-reflection is pivotal in nurturing our spiritual bond. Dedicate time to ponder your beliefs, values, and life experiences, extracting lessons and wisdom from them. Self-reflection enables us to identify areas for growth and areas where our faith may need tending. It's in this introspective journey that we confront doubts, fears, and uncertainties, emerging stronger on the other side. Embrace moments of stillness and solitude, allowing your soul's voice to illuminate your path.

Service is the embodiment of faith in action. Engaging in acts of kindness and compassion not only bolsters our faith but also enriches the lives of others. Whether it's volunteering at a local charity, lending a helping hand to a neighbor, or simply being there for a friend in need, acts of service underscore the interconnectedness of humanity and the potency of love. Seek out opportunities to make a positive impact on others' lives and experience the fulfillment that comes from aligning your deeds with your faith.

As you integrate these practices into your life, remember that faith is a lifelong journey, not a one-time achievement.

There will be moments of doubt, setbacks, and challenges along the way. Embrace these trials as avenues for growth and lean into your faith with unwavering conviction. Faith isn't about having all the answers but about entrusting ourselves to something beyond ourselves. Trust that your higher power is ever-present, even amid uncertainty.

Amid life's challenges, may you find comfort in the unyielding bond between your faith and your inner strength. As you journey forward, remain receptive to the divine whispers that guide you, inspiring you to greater heights. May your faith deepen, your spirit soar, and your inner resilience flourish, enabling you to conquer any hurdle in your path.

Nurturing your faith is an ongoing endeavor, demanding commitment, introspection, and action. Embrace rituals to forge sacred connections and commune with the divine. Dedicate time to self-reflection, unearthing insights, and nurturing your spiritual growth. Embrace acts of service as manifestations of your beliefs. Remember, setbacks and uncertainties are part of the journey, but trust in the guidance of your higher power. As you progress along this transformative path, may you unlock your inner strength and triumph over any challenge that crosses your way.

Embrace The Journey: Transforming Through Change

Change is an inevitable part of life's journey. At every turn, we encounter moments where the familiar shifts, propelling us into uncharted territory. While the idea of change may stir up feelings of uncertainty and fear, embracing it can be truly transformative. It's an opportunity to unlock our inner strength and overcome the obstacles that lie ahead.

Amidst change, there's room for growth. Stepping out of our comfort zones allows us to explore new possibilities and unearth hidden talents. Embracing change means embracing new aspects of ourselves, revealing resilience and adaptability we never knew we had. Instead of resisting change, we can choose to see it as a gateway to personal evolution, propelling us toward greater heights.

Adaptability is key when navigating change's twists and turns. Just as the seasons transition, life presents its own periods of change. Each shift offers a chance to flex our adaptability muscles and find fresh meaning in our experiences. It's all about mindset—seeing change not as a threat but as an opportunity to chart new paths and uncover untapped potential.

Embracing change broadens our horizons and offers new perspectives. Holding onto the familiar limits our worldview, but welcoming change enriches us with fresh insights and experiences. It serves as a catalyst for personal growth, fostering qualities like compassion and empathy.

While change isn't always easy, it requires courage and determination. Yet, within its challenges lies our hidden strength—the power to adapt and overcome. Each obstacle we encounter is a stepping stone toward our true potential.

The path of embracing change may seem unclear and daunting, but with each challenge, we unlock our inner resilience. We learn to trust in ourselves and our ability to adapt, transforming change from a foe into an ally.

As we navigate change and nurture our inner strengths, we become prayer warriors—individuals who draw upon faith and resilience to conquer any obstacle. With a positive mindset, we turn change into an opportunity for growth and self-discovery.

In times of uncertainty, remember that change isn't something to fear but something to welcome. Without change, our growth is stunted. So, let's embrace change wholeheartedly. As we embark on this journey, we discover more about ourselves, find empowerment, and open ourselves to endless possibilities.

As we journey through change, it's important to understand that it's not a straight path. Change comes with its share of setbacks and challenges, testing our determination. Yet, it's in these tough moments that our inner strength truly shines. With each obstacle we conquer, we grow more resilient and better equipped to handle life's twists and turns.

Embracing change means being willing to let go of the past. Clinging to what's familiar can stunt our growth and block the new opportunities waiting for us. By releasing our grip on the past, we make room for fresh starts and unexpected blessings. When we accept change as inevitable, we open ourselves to endless possibilities.

In the realm of change, surrender plays a vital role. Surrendering to life's flow connects us to a greater power that guides us through uncertainty. Letting go of the urge to control every detail allows us to be carried by the current of change, trusting it to lead us where we need to be.

During times of change, it's crucial to lean on our support networks and seek guidance. Change isn't meant to be faced alone. Drawing strength and comfort from loved ones, mentors, and kindred spirits helps us feel supported and less isolated amid uncertainty. Sharing our journey with others fosters a sense of connection and belonging.

In times of change, self-care is crucial. Prioritizing our physical, mental, and emotional well-being is essential. Taking moments for rest, reflection, and activities that bring joy helps us navigate change with clarity and resilience. Whether it's through meditation, exercise, or simply doing what makes us happy, self-care forms the bedrock of our growth and adaptability.

Let's remember that change isn't a one-time event or a destination; it's an ongoing journey. It's a lifelong process of discovering ourselves and evolving personally. By embracing change with open hearts and minds, we embark on a path of continuous growth and transformation.

With every stride forward, we tap into our inner strength and conquer hurdles that once felt overwhelming. As prayer warriors, we wield the power of faith and resilience to rise above challenges. We become beacons of hope and encouragement, demonstrating that change isn't something to dread but an opportunity for self-realization and growth.

So, let's march forward, fellow prayer warriors, with courage and determination. Within us lies the strength to embrace change and overcome any obstacle. Together, we can navigate life's uncertainties, thrive in the face of change, and unlock our full potential.

Raising A Village: Fostering Supportive Communities

The strength of a supportive community is undeniable. When life throws challenges our way, having a group of people who believe in us, encourage us, and stand by our side can make a world of difference.

In this discussion, we'll delve into why surrounding yourself with a supportive community is essential and how it can truly unlock your inner strength to conquer any adversity.

Life isn't meant to be lived in solitude. We're social creatures, craving connection and a sense of belonging. Cultivating a supportive community enables us to tap into the collective strength and wisdom of others. When we join forces with like-minded individuals who share similar passions and aspirations, we create an environment where mutual support flourishes.

One of the primary benefits of a supportive community is the encouragement it offers. During moments of self-doubt or when facing setbacks, having people who genuinely believe in us can boost our confidence and reignite our inner drive. Their words of encouragement serve as reminders of our potential and motivate us to continue striving for greatness.

Furthermore, a supportive community provides a safe haven for vulnerability. By openly sharing our struggles and challenges, we foster an atmosphere of trust and empathy. In this environment, we come to realize that we're not alone in our difficulties and that others have encountered similar obstacles. The shared experiences and tales of resilience become a well of inspiration, demonstrating that we too possess the strength to prevail.

Unity and collaboration are essential components of a supportive community. When we unite with others who share our vision, we can achieve much more than we could alone. Each individual brings unique skills, knowledge, and perspectives to the table, resulting in a collective brilliance that drives us forward. Together, we can dream bigger, innovate, and unleash our full potential.

Picture a community where everyone supports one another, lifting each other up and rejoicing in each other's successes. It's a place devoid of judgment and competition, where teamwork and cooperation thrive. This is the type of community that not only helps individuals overcome obstacles but also fosters personal growth and transformation.

Once you embrace the power of surrounding yourself with a supportive community, the possibilities become limitless. You no longer have to tackle challenges solo or feel burdened by the weight of your aspirations. The combined strength and encouragement of your community become a formidable force that propels you toward your objectives.

As we embark on the journey of cultivating a supportive community, let's start with a simple step. Seek out those who share your passions and goals, engaging in activities and groups that reflect your values. Extend a hand of support to those around you, reaching out to connect with like-minded individuals.

Here, we'll explore practical strategies for building and nurturing a supportive community. We'll discuss how to find and connect with people who resonate with your vision, as well as ways to develop genuine relationships.

But for now, let's ponder the strength that comes from a supportive community. Remember, you're never alone on this journey. Together, we can conquer any challenge and unleash our inner warriors.

We'll also dive into practical ways to build and nurture a supportive community. We'll discuss how to find and connect with individuals who share your vision, as well as different approaches to fostering genuine relationships.

To create a supportive community, it's important to find like-minded individuals who share your passions and goals. Start by exploring groups or organizations that match your interests. Whether it's a local charity, a hobby club, or a professional network, these communities can be a great place to meet people who understand and support your journey.

Attending events, workshops, and conferences related to your interests can also help you connect with like-minded individuals. Engage in meaningful conversations, listen to others' experiences, and be open to forming connections. Remember, building a supportive community isn't just about finding people who can benefit you but also about being genuinely interested in others and offering your support to them.

In addition to physical communities, the digital world offers a vast array of opportunities. Online forums, social media groups, and platforms dedicated to specific interests enable us to connect with people from diverse backgrounds, transcending geographical boundaries. Engage in conversations, share your experiences, and offer support and encouragement to those in need. The beauty of these virtual communities lies in the diversity of perspectives they offer, enriching our understanding and broadening our horizons.

When cultivating a supportive community, fostering genuine relationships is paramount. This entails actively listening to others, respecting their viewpoints, and extending a helping hand when necessary. By consistently showing up and being present for others, we not only strengthen our connections but also create a safe environment for vulnerability and personal growth.

Moreover, collaboration plays a pivotal role in nurturing a supportive community. Look for opportunities to collaborate on projects, exchange ideas, and share resources. Embrace a spirit of cooperation rather than competition, as it allows everyone to thrive and achieve collective success.

As you continue to build your supportive community, remember to prioritize authenticity above all else. Surround yourself with individuals who celebrate your victories, support you during setbacks, and uplift your spirit. These are the people who will empower you to unleash your inner strength and overcome any obstacle life throws your way.

Building a supportive community is a powerful tool for unleashing your inner strength and overcoming obstacles. By surrounding yourself with like-minded individuals who believe in you and provide encouragement, empathy, and collaboration, you can tap into a wellspring of inspiration and achieve personal growth and transformation.

As we conclude this portion of the chapter, always remember that you are never alone on this journey. Together, we can triumph over adversity and unleash our inner warriors. So, take that first step, seek out genuine connections, and embrace the power of a supportive community. The possibilities are endless, and the strength of unity is unbreakable. Keep moving forward, and let the power of your community guide you toward fulfilling your dreams.

Weathering The Storm: Overcoming Obstacles Together In Your Relationship

Effective communication is vital for healthy relationships, forming the bedrock of trust, understanding, and connection. Yet, obstacles often arise, leading to frustration and distance. But these challenges offer opportunities for growth.

In this chapter, we'll explore strategies to overcome obstacles and foster healthier, more fulfilling relationships.

Active listening is crucial. Often, we're so focused on our own thoughts that we neglect to truly hear others. Actively listening shows genuine interest in their feelings and perspectives. Set aside judgments and focus on understanding their needs, fostering empathy, and creating a safe space for open communication.

Effective communication goes beyond active listening; it involves expressing yourself clearly and assertively. Often, we hold back our true thoughts and feelings, fearing conflict or rejection. But doing so compromises relationship authenticity. It's vital to strike a balance between assertiveness and respect, articulating thoughts and emotions respectfully. This not only fosters understanding but ensures your needs are acknowledged.

Addressing miscommunication is another crucial aspect. Misunderstandings arise due to diverse communication styles, cultural backgrounds, or personal histories. Rather than letting them fester, seek clarification by asking open-ended questions and paraphrasing. This prevents unnecessary conflicts, fostering harmony.

Empathy and compassion are essential in overcoming relationship obstacles. Each person carries their own baggage and perspectives. Empathy allows you to understand their feelings, fostering a deeper connection. Responding with compassion builds trust and respect, bridging gaps and strengthening relationships.

Engaging in self-reflection and personal growth is crucial when facing relationship obstacles. Each relationship offers a chance for self-discovery. Reflect on your thoughts, beliefs, and behaviors that may affect your relationships. Being self-aware and open to change helps break negative patterns and foster healthier dynamics.

Remember, transformation takes time and effort. Every step toward effective communication and personal growth is an investment in your relationships. We'll explore more strategies to deepen connections and build stronger, fulfilling relationships.

Forgiveness and letting go are paramount in overcoming relationship obstacles. Holding onto grudges poisons relationships and perpetuates negativity. Forgiveness isn't about condoning or forgetting; it's a choice to release negative emotions and opt for compassion. Acknowledge the pain, allow yourself to feel it, and then consciously choose to let it go. This process is challenging but vital for your well-being and relationship health.

In forgiving, remember it's a journey, not a destination. Healing from past hurts takes time and effort. Be patient with yourself and others, allowing space for natural healing. Forgiveness is a gift to yourself, promoting personal growth and restoring relationships.

Gratitude is another powerful tool for overcoming relationship obstacles. Instead of dwelling on the negatives, focus on the positives. Cultivating gratitude shifts perspective to appreciate the strengths and positive aspects of relationships.

Expressing gratitude fosters appreciation and strengthens emotional bonds. Take time to acknowledge and verbalize gratitude for people in your life. Share qualities and actions you appreciate and how they've positively impacted you. This practice strengthens relationships and uplifts spirits, nurturing a positive mindset.

In addition to forgiveness and gratitude, it's crucial to establish healthy boundaries in your relationships. Boundaries act as a guide, helping you navigate interactions with others and creating a safe space for genuine connection.

Setting boundaries requires clear and open communication. Respectfully express your needs and expectations while also being receptive to the boundaries of others. Remember, boundaries promote respect, emotional well-being, and healthier dynamics within relationships.

Lastly, self-care should be prioritized as a vital aspect of overcoming relationship obstacles. Neglecting your well-being makes it challenging to invest fully in your relationships. Dedicate time to activities that nurture your physical, mental, and emotional health.

Self-care varies for each person—whether it's pursuing joyful activities, practicing mindfulness, prioritizing rest, or seeking support from loved ones. By prioritizing self-care, you replenish your resources and create a strong foundation to nurture your relationships.

As you continue on your journey to overcome relationship obstacles, remember that it's an ongoing process. Embrace these strategies with an open heart and mind, paving the way for healthier, more fulfilling connections each day.

Unleashing The Warrior Spirit: Overcoming Obstacles With Tenacity

As we delve further into the realm of prayer warriors, it's vital to recognize that sustaining the warrior spirit isn't a one-time achievement. Just like physical strength demands consistent exercise and nourishment, our inner strength requires continual care and attention.

Previously, we explored various principles and strategies to conquer our obstacles and tap into our innate power. Now, let's focus on applying these principles for ongoing personal growth and future triumphs.

A Prayer warrior actively engages with their spirituality, harnessing the power of prayer to overcome challenges and achieve goals. However, this journey extends beyond individual battles. It's a lifelong commitment to continuous growth, development, and overcoming whatever hurdles may come our way.

One crucial aspect of sustaining the warrior spirit is a dedication to personal growth. Just as the physical body needs nourishment, our minds and souls need ongoing nourishment, too. We must remain open to learning and growing, embracing new knowledge and perspectives. By expanding our understanding of ourselves and the world, we equip ourselves with the wisdom needed to face any obstacle.

Another essential strategy in sustaining the warrior spirit is to remain adaptable. Life is unpredictable, and challenges can arise unexpectedly. By cultivating flexibility, we become better equipped to adapt to changing circumstances.

As prayer warriors, we must be willing to adjust our approach, adopt new perspectives, and find creative solutions to the trials that come our way.

Resilience is another critical component of sustaining the warrior spirit. It's not about the absence of obstacles but rather the ability to bounce back from adversity. It's the inner strength that enables us to rise above our circumstances, regardless of their difficulty. Cultivating resilience involves recognizing our inherent power, understanding that we're not defined by our circumstances, and choosing to persevere even in the face of adversity.

As prayer warriors, we find our strength in faith and our connection to a higher power. This belief in something greater than ourselves sustains us through tough times. Knowing we're not alone in our struggles, we find comfort in the divine presence guiding and supporting us. Through prayer and seeking spiritual guidance, we tap into this wellspring of strength and fortitude.

So, fellow prayer warriors, as you embark on the journey of sustaining the warrior spirit, remember to nurture your mind, body, and soul. Seek opportunities for personal growth, embrace adaptability, cultivate resilience, and draw strength from your faith. The path of the prayer warrior isn't always smooth, but the rewards are unmatched—a life filled with purpose, strength, and the ability to overcome any obstacle.

Stay tuned as we explore specific strategies and techniques to sustain the warrior spirit in our daily lives. Get ready to unlock even more of your inner power and conquer future obstacles with unwavering faith and determination. The journey continues, and the best is yet to come.

In the face of adversity, it's easy to forget our inner strength and the progress we've made. As prayer warriors, it's vital to have a supportive community that uplifts and encourages us. Our fellow warriors offer empathy, understanding, and a sense of belonging, reminding us we're not alone on this journey.

By forming deep connections with like-minded individuals who share our faith and values, we create a supportive network that sustains our warrior spirit. Together, we can lean on each other during tough times and celebrate victories as one. United, we're stronger and can overcome any obstacle.

Moreover, sustaining the warrior spirit means cultivating self-compassion and practicing self-care. Amid life's challenges, it's crucial to prioritize our physical, mental, and emotional well-being. This involves setting healthy boundaries, making time for rest and rejuvenation, and engaging in activities that bring us joy and fulfillment.

Remember, self-care isn't selfish; it's essential for preserving ourselves. Just as we can't pour from an empty cup, neglecting our needs hinders our warrior spirit. Prioritizing self-care replenishes our energy, heals our wounds, and empowers us to face each battle with renewed strength.

In our quest for ongoing growth, we must challenge ourselves and step beyond our comfort zones. Growth happens when we push our limits and embrace discomfort. Trying new experiences, seeking further education, or tackling challenging projects all expand our potential and reveal hidden reserves of strength.

However, sustaining the warrior spirit also means recognizing the value of rest and reflection. We need a balance between growth and giving ourselves space to absorb lessons. Introspection lets us understand our strengths and weaknesses, identify areas to improve, and reignite our sense of purpose.

As our journey as prayer warriors continues, it's crucial to stay rooted in gratitude. Gratitude is a powerful tool that helps us shift our focus from scarcity to abundance. By appreciating the blessings in our lives, both big and small, we nurture a sense of contentment and fulfillment.

Gratitude reminds us of our progress, the obstacles we've overcome, and the support we've received. It strengthens our spiritual connection and fills us with purpose and hope, even in challenging times.

As we conclude this chapter on sustaining the warrior spirit, I urge you to embrace your unwavering faith and trust in your inner strength. Remember, this journey is ongoing, a commitment to nurturing our minds, bodies, and souls for the challenges ahead.

Forge ahead with courage and resilience, fueled by a heart brimming with gratitude. You have the capacity for greatness, and through your steadfast dedication, you'll overcome every obstacle in your path. Stay true to yourself, embrace the journey, and unleash the power within you.

May the strength of the warrior spirit light your way to victory.

CHAPTER 10
"Trust And Surrender"

Embrace Your Story: A Journey Of Self-Exploration

Discover the profound strength found in embracing life's mysteries and surrendering to the divine plan, unlocking a journey of profound fulfillment and purpose.

Life is an intricate tapestry woven with unexpected twists and turns, a labyrinth of choices. At a pivotal crossroads, uncertainty looms like a shadow, testing the very essence of our being. Yet, within these moments lies a pivotal choice – to cower in fear of the unknown or to embrace it unreservedly.

Embracing the unknown is no simple feat. Our innate desire for stability and predictability clashes with the chaotic dance of existence. We crave control, yearning to script every chapter of our story. But it's when we relinquish this grasp that life's true blessings reveal themselves.

In surrendering to the divine orchestration, we concede our finite control, acknowledging a force greater than ourselves. We humbly recognize the guiding hand of providence, steering us towards a higher purpose. As we release the reins of control, we open the floodgates to a realm of boundless possibilities and serendipitous encounters.

Surrendering to God's plan isn't about giving up control or feeling powerless. It's about understanding that there's a bigger picture beyond our understanding and trusting that God knows what's best for us, even when we don't.

When we trust in God's plan, we feel a sense of freedom. We no longer carry the burden of figuring everything out by ourselves. Instead, we can let go of our worries, knowing that God is with us every step of the way.

Embracing the unknown takes bravery – it means taking a leap of faith, letting go of our need to be in charge, and believing that God has a purpose for us. It's a choice to follow God's lead, which leads us to discover our true calling and find fulfillment.

By embracing the unknown, we open ourselves up to new experiences and opportunities to learn and grow. We become more flexible and able to handle life's challenges with resilience. Instead of seeing setbacks as obstacles, we view them as chances to grow and change.

But embracing the unknown isn't always easy. It means stepping out of our comfort zones and facing uncertainty. Yet, it's in these moments of uncertainty where we find the most growth and transformation, drawing us closer to the life that God has planned for us.

As we embark on this journey together, let's embrace the unknown and surrender to God's plan, knowing it holds incredible beauty and purpose for us. Though the path may seem uncertain, it offers us opportunities for profound growth and fulfillment.

As we explore the mysteries of embracing the unknown, we'll uncover inspiring insights and stories to guide us. But for now, let's stand at the threshold of the unknown, ready to step into a world of endless possibilities.

In this vast unknown, we're not alone. There's a divine presence guiding us, surrounding us with love and wisdom. By surrendering to God's plan, we trust in his greater purpose for our lives, letting go of our need for control and embracing the journey with open hearts.

With each step, the path becomes clearer. The fears and anxieties that once burdened us begin to fade, replaced by a profound sense of peace and trust. We realize that surrendering to God isn't about losing ourselves; it's about courageously aligning our will with his divine guidance.

In surrender, we discover freedom. We're relieved of the heavy burden of trying to navigate life's twists and turns alone. We find comfort in knowing we're supported in ways beyond our understanding. As we let go, we create space for miracles to unfold and blessings to shower upon us.

Embracing the unknown demands unwavering faith. It requires courage to silence the doubts and fears that linger within us. But as we wholeheartedly surrender, we tap into a wellspring of strength that empowers us to face each day with renewed determination.

So, I invite you to release your grasp on the familiar. Step beyond your comfort zone into a world of boundless possibilities. Understand that setbacks are opportunities for growth, and detours lead to valuable lessons. Embracing the unknown isn't a one-time decision but an ongoing journey toward profound transformation.

As we journey together, we'll encounter challenges and victories, moments of joy and sorrow. Each experience will teach us valuable lessons, shaping us into who we're meant to be. We'll form connections and support one another through uncharted territories.

Remember, in moments of doubt, you're not alone. God walks beside you, guiding and protecting you at every turn.

His plan for your life is filled with beauty and purpose beyond imagination, waiting to unfold. Embrace the journey with open arms, for the unknown holds treasures of growth and discovery that will transform you from within.

Let's look forward to the wonders ahead and treasure the lessons we've learned. With each page turned, continue to embrace the unknown, knowing you walk hand in hand with God, experiencing life's mysterious and awe-inspiring journey to the fullest.

Breaking Chains: The Art Of Liberating Your Life

In a world that prizes certainty and control, embracing the unknown and surrendering to a higher power's plan can feel daunting. We often crave security and assurance in the outcomes we desire. Yet, life's unpredictable nature presents us with twists and turns we can't foresee. It's in these moments that we must learn to let go of control and place our trust in God's guidance, even amidst uncertainty.

Control is deeply rooted in our human nature, offering a sense of power and stability. We believe managing every aspect of life shields us from disappointment and heartache. But life's complexities defy our control, weaving a tapestry of experiences beyond our grasp.

When we release this need for control and embrace God's plan, something transformative occurs. We find freedom. Surrendering lifts burdens, bringing peace beyond comprehension. Trust replaces anxiety, and hope supplants fear.

Letting go doesn't mean we shirk responsibility or become passive observers in our lives. It means acknowledging a divine order beyond our understanding and aligning ourselves with a higher purpose. We become active participants, co-creating our destinies with God rather than struggling to navigate alone.

Embracing trust in God's guidance demands a shift in perspective. We must learn to see uncertainty as an opportunity for growth rather than a threat to our stability. It's when we face the unknown that our faith is tested, and our character is shaped. Trusting God in uncertain times enables us to develop resilience, perseverance, and unwavering hope.

Take the story of Abraham, for instance, who was called upon to sacrifice his son Isaac. In that moment of unimaginable uncertainty and heartache, Abraham chose to trust in God's plan. He let go of control, believing that God would provide. Through his trust and surrender, he witnessed divine intervention, saving Isaac and strengthening Abraham's faith.

In our own lives, we'll encounter situations where we long for control, where the path ahead is obscured by uncertainty. In these moments, we must remind ourselves to release, surrender, and trust. Trust that even in the darkest times, God is guiding us toward a greater purpose.

So, as we navigate life's uncertainties, let's find comfort in surrender. Let's embrace the certainty within the unknown, knowing that relinquishing control creates space for miracles to unfold. Trust in God's guidance and believe that beyond our understanding, there's a plan far greater than we can imagine.

With this understanding, we embark on a journey of faith, eagerly anticipating the next chapter, where we delve deeper into practical steps to cultivate trust and surrender. Hold onto hope, for the best is yet to come.

As we explore letting go of control and trusting in God's guidance, it's essential to acknowledge that this journey isn't always easy. It requires us to confront fears, step out of our comfort zones, and surrender our own plans. But remember, we're not alone on this path.

In our journey, God walks alongside us, offering unwavering guidance and support with every step. When doubts cloud our minds or confusion grips our hearts, we turn to prayer, seeking solace and clarity in the boundless wisdom of the Divine. Through prayer, we open ourselves to receive divine guidance, inviting God to unveil his purpose for our lives.

Prayer stands as a mighty force, allowing us to release our grip on control. It serves as a direct conduit to our Creator, a channel through which we surrender our worries and burdens. By entrusting our concerns to God, we acknowledge his omniscience and willingly submit to his divine will.

As we embrace trust in God's guidance, patience becomes paramount. The path ahead may be shrouded in uncertainty, tempting us to succumb to restlessness in our quest for answers. Yet, we must remember that God operates on his own timetable. He orchestrates the tapestry of our lives with divine precision, even when the threads of his plan seem invisible to our eyes.

In moments of waiting and ambiguity, we are called to nurture patience and fortify our faith. It is through patience that we learn to relinquish our grasp on control and surrender to the rhythm of God's timing. Instead of rushing forward, let us find solace in the journey itself, trusting implicitly in the flawless cadence of God's perfect timing.

In addition to prayer and patience, surrounding ourselves with a supportive community is another practical step toward building trust and surrender. When we share our fears, doubts, and dreams with others who share our faith journey, we find strength in unity.

Connect with people or groups who share your beliefs, where you can have open and honest conversations about your struggles and successes. Together, you can pray, study scripture, and uplift each other as you navigate life's uncertainties. This community reminds us that we're not alone and that God's plan is unfolding for everyone.

Let's continue to embrace the unknown and trust in God's plan with open hearts. Through prayer, patience, and support from our community, we can let go of the need for control and find comfort in knowing that God is guiding us toward a greater purpose.

As we journey in surrender, hold onto hope and faith, knowing that every twist and turn is an opportunity for growth and miracles. Trust in God's guidance, and be open to divine blessings beyond imagination.

May you find peace in surrender and look forward to the chapters ahead with anticipation. Though the path may not always be clear, with God as our guide, the best is yet to come.

The Stillness Within: Finding Peace Amidst The Unknown

In the whirlwind of our busy lives, finding peace can be a challenge. Pressures from work and personal life, coupled with uncertainty about the future, often leave us feeling overwhelmed. But what if we could find a way to stay calm amidst life's chaos? In this chapter, we'll explore simple strategies to help us embrace uncertainty and discover inner peace.

Central to finding peace in uncertainty is accepting life's unpredictability. No matter how much we plan, unexpected twists are inevitable. Instead of resisting these uncertainties, we can shift our perspective and trust in a higher plan. Embracing the unknown opens doors to growth, self-discovery, and a deeper connection with the universe.

One effective way to find peace in uncertainty is practicing mindfulness. Mindfulness means being fully present in the moment, observing our thoughts and feelings without judgment. By staying present, we let go of worries about the future and regrets from the past, finding comfort in the here and now. This practice helps us develop inner calmness, allowing us to navigate life's uncertainties with ease.

The past is behind us, unchangeable. Dwelling on it serves no purpose. All secrets belong to God, and our future remains unknown. Living in the present moment is where God wants us to be. The struggle to trust God is ongoing in our daily lives. Today brings its own challenges that require our trust in God.

Another practical strategy is letting go of the need for constant control. Our desire for certainty often stems from fear of the unknown. Resisting change and insisting on having everything figured out only adds stress. Surrendering to a greater plan frees us from unnecessary worry and opens us to new possibilities. Trusting in life's unfolding brings comfort, knowing there's a guiding force beyond our understanding.

Building a supportive network of like-minded individuals can also help us find peace in uncertainty. Surrounding ourselves with people who share our mindset fosters a sense of belonging and strengthens our resilience. Through honest conversations and shared experiences, we realize we're not alone in our journey, enhancing our inner peace.

Nature offers solace in embracing the unknown. Its beauty induces calmness and reminds us of life's grandeur. Whether walking in the woods, by the ocean, or simply appreciating a flower's bloom, nature's majesty puts our worries into perspective. Immersing ourselves in nature's beauty reveals the insignificance of our concerns in the grand scheme of things.

As we venture into the journey of finding peace amidst uncertainty, it's crucial to approach it with openness. Embracing the unknown isn't a one-time event but a continuous process of growth. Through mindfulness, letting go of control, nurturing relationships, and connecting with nature, we gradually build inner peace.

Let's delve into additional strategies to deepen our peace in uncertainty. These practices help us continue embracing life's uncertainties with an open heart and mind.

Self-reflection is a potent strategy. Delving into our inner world—our thoughts, emotions, and desires—offers insights into our journey. By understanding our fears, hopes, and dreams, we better grasp how they influence our response to uncertainty. Self-reflection fosters clarity and inner peace. Journaling, meditation, and therapy serve as effective tools for this journey of self-discovery.

Another vital element of finding peace amid uncertainty is embracing gratitude. It's easy to dwell on what we lack or the hurdles we encounter, but shifting our focus to gratitude can change our perspective profoundly. When we consciously recognize and appreciate the blessings and positives in our lives, we foster a sense of abundance and contentment. Gratitude reminds us of the richness surrounding us, even in uncertain times.

Incorporating a gratitude practice into our daily routine, like jotting down three things we're thankful for each day, significantly boosts our well-being and peace of mind.

Developing resilience is equally crucial in navigating the unknown. Resilience empowers us to bounce back from challenges, setbacks, and surprises, fostering growth amidst uncertainty. Cultivating resilience involves nurturing self-belief, maintaining a positive outlook, and adopting healthy coping strategies. Engaging in activities that enhance resilience, such as exercise, mindfulness, and seeking support from loved ones, helps us face the unknown with confidence and grace.

Lastly, embracing the unknown means releasing attachments and accepting impermanence. Life is ever-changing, and clinging to rigid expectations only leads to suffering. By acknowledging that change is inevitable and everything is fleeting, we free ourselves from the burden of control. Instead, we learn to flow with life's shifts and appreciate its dynamic nature. Letting go and welcoming the unknown's possibilities brings a deeper sense of freedom and inner peace.

Throughout this book, we've explored strategies to find peace amid uncertainty. By embracing life's uncertainties, practicing mindfulness, letting go of control, nurturing relationships, connecting with nature, reflecting on ourselves, cultivating gratitude, building resilience, and accepting impermanence, we embark on a transformative journey toward profound peace.

Remember, this journey is unique for each of us. There's no one-size-fits-all approach, but combining these strategies and finding what resonates with your heart creates a personal roadmap. Embrace the beauty of the unknown, for it reveals our true selves and purpose.

I pray you embark on this journey with an open heart and mind, trusting in your ability to find peace. Embrace the uncertainties, surrender to your divine path, and know that you are capable, resilient, and deserving of a peaceful life.

Finding Courage: Navigating Through Fear's Terrain

Fear resides deep within us all, often holding us back from embracing the unknown and surrendering to God's plan. When uncertainty looms, fear surfaces, bringing doubt, anxiety, and even paralysis. But as we explore navigating through fear, we'll find that faith can conquer even the most daunting fears.

In uncertainty, fear often masquerades as fear of failure. We worry that surrendering to God's plan will lead us astray or result in mistakes. It's natural to hesitate when the future is unclear. Yet, God's plan surpasses our understanding. Sometimes, surrendering leads us to our true purpose.

To overcome the fear of failure, we must shift our perspective. Failure isn't the end but a step toward growth and learning. Through failure, we gain wisdom and the courage to press on. Trusting in God's plan means trusting that even amidst unexpected outcomes, he guides us toward something greater.

Another common fear in embracing the unknown is the fear of judgment. We worry about others' opinions of our choices, fearing criticism or misunderstanding. This fear can paralyze us, hindering our surrender to God's plan. Yet, our true worth lies in our relationship with God, not in others' judgments.

Overcoming the fear of judgment means understanding our self-worth deeply. When we grasp that we're unconditionally loved by our Creator, others' opinions lose their power. We hold onto the truth that we're on a unique path, guided by a loving God who knows our hearts and sees our potential.

Moreover, fear often stems from doubting ourselves. We question our abilities and wonder if we're capable of navigating the unknown. But in uncertainty, we're not alone. God is with us, providing strength and guidance every step of the way.

To overcome self-doubt, we must nurture faith in ourselves. Acknowledging our strengths and talents as gifts from God, we take a leap of faith, believing in our capacity to face challenges. Embracing the unknown requires trust in ourselves and in the divine plan unfolding before us.

Addressing the fears that often arise when surrendering to the unknown requires us to have faith in God's plan. Understanding that failure is not the end and finding confidence in our own worth are crucial steps. By trusting in our abilities, we can navigate through fear with unwavering faith. In this exploration, we will delve into practical steps to overcome specific fears and embrace the unknown.

One effective technique for confronting fear is to visualize success. When fear grips us, we tend to envision all the ways things could go wrong. However, if we shift our focus toward imagining positive outcomes and envisioning ourselves confidently navigating through challenges, we can rewire our minds for success. Visualizing the path ahead and seeing ourselves walking in faith, guided by God's loving hand, strengthens our belief in our ability to handle uncertainty.

Prayer is another powerful tool to overcome fear. When we surrender our fears and doubts to God through prayer, we invite Him to work in our lives and guide us through the unknown. Prayer strengthens our connection with God, reminding us of His presence and His promise to never leave us nor forsake us. As we pray, we can specifically ask for courage, wisdom, and trust in God's plan. Through prayer, we find peace in knowing that God's faithfulness will sustain us throughout our journey.

Additionally, surrounding ourselves with a supportive community can provide both security and encouragement. Sharing our fears and anxieties with trusted friends or mentors can offer valuable perspectives and insights. Learning from others who have faced similar challenges and drawing strength from their triumphs can be immensely beneficial. Together, we can uplift and inspire one another as we navigate uncharted territory.

Taking action is crucial in overcoming fear. Often, fear paralyzes us, trapping us in indecision. Yet, it's through action that we gain momentum and create opportunities for growth. Stepping into the unknown with boldness demonstrates our trust in God's plan and opens doors for divine guidance. Even small steps forward can lead to significant breakthroughs.

Lastly, fostering a grateful heart can reshape our perspective and weaken fear's grip. By focusing on the blessings in our lives rather than potential failures, we shift from scarcity to abundance. Gratitude allows us to receive God's love and provision, affirming His faithfulness and provision for our needs.

As we embrace these practical steps, we can navigate fear and fully embrace the unknown. While fear may surface, it doesn't have to define our journey. With faith as our compass, we can confidently surrender to God's plan, trusting that He leads us toward greater things.

Through visualizing success, seeking support from our community, taking action, and cultivating gratitude, we can conquer specific fears and welcome the unknown. As we turn the pages of this book, may we find strength and encouragement to navigate fear with unwavering faith. Embracing the unknown reveals the beauty of God's unfolding plan in our lives.

Resilience: The Power Within

Explore the strength of resilience in confronting challenges and setbacks and how embracing God's plan can bolster our ability to bounce back.

Resilience, the ability to recover swiftly from hardships, setbacks, or difficulties, is a quality of immense value in life's journey. Life's twists and turns are unpredictable, and despite our best efforts to plan and prepare, we inevitably encounter obstacles along the way. It's our response to these challenges that truly shapes our character and charts our course.

In the face of adversity, resilience serves as our inner anchor, guiding us through life's turbulent seas with courage, hope, and faith. It's during tough times that we often discover our true selves and unearth the depths of our capabilities. While setbacks may momentarily knock us down, resilience empowers us to rise again, fortified and even stronger than before.

By surrendering ourselves to God's plan, we acknowledge that there's a higher purpose at play, even amidst adversity. In surrender, we find comfort, knowing that God walks alongside us, offering guidance and strength to navigate life's trials. Surrendering to God's plan isn't passive resignation to difficult circumstances; rather, it's an active embrace of seeking God's wisdom and relying on His strength.

To build resilience, fostering a mindset of trust and surrender is vital. Entrusting the unknown may seem daunting, yet when we release control and yield our plans to

God; we embrace the beauty of His divine guidance. We learn to rely on His wisdom instead of solely on our own, shedding the burden of trying to control every aspect of our lives. This surrender allows us to receive the peace and strength that God freely offers.

Moreover, surrendering to God's plan grants us a broader perspective beyond our immediate circumstances. It empowers us to view challenges and setbacks as stepping stones rather than stumbling blocks. Trusting in God's sovereignty, we recognize that every trial is an opportunity for growth, transformation, and a deeper reliance on His grace.

The journey of surrender and resilience isn't without its challenges. Moments of doubt, fear, and uncertainty will arise. We may stumble and question whether yielding to an unseen plan is truly worthwhile. Yet, it's precisely in these moments that our faith is strengthened. As we surrender our doubts, fears, and limitations to God, He fills us with unwavering strength and peace, enabling us to move forward with resilience.

Resilience, when fueled by surrender to God's plan, becomes a powerful force in our lives. It molds our character, strengthens our faith, and emboldens us to confront life's trials head-on. Through surrender, we tap into a wellspring of resilience that surpasses our human limitations. Armed with this resilience, we can rebound from setbacks and navigate difficult situations with newfound courage, hope, and the assurance that we are never alone in our struggles.

As we embark on the latter part of this chapter, we'll delve into practical ways to cultivate resilience and how surrendering to God's plan can further bolster our capabilities. But for now, let's take a moment to reflect on our own experiences of resilience and surrender. Recall the times when facing adversity, surrendering to God's plan enabled you to persevere. As we delve deeper, be prepared to uncover strategies and insights that will empower you to nurture a resilient spirit, relying on God's guidance as you embrace the unknown with courage and hope.

A simple yet effective way to cultivate resilience is by fostering a mindset of gratitude. Shifting our focus from what we lack to what we have opens our hearts to a sense of abundance and contentment. Gratitude enables us to recognize the blessings in our lives, even amidst challenging circumstances. By expressing gratitude to God for His guidance and provision, we invite His presence into our struggles, discovering strength we never knew existed.

Moreover, establishing connections within a supportive community significantly contributes to resilience. Surrounding ourselves with like-minded individuals who share our faith and values fosters a sense of belonging and solidarity. When faced with challenges, turning to this community provides comfort, encouragement, and diverse perspectives that aid us in navigating through adversity. Together, we confront life's trials with collective strength and shared wisdom.

In our journey of surrender and resilience, prioritizing self-care is paramount. Nurturing our physical, mental, and emotional well-being replenishes our reserves, enabling us to tackle challenges with clarity and vigor. Engaging in activities that bring joy, such as hobbies, exercise, or spending time outdoors, rejuvenates our spirits and offers respite from life's demands.

Additionally, developing resilience entails challenging negative thoughts and beliefs. In times of hardship, self-doubt, fear, and limiting beliefs may creep in. Yet, consciously replacing negative thoughts with positive affirmations fosters a resilient mindset. Recognizing our strengths, talents, and past successes empowers us to confront challenges with confidence and fortitude.

Finally, surrendering to God's plan entails embracing the process of letting go. At times, we may cling to past failures, regrets, or bitterness, hindering our ability to recover from setbacks. Releasing these burdens and extending forgiveness to ourselves and others creates space for God's transformative work in our lives, molding us into stronger and more resilient individuals.

Reflecting on this chapter, let's earnestly consider practical strategies and insights to integrate into our lives. Acknowledge the power of gratitude, the support found in the community, and the importance of self-care. Challenge negative thoughts and beliefs, and practice the art of letting go. Embracing these principles, we cultivate resilience and surrender to God's plan, knowing we are never alone.

In conclusion, resilience and surrender are intertwined, empowering us to confront life's challenges with steadfast faith. Through setbacks and difficulties, we've emerged as stronger, wiser, and more compassionate individuals. By nurturing resilience and embracing the unknown, we position ourselves to receive God's guidance and the transformative essence of surrender. Let's continue nurturing a resilient spirit, relying on God's wisdom, and embracing surrender's beauty as we journey through life.

Perfect Timing: Embracing the Divine Plan Titles

In the intricate fabric of life, there are moments when our plans seem to collide with an unseen force. We find ourselves swept up in unexpected twists, uncertain outcomes, and a future veiled in mystery. It's in these times that we must learn the art of trusting in God's perfect timing.

How often have we painstakingly crafted our dreams, only to face delays, disappointments, and prayers that seem unanswered? Frustration and doubt are natural in these moments. Yet, it's precisely then that we're called to embrace the unknown and surrender to a higher plan beyond our comprehension.

Trusting divine timing requires a shift in perspective, moving from our limited view of what should be to an understanding that the universe operates in a harmonious rhythm. Picture a grand symphony where each musician plays their part, trusting the conductor's guidance and awaiting their cue. We, too, must trust that every note, every opportunity, and every breakthrough in our lives has its appointed time.

When our plans diverge from God's, it's hard to grasp the bigger picture. We're ensnared in questions of why and how seeking immediate answers. But perhaps, just perhaps, it's in the waiting, in the surrender, that we discover life's true beauty unfolding.

Trusting divine timing demands a faith that transcends human logic, acknowledging a purpose and wisdom beyond our own. It calls us to release our grip on control and embrace the possibility that what lies ahead holds greater magnificence than we can imagine.

In moments of uncertainty, it's easy to lose sight of the miracles awaiting us. We may question our worth, wondering if we're deserving of God's blessings. But remember, you are a cherished creation, intricately woven into this vast universe. Just as a loving parent knows the perfect time to give a gift, so does God know the ideal moment to abundantly bless you.

Trusting divine timing means releasing the weight of our expectations and surrendering to life's unfolding plan. It teaches us patience, resilience, and steadfast faith. It's a call to let go of the need for instant gratification and find comfort in the belief that everything happens for a reason, in its own time.

As we embark on this journey of trust, remember that beauty lies not just in the destination but in the process itself. The winding path may lead through valleys of uncertainty and mountains of challenges, but it's in these moments that we grow stronger, resilient, and spiritually enriched. So, may you find peace in surrender, and may your trust in divine timing lead you to a life beyond your imagination.

And with that, I leave you in anticipation, awaiting the unveiling of remarkable stories and profound insights that illuminate the path of trusting divine timing. Stay tuned, for the grand reveal is just around the corner. In times of uncertainty, when doubt clouds our faith in divine timing, remember that our journey is not in vain. In moments of surrender, there is a beacon of hope that pierces through the darkness, guiding us forward.

Throughout history, countless individuals have faced inexplicable challenges yet placed their trust in something greater than themselves. Their stories remind us that even amid adversity, divine timing orchestrates miracles.

Consider Helen Keller, who lost her sight and hearing at just 19 months old. In a silent and dark world, despair could have easily consumed her. Yet, Helen held steadfast trust in divine timing. Through her teacher, Anne Sullivan's love and perseverance, Helen learned to communicate and surpass her perceived limitations. She became an esteemed author, activist, and lecturer, inspiring millions. Helen's journey shows that even in darkness, divine timing can turn the impossible into the extraordinary.

Now, think of Nelson Mandela, imprisoned for 27 years for his anti-apartheid efforts. Despite facing injustice, Mandela clung to faith in divine timing. Upon release, he emerged as a symbol of unity, guiding South Africa towards reconciliation. Mandela's story illustrates the transformative power of patience and trust, revealing that divine timing fuels profound change.

These examples teach us that purpose exists in waiting, even when reasons elude us. Divine timing's unseen threads intricately connect us to opportunities, growth, and blessings beyond comprehension.

As you navigate surrendering to divine timing, embrace the unknown. Trust that God's plan, though unseen, is grander than imagined. Have faith that when the time is right, the universe aligns to manifest your destiny.

Cultivate this trust, but be gentle with yourself. Moments of doubt and impatience are natural. Remember, divine timing operates beyond our understanding. Every detour, disappointment, and unanswered prayer brings you closer to a purposeful, joyful destiny.

Trusting divine timing isn't easy. It demands unwavering faith and the courage to surrender control. Yet, within surrender lies life's true beauty unfolding. Trust that the universe conspires in your favor, and embrace the exquisite surprises awaiting you. Surrender to God's plan, and witness the miracles of divine timing unfurl before your eyes.

Through The Storm: Finding Silver Linings

In life's journey, we often encounter unexpected challenges and uncertainties. We question why things unfold as they do, seeking clarity and reassurance. It's in these moments of confusion and doubt that we're urged to embrace the unknown and surrender to a higher power – God's plan.

Surrendering to God's plan opens us to hidden blessings, especially in our toughest times, offering opportunities for growth and transformation. While the purpose behind difficulties may not be immediately clear, trusting in a greater purpose is essential.

Amid trials, we wrestle with a range of emotions, from fear and sadness to anger and frustration. These feelings can overwhelm us, leaving us disheartened and alone. Yet, surrendering to God's plan invites peace and hope into our lives. We lean on faith, trusting in a plan even when it's unseen.

Embracing the unknown means relinquishing control over our desires and handing them over to a higher power. Though daunting, this act of surrender is a potent display of faith, leading to unforeseen joys.

Through surrender, we open ourselves to new possibilities and perspectives, seeing blessings we might have missed otherwise. In challenging times, we unearth strength we didn't know we possessed, persevering with newfound resilience.

In surrendering, we may realize that our envisioned path isn't always aligned with God's plan. Our understanding may be limited, but God's plan knows no bounds. Surrendering allows us to be guided by a wisdom beyond our own.

Navigating the unknown, we encounter unexpected twists and turns. These challenges refine us, offering valuable lessons and shaping us into who we're meant to be. Though tough at the moment, these detours often lead to unforeseen blessings.

Amid difficulties, we crave clarity and answers. We seek a swift resolution and a clear path forward. Yet, it's often in the waiting and uncertainty that we experience profound growth and deepen our trust in God's plan.

Embracing the unknown, we stay open to unexpected blessings ahead. Even in dark times, there's light waiting to be revealed. In this chapter, we'll explore how surrendering to God's plan unveils hidden blessings and joys. For now, let's immerse ourselves in the beauty of the unknown, trusting that the journey is just beginning.

Here, we'll delve deeper into how surrendering to God's plan leads us to discover hidden blessings and joys. Navigating the unknown, it's vital to keep our hearts and minds open to the miracles awaiting us.

Surrendering to God's plan has a profound impact on our perspective. When we let go of our desires and expectations, it creates space for God to work in ways we may never have imagined. Through this surrender, we open ourselves up to the divine orchestration of events in our lives.

In difficult situations, we may feel overwhelmed. However, as we submit to God's plan and trust in His timing, we discover the strength and resilience within us. Drawing from our faith, even the most challenging periods serve a purpose in shaping us into the individuals we are meant to be.

By surrendering to God's plan, we relinquish control and embrace divine guidance. As we release our grip on the reins, we begin to witness miracles unfolding before our eyes. Closed doors suddenly open, and new opportunities present themselves. This surrender marks the beginning of a journey of discovery and growth.

As we navigate through the unknown, we may encounter unexpected detours and roadblocks. These detours are not setbacks; rather, they offer redirection towards a path more aligned with God's intentions for us. Embracing these detours leads us to hidden blessings that we could not have anticipated or planned for ourselves.

During times of waiting and uncertainty, impatience may arise. However, surrendering to God's plan teaches us the value of patience and trust. It is in the waiting that we learn to rely on God's perfect timing, and it is in the uncertainty that we cultivate a deeper sense of faith. These periods of anticipation become the fertile ground in which our character and trust in God's plan are strengthened.

Even in the darkest of times, there is a glimmer of hope, for God's light is always present. We must hold on to this hope, knowing that no matter how daunting the journey may seem, there are hidden blessings waiting to be revealed. Embracing the unknown requires courage—to let go, to surrender our fears, and to trust in the path that God has laid out for us.

In conclusion, discovering hidden blessings through surrender reminds us that God's plan is far greater than anything we could have ever imagined. As we step forth into the next chapters of our lives, may we carry with us the faith and hope found in embracing God's plan.

Faith In The Unknown: Nurturing Belief Amidst Uncertainty

The journey of faith often leads us into unfamiliar territories where the path is unclear and the destination unknown. It's in these moments of uncertainty that our faith is truly tested. How do we navigate through such depths of the unknown? How do we cultivate a faith that not only survives but thrives amidst uncertainty? The answer lies in embracing the unknown and surrendering to God's plan.

In a world that constantly emphasizes control and certainty, letting go and trusting in God's wisdom can be challenging. We're urged to have all the answers, to plan meticulously, and to avoid ambiguity. However, by clinging to control, we inadvertently limit our growth potential.

The unknown isn't something to fear; it's an opportunity for faith to blossom. In these moments of uncertainty, we're called to surrender our plans and desires, leaning into God's plan instead. Though difficult, embracing the unknown means releasing control and placing our trust in a higher power.

Surrendering to God's plan isn't about giving up on our dreams; it's about aligning our will with His, trusting His wisdom even when we can't see the full picture. When we surrender, we admit that our understanding is limited compared to God's boundless wisdom. We recognize His plans surpass ours and that the unknown holds blessings beyond our imagination.

Deepening our faith amid uncertainty involves letting go of our expectations and being open to divine guidance.

Through surrender, we discover our inner strength and resilience, nurturing our relationship with God. We learn to rely on His grace, wisdom, and unwavering love, knowing He'll never abandon us, even on the most challenging paths.

Amidst the unknown, we're called to nurture patience and perseverance. Just like a seed requires time to grow, our faith needs care and time. We must be patient, trusting in God's perfect timing. Even when it seems like our prayers go unanswered or our dreams linger beyond reach, we find comfort in knowing God is at work, orchestrating every detail according to His plan.

Embracing the unknown and surrendering to God's plan isn't a one-time event. It's an ongoing journey, a process of deepening our faith and strengthening our bond with Him. As we navigate life's uncertainties, let's cling to the comforting truth that God's promises endure, and His love never wavers.

As we press forward, consider these questions: How can you embrace uncertainty in your life? What areas do you struggle to surrender to God's plan? Take a moment to ponder these questions; let them guide us deeper into cultivating faith amidst uncertainty.

In our journey to foster faith amidst uncertainty, we often encounter challenges and obstacles. These trials test our faith's resilience, prompting doubts about embracing the unknown. However, it's precisely in these moments of doubt that our faith has room to grow and blossom.

A crucial aspect of nurturing faith amidst uncertainty is letting go of the urge to control. Our society prizes planning and predictability, leading us to believe we can dictate every aspect of our lives. But when faced with the unknown, this facade crumbles.

To truly embrace uncertainty, we must relinquish control and trust in God's guidance. We acknowledge that some things are beyond our control, finding liberation and peace in surrendering to His will.

Surrendering to God doesn't mean abandoning our dreams or plans; it means releasing our attachment to specific outcomes. We humbly accept that God's wisdom surpasses our own, trusting His direction over our limited understanding.

Amid the uncertainty, it's tempting to seek security in worldly comforts. Yet, true faith urges us to find solace solely in God. Our value isn't defined by circumstances or possessions but by our connection with Him.

As we navigate through life's uncertainties, it's crucial to have a supportive community of believers around us. Sharing our doubts, fears, and hopes with others strengthens our faith and reminds us that we're not alone.

In uncertain times, we find comfort in knowing that God is always by our side. His love is unwavering, and His promises are steadfast. Even when the path ahead seems unclear, we can trust in His guidance.

As we wrap up this chapter, take time to reflect on your own journey of embracing uncertainty. Consider areas where you struggle to surrender to God's plan, and bring them to Him in prayer. Trust that He is guiding you, even when the way forward is unclear.

Remember, cultivating faith in uncertainty is an ongoing process. It requires daily surrender, trust, and reliance on God's wisdom and love. May your faith deepen, your trust strengthen, and your relationship with God flourish as you continue on this journey.

Unstoppable: Rising Above Resistance To Achieve

In times of uncertainty, it's common to face resistance and doubt, which can feel like significant hurdles. When we encounter the unknown, fear and apprehension often bubble up within us. However, it's precisely during these moments that we need to summon the courage to push through resistance and accept the divine plan that lies ahead.

A fundamental step in overcoming resistance is to nurture a mindset of trust and surrender. Whether we call it God, the universe, or something else, surrendering to a higher power acknowledges that there's a greater wisdom guiding us. It's an acknowledgment that we're not alone in our journey and that unseen forces are working in our favor. Letting go of our need for control and embracing this higher power opens us to endless possibilities.

To truly embrace God's plan, we must release our attachment to specific outcomes. Resistance often stems from our strong desire for things to unfold exactly as we imagine. We become fixated on a particular path, unable to see the alternate routes that the divine plan might offer. Yet, sometimes, the unexpected twists and turns are necessary for our growth and fulfillment.

Overcoming resistance involves delving inward and tapping into our inner strength. Establishing a daily practice of self-reflection and meditation can be immensely helpful. Creating mental space allows us to observe our resistance and doubt without judgment. Through mindfulness, we gradually uncover the underlying beliefs and fears contributing to our resistance, enabling us to work through them.

Additionally, surrounding ourselves with a supportive community can be invaluable. Seek out like-minded individuals who are also navigating the unknown. Together, you can share experiences, offer encouragement, and gain insights. Remember, community isn't just about receiving support but also about providing it. By uplifting each other, we create a network of resilience and strength.

It's important to recognize that resistance and doubt aren't reflections of our potential or worthiness. Instead, they're simply part of the journey of growth. Rather than letting them throw us off course, we should see them as opportunities for inner transformation. Embracing the unknown means facing our fears directly and understanding them as chances for growth and expansion.

As we navigate life's uncharted territories, embracing God's plan means surrendering to a greater unfolding. It's about trusting in a divine wisdom that goes beyond our limited understanding. By surrendering to this higher power, we give ourselves the freedom to fully embrace the unknown and all its possibilities.

As we delve deeper into embracing the unknown, we should expect to encounter resistance and doubt. But by nurturing trust and surrender, letting go of attachments, and seeking support from communities, we can overcome these obstacles. Remember, resistance isn't a roadblock but a chance for growth. Embrace the unknown wholeheartedly, and let God's plan reveal the extraordinary possibilities ahead.

A key strategy in overcoming resistance is practicing gratitude. Gratitude shifts our focus from what's lacking to what we have, fostering a mindset of abundance and trust in the divine plan. By practicing gratitude daily, we train our minds to see the blessings and gifts around us, even in uncertain times. It reminds us that we're supported and loved by a higher power and that everything we need will come at the right time.

Another powerful tool for overcoming resistance is cultivating patience and faith. When faced with the unknown, it's tempting to become impatient and seek quick solutions. However, embracing God's plan requires trusting in divine timing and believing that everything is unfolding as it should. Patience allows us to surrender control and flow with the divine plan, knowing that things are happening according to a greater design beyond our understanding. Even in uncertainty, we can find comfort in the knowledge that God is guiding us every step of the way.

It's crucial to remember that self-compassion plays a key role in overcoming resistance. When we face challenges or setbacks, it's easy to be hard on ourselves. But by offering love and kindness to ourselves, we build resilience and strength to keep moving forward. Embracing the unknown isn't a straight path; we might stumble along the way. But by treating ourselves gently, we lay a solid foundation of self-belief and confidence that helps us embrace God's plan wholeheartedly.

As we journey through surrender and overcoming resistance, it's vital to stay open-minded. The unknown is full of possibilities and chances for growth. By staying curious and open to wonder, we allow ourselves to experience life's beauty and magic. Embracing the unknown means shifting our perspective, welcoming surprises, and finding joy in the journey of exploration.

Lastly, remember that this journey is unique to each person. While the strategies mentioned here work, they may look different for everyone. Trust your intuition and inner guidance to lead you to the tools and practices that support your growth and surrender to God's plan.

Overcoming resistance isn't a one-time thing; it's a lifelong practice. It's a continuous journey of surrender, trust, and self-reflection. As we navigate the uncertainties of life, we find comfort in knowing we're not alone. God's plan unfolds for each of us, and by embracing the unknown, we connect with divine wisdom and unlock our limitless potential. With faith, resilience, and a commitment to surrender, we can overcome any obstacle and fully embrace the extraordinary path ahead.

Mission Accomplished: Living With Purpose And Fulfillment

Discover your true potential and step into a life of purpose and fulfillment by embracing God's plan and trusting in His greater vision for your life.

Life often throws us into uncharted territories, challenging us to navigate through uncertainty. It can be overwhelming, leaving us questioning our purpose and where we truly belong. Yet, embracing the unknown and surrendering to God's plan opens the door to a life filled with meaning, joy, and fulfillment.

Amidst the chaos of daily life, it's easy to lose sight of our purpose. We get caught up in the pursuit of success, wealth, and material possessions, forgetting that true fulfillment lies in embracing God's plan for our lives. It's crucial to pause, reflect, and ask ourselves if we are truly living a purpose-driven life.

Surrendering to God's plan requires faith, trust, and a willingness to let go of our own desires and ambitions. It means acknowledging that God's vision for our lives surpasses our limited understanding. By surrendering to His plan, we open ourselves up to His divine guidance, allowing Him to mold us into the best version of ourselves.

When we surrender to God's plan, we embark on a journey towards self-discovery. We begin to understand our true potential and uncover the unique gifts and talents that God has bestowed upon us. Through surrender, we find our purpose, letting go of our own agenda and aligning ourselves with God's higher purpose.

Living with purpose isn't about chasing worldly success or meeting societal expectations. It's about recognizing and utilizing our gifts to positively impact the lives of others. When we surrender to God's plan, He reveals our purpose, guiding us toward opportunities where we can make a difference in the lives of those around us.

Moreover, embracing God's plan brings a sense of peace and contentment. It eliminates the constant pursuit of more and shifts our focus to what truly matters. We find fulfillment in serving others, spreading love and kindness, and living a life aligned with our core values.

As we embrace God's plan, we realize that our purpose extends beyond ourselves. We're part of a larger picture, connected with others in a web of divine providence. Each of us has a unique role to play, and only by surrendering to God's plan can we truly fulfill our part.

So, as you journey through the unknown in search of purpose, I encourage you to embrace God's plan. Let go of the illusion of control and surrender to His divine guidance. Trust that He has a greater vision for your life, one that surpasses anything you could imagine.

In the upcoming discussions, we'll delve into practical steps for living a purpose-driven life. We'll explore how to align your actions with God's plan and discover the beauty in surrendering to His will. Until then, hold onto the faith that embracing the unknown and living with purpose will lead you to a life filled with blessings.

As we continue our exploration of living with purpose and embracing God's plan, it's important to grasp the practical steps that can guide us toward a meaningful and fulfilling life. These steps will help us align our actions with God's will and uncover the beauty of surrendering to His divine guidance.

Firstly, it's crucial to nurture a deep relationship with God. Through prayer, meditation, and reflection, we connect with our Creator, seeking His guidance. This bond lays the groundwork for understanding His plan for our lives. Spending time in His presence tunes us into His voice and prompts. It helps us discern the best path, knowing His guidance never steers us wrong.

Secondly, we must embrace change and let go of our own agendas. Surrendering to God's plan demands humility and a release of control. It means being open to the unknown and trusting His purpose for us surpasses our imagination. It might mean stepping out of comfort zones, taking risks, and embracing new opportunities aligned with His will. This openness allows God to shape us into the individuals He intended.

Thirdly, living with purpose involves using our gifts to serve others. God has entrusted each of us with unique abilities and passions. When we use them to serve others, we bring positive change. Whether through careers, volunteer work, or relationships, we can make a difference by showing compassion, kindness, and love. Being purpose-driven means aligning actions with core values and beliefs.

Furthermore, surrounding ourselves with a supportive community is crucial. Connecting with like-minded individuals pursuing purpose-driven lives offers encouragement, accountability, and inspiration. Together, we can share journeys, learn from experiences, and grow. Seeking guidance from mentors or spiritual leaders can also provide valuable insight and wisdom.

Lastly, living with purpose is an ongoing journey. It requires continual self-reflection, evaluation, and adjustment. Our understanding of God's plan may evolve as we mature spiritually. Remaining flexible and adaptable to the Holy Spirit's guidance is essential, allowing Him to lead us in each new season of life.

As you journey toward embracing the unknown and living with purpose, may you remain steadfast in faith and trust in God's plan. Embrace growth opportunities, surrender to His will, and open yourself to a life filled with blessings and fulfillment. *May your purpose shine, illuminating the lives of those around you!*

ABOUT THE AUTHOR

I am Joseph Christopher Stemple, born and raised in Arizona among six siblings in a devout Catholic household. After studying political science at Cochise College and the University of Arizona, I spent over three decades with the Arizona Department of Corrections, eventually becoming a Correctional Lieutenant. Throughout my career, I honed my writing skills, influenced by leadership roles in lodges, emphasizing the importance of clear communication. Now, as an author, I aim to inspire faith, trust, and spiritual growth through my writings. My hope is that my words serve as a beacon of enlightenment for those who seek solace and guidance on their own path.